3D PHOTOREALISTIC RENDERING

VOLUME 1: INTERIORS & EXTERIORS WITH **V-RAY** & **3DS MAX**

3D PHOTOREALISTIC RENDERING

VOLUME 1: INTERIORS
& EXTERIORS
WITH **V-RAY**
& **3DS MAX**

JAMIE
CARDOSO

CRC Press
Taylor & Francis Group
Boca Raton London New York

CRC Press is an imprint of the
Taylor & Francis Group, an **informa** business

CRC Press
Taylor & Francis Group
6000 Broken Sound Parkway NW, Suite 300
Boca Raton, FL 33487-2742

© 2017 by Taylor & Francis Group, LLC
CRC Press is an imprint of Taylor & Francis Group, an Informa business

No claim to original U.S. Government works

Printed in Canada on acid-free paper
Version Date: 20160921

International Standard Book Number-13: 978-1-1387-8072-9 (Hardback)

Library of Congress Cataloging-in-Publication Data

Names: Cardoso, Jamie, author.
Title: 3D photorealistic rendering : interiors & exteriors with V-Ray and 3ds
Max / Jamie Cardoso.
Description: Boca Raton : CRC Press, 2016.
Identifiers: LCCN 2016034690 | ISBN 9781138780729 (pbk. : alk. paper)
Subjects: LCSH: Architectural rendering--Data processing. | V-ray. | 3ds max
(Computer file)
Classification: LCC NA2728 .C37 2016 | DDC 006.6/93--dc23
LC record available at https://lccn.loc.gov/2016034690

**Visit the Taylor & Francis Web site at
http://www.taylorandfrancis.com**

**and the CRC Press Web site at
http://www.crcpress.com**

Contents

Preface

V-Ray is a rendering engine created by Chaos Group in 1997. It was originally created as a rendering plug-in for 3ds Max only and later integrated into other platforms such as Cinema 4D, Maya and SketchUp.

In its early beginnings, there were other strong rival rendering engines such as finalRender, Brazil and mental ray, but V-Ray somehow managed to captivate the imagination of most users across the globe over the years to become the most popular rendering engine today.

Its current popularity is such among novices and professionals that even well-known Oscar-winning film studios such as ILM (Industry of Light & Magic) have incorporated it into their rendering pipeline.

Recent reports suggest that around 90% of companies and/or industries using rendering applications have at least one copy of V-Ray in their rendering pipeline.

V-Ray's meteoric rise is mostly attributed to its ease of use, support group, constant updates and improvements, and its rendering speed.

Jamie Cardoso
Senior 3D Artist

Additional material is available from the CRC website: http://www.crcpress.com/product/isbn/9781138780729

Acknowledgements

I would like to take this opportunity to personally thank Sean Connelly for the amazing opportunity to be involved with his team at Taylor & Francis and for being ever so patient with me throughout the entire process!

In addition, I would like to thank my family and friends, who have been my greatest supporters.

Furthermore, I thank everyone who contributed, directly or indirectly, to the production and completion of this book:

Special thanks to Elitsa Dimitrova and Graham Macfarlane (for their continuous technical and artistic support), James Goodman, Marcin Piotrowski, FoxRenderfarm, Nadeem Bhatti, Nick Nyon, Maher Zebian, Geoff Chilvers, Renderpeople, Andrew Gibbon, gobotree.com, Giacomo Arteconi, Arroway Textures, Henry Yu, Alan Coleman, Rita Gulyas, Olivier Ladeuix, Jacob Adamiec, Simon Keay, Mateusz Wawrzyniak, Mark Simpkin, Simone Cabras, Eamonn Mohieldean and Dario De Paoli.

Finally, I would like to express my eternal gratitude for the continuous support from friends, family, esteemed colleagues, my book readers, my LinkedIn connections, followers and my blog viewers: You rock!

Author

Jamie Cardoso is an innovative and intelligent senior computer artist, technologist, author and reviewer, whose first-rate experience has been gained by designing and producing work since 1996 for a wide range of clients worldwide.

In collaboration with well-established marketing/design agencies and visualization companies, he has helped design iconic buildings and spaces such as the Gherkin, the Shard, the Welsh Assembly, 1 Cheapside, Heron Tower, Jaguar headquarters, Virgin cruise ship, One Hyde Park, Google, etc.

Skilled at evaluating and resolving problems creatively, Jamie is also adept at working with a wide variety of people effectively and good-humouredly in situations that are sometimes highly demanding.

Much of Jamie's work and contributions have been featured in books and magazines such as the *3D World*, *3D Artist*, *CGSociety*, *TutsPlus* and *3D Total*, to name a few. Furthermore, he is the co-author of two successful books, entitled *Realistic Architectural Visualization with 3Ds Max* and *mental ray*.

Finally, Jamie regularly shares his knowledge with users by constantly updating his blog, http://jamiecardoso-mentalray.blogspot.com/. More information about him is available through an Internet search.

1

Pre-production, Production and Post-production Overview

1.1 Pre-production Overview

The pre-production process is one of the most important steps of an entire project, as it lays the foundation for all subsequent steps (i.e. production and post-production).

To ensure the entire project runs smoothly and on schedule, the following steps are recommended:

1. Check the drawings and/or the 3D models thoroughly, prior to committing to a budget or deadline. ▶1.1 and 1.2

1.1

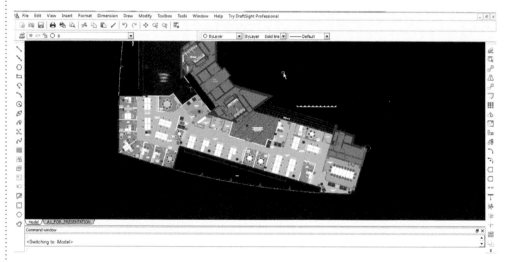

1.2

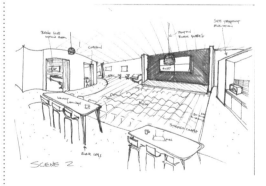

This precautionary measure is important, as there will be instances when assets are riddled with artefacts or are incomplete (e.g. missing textures), which may subsequently affect the original budget and/or the deadline.

In addition, there will be times when delays may occur due to *not* fully understanding the drawings or design and hence creating incorrect models.

These preliminary checks are safeguards to ensure both the client and the user have a good understanding of what they are committing themselves to, in order to prevent any potential shortcomings.

2. After checking the models, drawings and brief, begin discussing and marking up (on the printed CAD drawings) where the potential 3D cameras may be pointed. The camera positions will help you estimate the amount of time involved in creating the 3D assets and the image composition. ▶1.3

1.3

3. Once the above steps have been ironed out, the budget and the project deadline can be set, based on your expertise and available resources.

The pricing of an entire project is always based on the number of hours or days necessary for one person to finish the project (hence the term *man days/hours*). For instance, if it would take 6 months for one person to finish a project, but the project deadline is within 30 days, the job should be priced as if it were one person working for 6 months. Then work out how many people would be necessary to finish the same project in 30 days.

Some companies and users also take into consideration the cost of hiring freelancers, a render farm and buying 3D assets to calculate the final budget.

Moreover, the deadline and budget should also reflect the time it may take to sign off on the final art direction (e.g. a few hours or days, depending on the budget and time), the overall revisions by the client throughout the project and the test rendering times.

Finally, always try to persuade the client (politely) to be more prompt and decisive with general comments, in order to help move things faster. There are instances when clients expect the visualizers to aid them with their design concepts and colour decisions (mostly interior designers). In such exceptional cases try *not* to have a fixed budget, as costs will most likely rise exponentially.

4. Once all of the above-mentioned options and circumstances have been taken into consideration and there's a mutual agreement on the time and budget, begin discussing the art direction.

1.4

During this process, the user and/or the client should begin creating digital mood boards depicting suggestions about the colour of the artificial lights, natural light colour, time of day, light effects, camera angles, camera effects, overall colour/feel, etc.

The images or photos should resemble the render you are trying to create. These similarities should be in the composition, time of day and colours.

The proposed photo references should be striking enough to convince the client and/or the art director. ▶1.4, 1.5 and 1.6

3D Photorealistic Rendering

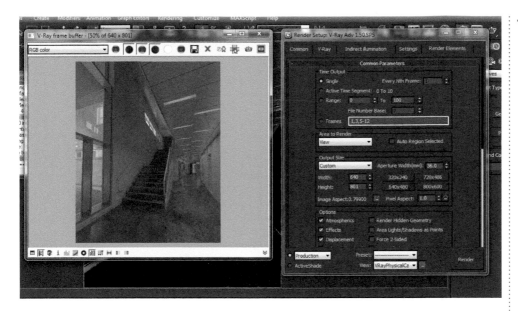

1.5

The following websites are excellent resources for online photo references:

> http://architecturepastebook.co.uk/

> http://www.barratthomes.co.uk/
> new-homes/greater-london/
> h634701-great-minster-house/
> gallery-set/gallery-pages/

> http://www.thecoolhunter.co.uk/
> offices

It's also common for clients to have their own set of photos as a guide and a source of inspiration.

As mentioned earlier, consensus on the art direction may take a few hours or days, depending on the client, budget or project in question.

1.6

It is worth noting that most of the above-mentioned steps are usually adopted by companies or users commissioned to produce compelling "hero shots" for marketing/campaign purposes. However, when working in a fast-paced environment where users are expected to model 3D scenes from scratch and create multiple camera renders on a daily basis, some of the pre-production steps, such as the art direction, might at times prove impossible due to time constraints. In such instances, users can still guide themselves through their own selection of private photo references and images whilst using their own artistic licence and trained eyes to produce the expected images and "manage" client expectations.

1.2 Production Overview

The production process is typically the stage where the user begins modelling/assembling the agreed 3D shots, followed by shading/texturing and rendering the views. This process generally consists of the following steps:

1. Create the 3D model from the drawings supplied by the client while focusing solely on areas within camera boundaries, previously agreed upon.

1.7

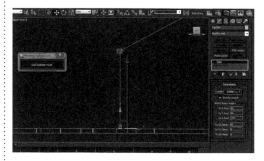

Some users prefer to create and place the camera (at a typical human eye height – 1.65 m) halfway through the modelling process. Others prefer to create the camera after the modelling of the relevant areas is complete. ▶1.7

2. Adjust the camera and the composition to make the overall image more appealing. As mentioned earlier, good photo references can be a useful guide to make the final renders more interesting.

    Next, create/place artificial lights and/or the daylight system in the scene to help sign off the camera composition and most of the 3D model. During this stage, users can produce an appealing chalk render to help "sell" or sign off the chosen view. Chalk renders consist of a basic white material/texture applied as an override render material. ▶1.8

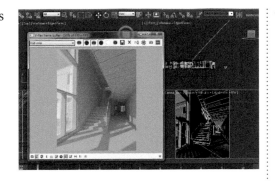

To produce appealing chalk renders, users often ensure that materials such as glass, water, transparent objects, window frames, picture frames, and objects with glow and bump/displacements are not part of the chalk override material/render. In addition, the final chalk renders should look interesting in modelling details – they should be well lit and have a good image sampler (antialiasing).

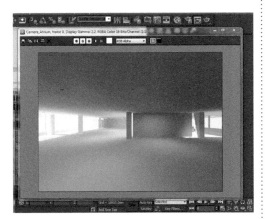

Lighting a scene realistically is one of the most important and crucial parts of the production. When lighting, the primary focus should be on ensuring that there's a clear definition between dark and bright areas in the scene (i.e. depth and contrast). Most scenes consist of sunlight, ambient/diffused light and interior artificial lights. Ambient/diffused light should be present in most lit scenes. ▶1.9

The sunlight can be recreated with a sunlit object. ▶1.10

1.8

1.9

1.10

Production Overview

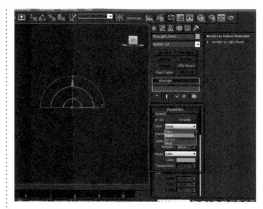

The ambient light is usually reproduced with a dome light and plane lights (for glass windows and openings). ▶1.11

The artificial lights can be recreated with IES (Illuminating Engineering Society) photometric lights. ▶1.12

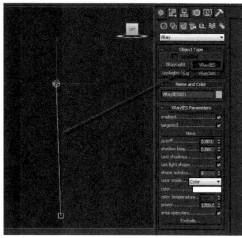

Always choose IES web files that cast pools of light, whenever possible. The 14.IES is widely used to generate such effects and can be found in the book's resource files. These pools of light will help create details, contrast and depth in the entire scene. In addition, ensure that these pools of light don't overlap with each other. To prevent overexposed hot spots generated by the pools of light, simply space each light adequately and periodically test render regions of the scene.

To add further light details in the scene, users usually position these lights close to the walls, so their IES web patterns can be cast onto the walls.

To create more realistic patterns of light, position/rotate some of the lights, so the pools of light are projected in an oblique direction. ▶1.13

The light colours also play an important role in making a scene look more appealing. Blue and yellow tones are often seen in most striking images/photos. Yellow light colours usually represent artificial lights, and blue colours represent ambient/diffused light. The sunlight colour is usually white, unless it's sunset.

Before illuminating a scene, always determine where the main light source should be coming from. This is often determined by the chosen camera view and the number of glass windows/openings close to the camera and/or visible in the shot. The rule of thumb is to always choose sunlight as the main light source in interior and exterior daylight scenes. In exterior daylight scenes, this choice is always a given.

In interior daylight scenes, choose sunlight as the main light source only when there are glass windows/openings visible and/or close to the camera view. In such cases, users should have strong direct/angled sunlight cast onto surfaces, with hints of blue on areas indirectly lit by the ambient/diffused light.

1.14

Artificial lights caught in sunlit areas should be dimmed or switched off, in order for the sunlight to have more prominence. Indirectly lit areas can have artificial lights switched on, with ambient light in the mix. ▶1.14 and 1.15

To add people, most studios mix between 2d and 3d people: 2d people are usually placed in the foreground, and 3d people in the mid and background.

1.15

For aerial and isometric views, 3d people are often used throughout.

1 Production Overview

Currently, Renderpeople models are the best in the industry; and often used by reputable studios and top artists.

Renderpeople models are broken down into three levels of detail: low, medium and high resolution models. The high resolution models can be used for close up shots/renders.

For more information about Renderpeople models, please go to: http://renderpeople.com/ ▶1.16 and 1.17

In all other interior daylight scenarios users frequently choose artificial lights and ambient/diffused light as the main light sources. When such happens, sunlight should ideally be casting direct light in the distance, so the ambient and artificial lights can have more dominance in the scene. ▶1.18

In exterior night scenes, the main light sources should be dome/ambient/diffused light and artificial lights. ▶1.19

1.16

1.17

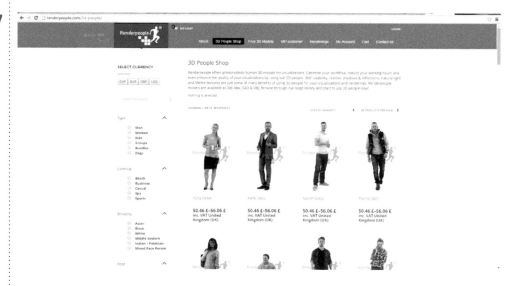

3D Photorealistic Rendering

1.18

1.19

3. Once the chalk views have been signed off on by the client, begin creating shaders and details in areas closer to the camera. These extra modelling details will help make the render appear more realistic.

    For instance, details such as shadow gaps, general table contents, carpet, fur, chamfered edges, realistic plants/trees/grass, slight uneven surfaces/tiles, creases, subtle asymmetry and clutter always make a 3D scene look more appealing and realistic. ▶1.20 and 1.21

1.20

1.21

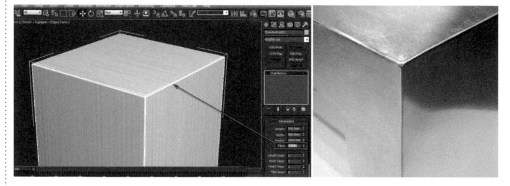

Having a vast library of pre-modelled assets from previous projects will help speed up the modelling process. Websites such as evermotion.org, designconnected.com and turbosquid.com are a good source for 3D assets.

3D Photorealistic Rendering

Below are some of the many guidelines to keep an eye out for while shading and texturing the scene:

1.22

1. Ensure there's a photorealistic texture applied to most objects in the scene (even when the material is white).

   Having a realistic texture applied to a white wall often makes a surface appear more realistic than otherwise. In real life, even pristine surfaces come with subtle details that we usually take for granted. ▶1.22

   When these subtle details are removed, our eyes may subsequently perceive the surface or the overall image to be unnatural, unrealistic or CG.

   These illusive details are generally captured in a photo of a texture.

   Websites such as http://www.arroway-textures.com/ have some of the most photorealistic textures in the industry.

   They have a host of hyper realistic collections such as, veneers, upholstery leather, gravel (3d), wood, stonework, concrete, bricks, tiles, flooring, cardboard, etc.

   For more information about Arroway Textures, please visit: http://www.arroway-textures.com/.

   Alternatively, you may create your own textures by photographing them yourself.

2. Bump/displacement maps usually add more realism to a surface/texture.

   To emulate and reinforce the appearance of a convincing bump/displacement surface, users frequently create and plug a greyscale version of the diffuse texture into the *Bump/Displacement* toggle. ▶1.23 and 1.24

1.23

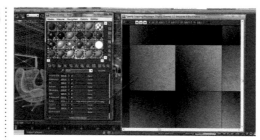

To create a greyscale version of the diffused map, simply open the texture in Photoshop. Next, desaturate and tweak with its contrast; save it with a separate file name. The more contrast between the black and white colours, the sharper the bump/displacement will be. ▶1.25

1.24

▼1.25

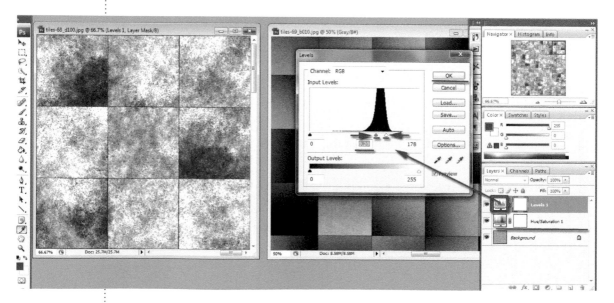

3D Photorealistic Rendering

While the bump effect adds more realism to a surface, the displacement will certainly increase its photorealism dramatically.

Displacing a 3D surface only adds value to a rendered image when the object in question is closer to the camera. The displacement details will go unnoticed on distant objects. ▶1.26

1.26

3. Add reflective or glossy surfaces whenever possible: Reflective or glossy surfaces generally make a scene more interesting and realistic.

High dynamic range images (HDRIs) can also help add extra reflection or glossy details. In an HDRI is being used for reflection purposes only, ensure it's plugged to the Environment reflection/refraction override toggle only. Otherwise it will also contribute to the overall illumination.

There will also be times when HDRI reflection values such as position, rotation and intensity may require drastic changes in order to be visible in the scene. ▶1.27 and 1.28

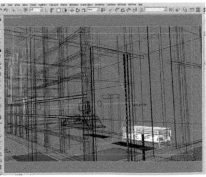

1.27

1.28

4. Uneven reflectivity: Most surfaces in real life reflect light unevenly. To emulate this effect, simply plug a greyscale version of the diffuse map texture onto the reflectivity toggle.

   As mentioned earlier, the grey-scaling process can be achieved in Photoshop. The higher the greyscale contrast, the sharper the reflections will be.

1.29

5. Highlight glossiness: Adding glossy highlights on surfaces frequently helps make a scene more interesting and realistic. ▶1.29

3D Photorealistic Rendering

Rendering

A variety of different test renders are carried out during the production stage. It is common practice to start with draft renders while setting up the lights and the chalk renders. While creating the chalk renders, the light samples and render settings should be low to start with. ▶1.30 and 1.31

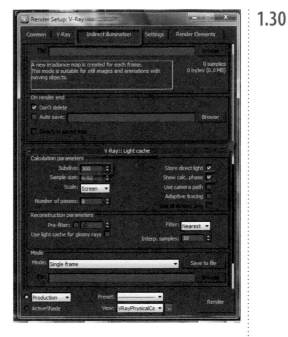

1.30

1.31

1.32

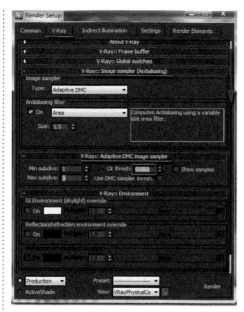

Once satisfied with the overall lighting and the image sampling, you can increase the light and render settings for the final high resolution chalk render (i.e. 3000 pixels). ▶1.32, 1.33, 1.34 and 1.35

1.33

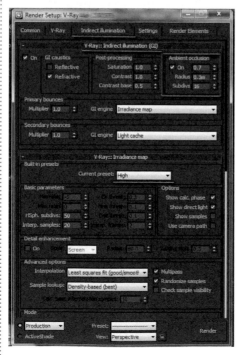

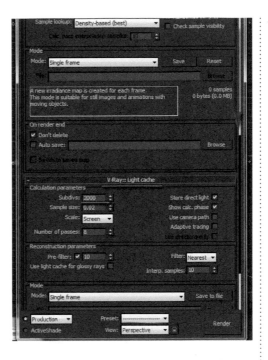

1.34

1.35

1.36

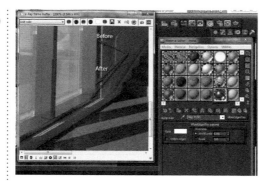

The following step is to carry out further region renders as a test, during the process of creating shaders/textures and the image sampling. ▶1.36

1.37

With the lighting, shaders and textures fine-tuned, begin adding the render elements and test rendering them (without saving). ▶1.37

Next, increase the render output size to 6000 pixels, further tweak the render parameters and render/save the file. ▶1.38

1.38

1.3 Post-production Overview

Post-production is often used to tweak specific materials, replace backgrounds and fine-tune the overall image.

While most users are recommended to get the raw renders looking as good as possible from 3ds Max, post-production work will always be necessary to take the final image to the next level. More often than not, even when the raw renders are already very good, adjusting render elements and the overall image in post-production will turn a good image into an excellent one.

To enhance materials in post-production, multiple render passes are frequently mixed with key Photoshop blending modes and adjustment layers. Some of the most popular render passes for post-production are specular, reflection, lightselect, reflection filter, diffuse material, MultiMatteElement and Refraction. ►1.39

1.39

For better control of each material in post-production, some render passes are copied and moved into one specific material group folder, with a mask attached to it. To blend multiple render passes within each material group folder, users choose blending modes such as screen, multiply and overlay.

As mentioned earlier, adjustment layers are also used within the group folders to control the material contrast and its colours. Some of the widely used adjustment layers are levels, curves, photo filter, exposure, colour balance, hue/saturation and brightness/contrast. These adjustment layers can also be used to grade and fine-tune the overall image. ►1.40 and 1.41

1.40

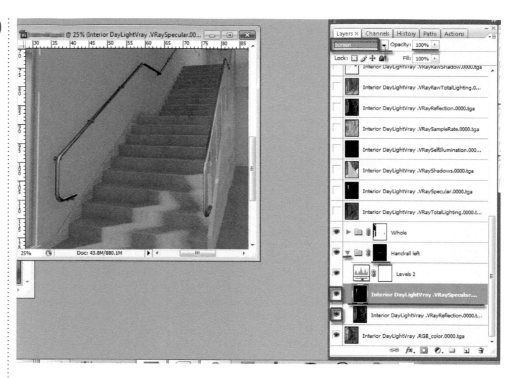

1.41

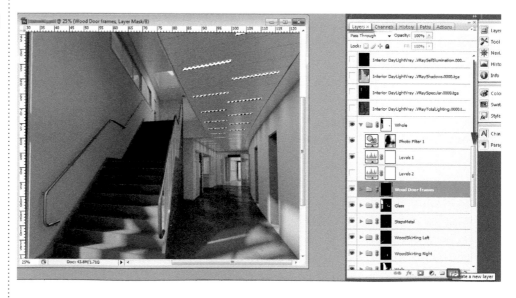

2

Creating Materials and Shaders in V-Ray

2 Materials and Shaders in V-Ray

V-Ray is fully integrated with 3ds Max and comes equipped with a list of robust and powerful procedural maps and shaders to help achieve complex and striking results.

2.1

By default, a number of its presets are set to draft quality, to ensure quick rendering times. However, users often find themselves having to fine-tune some of these preset parameters in order to achieve more photorealistic results.

In the discussions that follow, we focus primarily on the *VRayMtl* parameters, procedural maps and some of the most popular V-Ray shaders.

2.2

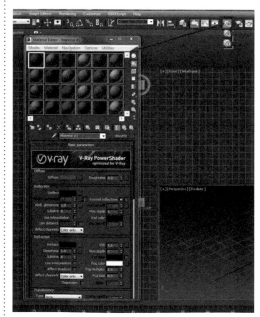

In order to access the *VRayMtl* parameters, the V-Ray renderer needs to be loaded first. To do so, press F10 to open the *Render Setup* dialogue. Alternatively, simply click on its main toolbar button. In the *Render Setup* dialogue, under the *Common* tab, scroll down and open the *Assign Renderer* roll-out parameters. Next, click on the *Production* toggle and pick the V-Ray renderer, in the *Choose Renderer* dialogue. The V-Ray renderer should be loaded automatically. ▶2.1

To begin using the *VRayMtl*, simply open the *Material Editor* (M). For the purpose of this discussion, we will be using the compact material editor version, as opposed to Slate (Node base). ▶2.2

To apply each V-Ray material, simply select a material slot and object(s) in the scene, followed by clicking on the *Assign Material to Selection* button. ▶2.3

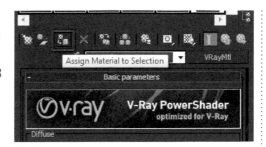

2.3

2.1 Diffuse Group

2.1.1 Diffuse Color

This colour swatch enables users to pick and choose a diffuse colour, by using the *Color Selector* dialogue. ▶2.4

2.4

To access the *Color Selector* dialogue, simply click on its colour swatch and hold down. Once the *Color Selector* dialogue appears, pick a colour or type in a specific value and adjust its *Whiteness* slider. ▶2.5

Alternatively, you can sample colours by selecting the *Sample Screen Color* picker and picking a colour inside or outside 3ds Max. ▶2.6

2.5

2.6

2 Materials and Shaders in V-Ray

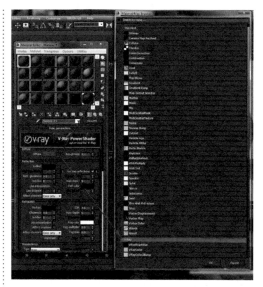

2.7

2.1.2 Diffuse Toggle

The *Diffuse* toggle allows users to apply standard/native and V-Ray procedural maps listed in the *Material Browser* dialog.

The bitmap procedural map is often used to apply textures to the diffuse surface. It's worth noting that reflective surfaces will affect the original diffuse colour and/or its texture. Some of the tutorials in the chapters ahead will show how to counteract this problem. ▶2.7

2.8

2.1.3 Roughness Value

This function determines how coarse a surface appears. ▶2.8

2.9

2.1.4 Roughness Toggle

The toggle enables users to plug textures and other procedural maps from the *Material/Map Browser* list. This toggle works best with greyscale textures/procedural maps. Once a texture is applied, it automatically overrides the numerical values. ▶2.9

3D Photorealistic Rendering

2.2 Reflection Group

2.2.1 Reflect Colour

This colour swatch allows users to pick and choose the Reflect intensity/colour, by using the *Color Selector* dialogue.

The default colour is black, which is equivalent to no reflections. Darker colours yield less reflection, and lighter colours (e.g. white) yield the opposite effect. It's also common for users to set specific colours (e.g. orange/brass colour), when creating metallic surfaces such as brass.

2.2.2 Reflect Toggle

This toggle enables users to set the reflectivity of the surface by plugging textures and other procedural maps from the *Material/Map Browser* list. It works best with greyscale textures. Artists often plug a grey texture into this toggle, to realistically emulate a surface reflecting light unevenly.

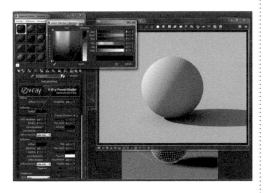

2.10

Once a texture/procedural map is applied to the toggle, it automatically overrides the colour swatch values.

Fresnel reflections: When enabled, the reflections are calculated automatically by the camera/viewing angle of the surface. This function is turned on by default. ▶2.10, 2.11, 2.12 and 2.13

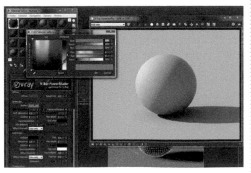

2.11

At times, having the *Reflect* toggle with a greyscale texture, in conjunction with enabling *Fresnel reflections*, can yield appealing results. It's just a matter of trying what works best (e.g. with or without Fresnel turned on).

2.12

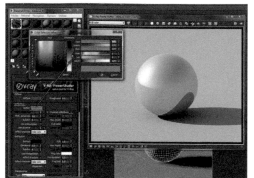

The more contrast the greyscale texture has, the sharper the reflections/glossiness will be. To achieve the opposite effect (e.g. more diffused results), the greyscale texture needs to have less contrast (e.g. more grey than black areas). ▶2.14

2.13

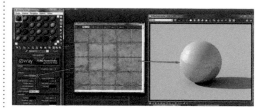

2.14

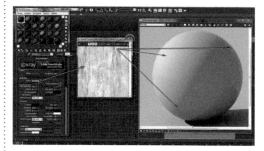

3D Photorealistic Rendering

There are also instances where users might be required to invert the greyscale texture inside the *Reflect* toggle, in order to achieve specific results. To do so, simply go inside the *Reflect map* coordinates and scroll down to the *Output* roll-out. In the *Output* roll-out parameters, enable the *Invert* function. It works in the exact same way as the *Invert* tool in Photoshop (Ctrl+I). ▶2.15

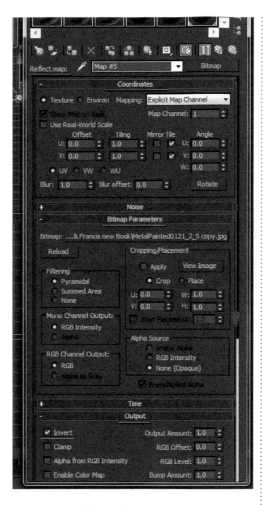

2.15

The *Reflect* toggle texture can also be mixed or blended with its colour swatch to produce specific results. To do so, simply scroll down to the *Maps* roll-out and reduce the *Reflect* toggle's numerical values. ▶2.16

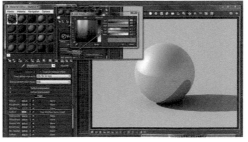

2.16

2.17

It is also common practice for users to apply the Falloff procedural map to help control the Fresnel effects manually. ▶2.17, 2.18, 2.19, 2.20 and 2.21

2.18

2.19

2.2.3 Fresnel IOR

The Fresnel IOR *(Index of Refraction)* function is padlocked with Fresnel reflections, and it's set to 1.6 by default. To manually change this value, simply click on the *L* (padlock) button. ▶2.22

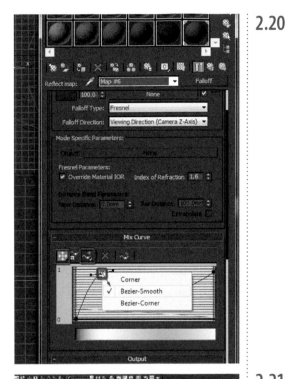

2.20

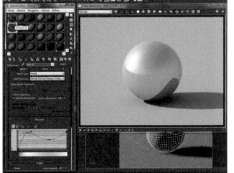

2.21

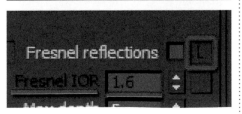

2.22

2.2.4 Hilight Glossiness

This function determines the appearance of glossy highlights. It is padlocked (greyed out) against the *Refl. glossiness* values, by default.

To manually control it, simply uncheck the adjacent padlock. Values range from 0.0 (e.g. diffused large highlights) to 1.0 (e.g. sharp small highlights). The default value is 1.0.

The *Hilight glossiness* values are more visible when the *Fresnel reflections* function is disabled.

2.23

When adjusting the reflectivity and the glossy highlights of a surface, it's always worth enabling the *Background* function in the *Material Editor*. This will provide you with a better material slot/thumbnail preview of its physical properties. ▶2.23

2.2.5 Hilight Glossiness Toggle

This toggle allows users to apply a greyscale texture and/or a procedural to it. Once applied, it automatically overrides its numerical values. ▶2.24

2.24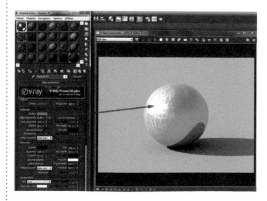

3D Photorealistic Rendering

2.2.6 Refl. Glossiness

This function determines the appearance of the reflections. Values range from 0.0 (e.g. diffused reflections) to 1.0 (e.g. sharp reflections). The default value is 1.0.

It's common practice to constantly refer to the *Material Editor* slot thumbnail, to preview how material parameters are behaving. ▶2.25 and 2.26

2.25

2.26

2.2.7 Refl. Glossiness toggle

The toggle enables users to plug a greyscale texture or/and a procedural map to it. Once applied, it automatically overrides its numerical values.

2.2.8 Subdivs

This function determines the quality of the reflections and glossiness. The default value is 8.

2.27

For surfaces such as plane glass, the default value is often fine. However, other types of reflective surfaces may require users to increase these values to 16 or higher, in order to correct glossy artefacts. Glossy artefacts are more apparent when the *Refl. glossiness* values are low, on a very reflective surface.

2.28

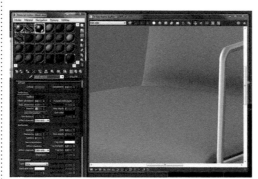

High *Subdivs* results are more noticeable when the *Image sampler (Antialiasing)* parameters are reasonably high. Increasing the *Subdivs* values will subsequently increase the rendering times of the surface slightly. ▶2.27 and 2.28

2.2.9 Use Interpolation

This function enables users to cache and speed up the glossy reflections process. It is disabled by default.

2.2.10 Dim Distance

When enabled, this function restricts the distance of traced rays, by entering the numerical radius. It is disabled by default.

2.2.11 Dim Fall Off

When enabled, this function sets the fall-off radius of Dim distance. It is automatically enabled when the Dim distance is turned on and is greyed out by default.

2.2.12 Affect Channels

This function determines render channels being affected by the reflection. It is set to colour only, by default.

2.2.13 Max Depth

This function sets the number of times a ray can be reflected before it stops and begins using the *Exit* colour. This function is quite useful for scenes with numerous reflections/refractions bouncing off each other. Increasing the *Max depth* value will eradicate any potential black areas in the reflections/refractions. However, it may increase the rendering times.

The *Max depth* value is set to 5 by default.

2.2.14 Exit Colour

This function determines the returning colour, once the *Max depth* value is reached (e.g. 5).

The default colour is black.

2.3 Refraction Group

2.3.1 Refract

The colour of this function controls the opacity of a surface, black (e.g. 0.0) being completely opaque and white (e.g. 255) being fully transparent.

The default colour value is 0.0 (fully opaque). When the *Refract* colour value is 0.0 (black), *VRayMtl* immediately uses the diffuse base colour instead.

2.29

2.3.2 Refract Toggle

The *Refract* toggle allows users to apply textures and/or procedural maps to it. Greyscale and black/white textures work best. ▶2.29 and 2.30

2.30

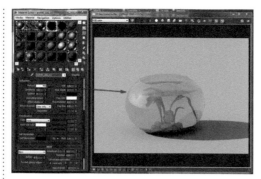

IOR: The IOR determines how light interacts or bends on or through a surface. An IOR value of 1.0 is equal to no refraction. The default value is 1.6. ▶2.31 and 2.32

For a more detailed list of refractive indices, visit the following website:

https://en.wikipedia.org/wiki/List_of_refractive_indices

2.31

2.32

3D Photorealistic Rendering

2.3.3 Glossiness

This function controls the sharpness of refractions. A value of 1.0 yields sharp refractions. A value of 0.0 is equivalent to completely diffused refractions. Users often decrease these values to emulate translucent surfaces. It's worth noting that decreasing these values will subsequently increase the rendering times of this surface. ▶2.33 and 2.34

2.33

2.34

2.3.4 Subdivs

This function controls the quality of the glossiness results. The Subdivs values are more apparent when the glossiness values are reasonably low.

The default value is 8. Increasing this value will subsequently increase the rendering times of the surface. ▶2.35 and 2.36

2.35

2.36

2.3.5   Use Interpolation

When enabled, it caches the rendering process of glossy refractions (similar to caching the irradiance map and/or the light cache). This function is disabled by default.

2.37

2.3.6   Affect Shadows

If turned on, this function allows the light to pass through transparent surfaces (e.g. refractive objects) and cast transparent shadows. The shadow colours may vary depending on the surface. This function is disabled by default. However, most users enable this function on refractive surfaces.
▶2.37 and 2.38

2.38

2.3.7   Max Depth

This function determines the number of times a ray can be refracted before it stops and begins using the *Exit* colour.

The *Max depth* value is set to 5 by default. Increasing it will subsequently increase the rendering times of this surface.

2.3.8 Exit Color

When enabled, this function sets the returning colour of refraction, once the Max depth value is reached (e.g. 5). This function is disabled by default.

2.3.9 Fog Color

This function enables users to change the colour of refractive objects and/or emulate the effect of a more opaque object, depending on its size. Darker colours make refractive objects look more opaque, and lighter colours yield the opposite effect. ▶2.39 and 2.40

2.39

2.3.10 Fog Multiplier

This function determines the density/influence of the fog. The default value is 0.1.

2.3.11 Fog Bias

This function allows users to control what areas of an object may look denser or otherwise. The default value is 0.0.

2.40

2.3.12 Affect Channels

This function allows users to choose the channels to be affected by the refraction in the rendering channels (e.g. alpha and *MultiMatteElement*).

2.41

Professionals often choose the *Color+alpha* option, as it helps to insert the background and other elements behind a refractive/transparent surface. ▶2.41, 2.42 and 2.43

2.3.13 Dispersion

When enabled, it computes the light wavelength dispersion more accurately or photorealistically. However, the rendering times may skyrocket drastically.

The results are more noticeable when used in conjunction with the Abbe function and its value is set to a minimum of 10. Abbe values help

2.42

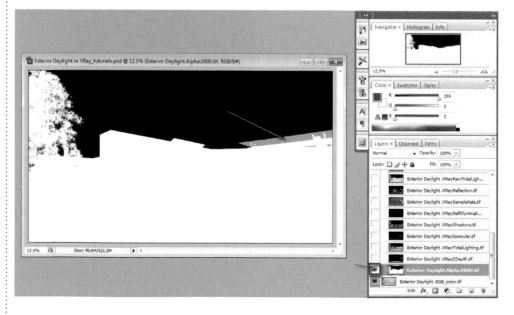

2.43

reinvigorate a spectrum's true light colours, which become apparent on the rim of objects and on caustic effects (if enabled).

This function is disabled by default. ▶2.44

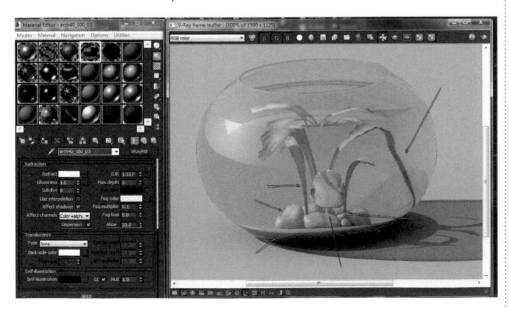

2.44

2.4 Self-Illumination Group

2.4.1 Self-Illumination

This function allows users to choose the self-illumination colour, from its colour swatch, or apply a texture and/or a procedural map to its toggle.

The self-illumination colour swatch is set to black by default.

2.4.2 GI

This function uses the global illumination (GI) settings to light up a scene. Otherwise, it will simply illuminate itself without contributing to the GI. This function is enabled by default.

2.4.3 Multiplier

This function sets the intensity of the self-illumination. The default value is 1.0. ▶2.45

2.45

When using a bitmap/texture in the *Self-illumination* toggle, ensure its colour swatch is black; otherwise the texture will not be visible in the viewport. ▶2.46 and 2.47

2.46

2.47

2.5 Bidirectional Reflectance Distribution Function rollout

The Bidirectional Reflectance Distribution Function (BRDF) parameters control the appearance of the glossy highlights and the reflections on a surface.

There are currently three types of BRDF.

2.48

2.5.1 Phong

This type of BRDF yields a small/sharp glossy highlight.

2.5.2 Blinn

The glossy highlights of this type of BRDF are wider and less sharp. ▶2.48

2.5.3 Ward

This BRDF produces even wider and more metallic glossy highlights. ▶2.49

2.49

2.5.4 Soften

Positive values soften the appearance of glossy highlights, from darker to brighter areas. The default value is 0.0.

2.5.5 Fix Dark Glossy Edges

Reflective objects at times generate dark glossy edges on their rims, especially spherical objects. Enabling this function corrects such artefacts. This function is disabled by default.

2.5.6 Anisotropy

This function dictates the direction of the glossy highlights. Users can also apply greyscale texture and/or a procedural map to its toggle. The default value is 0.0. ▶2.50

2.50

2.5.7 Rotation

This allows users to manually set the direction (in degrees) of the reflections and highlights.

Users can apply a greyscale texture and/or a procedural map in the *Rotation* toggle. The default value is 0.0. ▶2.51 and 2.52

2.51

2.52

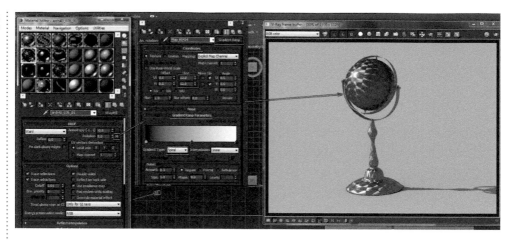

2.53

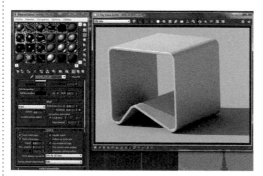

2.6 Options Roll-Out

2.6.1 Trace Reflections

This function enables reflections to be traced, when a surface is reflective. If reflections are not contributing much to a surface, this function can be disabled, to speed the rendering times. This function is enabled by default.

2.54

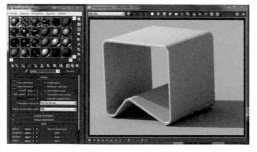

2.6.2 Trace Refractions

This allows refractions to be traced when a surface is reflective/refractive. In addition, if refractions are not contributing much to a surface, this function can be disabled, to speed the rendering times of the surface. Trace refractions are enabled by default.
▶2.53 and 2.54

2.6.3 Cutoff

This function sets the trace limit of reflections and refractions. High values reduce the tracing time (with a risk of artefacts), and low values increase the rendering times drastically (with more accuracy).

The default value is 0.01

2.6.4 Double-Sided

This function is quite useful to correct surfaces with one side or surfaces that require some of its faces' normals to be flipped (e.g. black/dark). Enabled by default.

2.6.5 Use Irradiance Map

This function uses the irradiance map computation to calculate its surface, if enabled in the GI render settings.

Otherwise it will automatically use the brute force (more accurate), if the GI is turned on. Enabled by default.

2.55

2.7 Maps Roll-Out

Most map toggles displayed under this roll-out are directly connected to the textures/procedural maps being used in the V-Ray basic parameters. ▶2.55

The toggles being used have a capital letter *M* in them, and the toggles not being used are empty (e.g. blank).

Increase or decrease the contribution of each toggle being used (in percentages) by typing in a value or using its adjacent spinner. The default value of each toggle is 100%.

2.56

In addition, it is possible to completely disable a toggle being used by simply disabling its adjacent tick box. When such happens, the toggle with the capital *M* will automatically become lowercase (e.g. *m*). ▶2.56

2.57

2.7.1 Bump

This function allows users to apply a texture and/or a procedural map to its toggle. It works best with greyscale and/or black and white bitmaps. ▶2.57 and 2.58

2.58

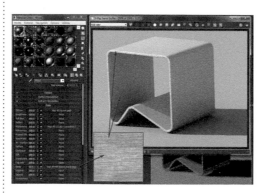

2.7.2 Displace

This function physically modifies a geometry according to its mapping coordinates. For accurate results, users are recommended to have a detailed geometry (many segments).

Users can apply a texture and/or a procedural map to its toggle. In addition, it works best with greyscale and/or black and white bitmaps.

Note that this type of displacement is very time-consuming to render. ▶2.59

2.59

2

2.60

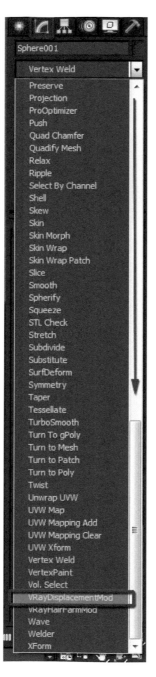

For relatively fast results, professionals tend to use the *VRayDisplacementMod* instead. When using this modifier, the *Displace* toggle needs to be disabled.

This V-Ray modifier can be accessed from the *Modify* list. ▶**2.60**

In addition, the 2D mapping (landscape) option is the fastest to render of the three types. To apply a greyscale texture or/and a procedural map, simply use the *Texmap* toggle. ▶**2.61**

To edit the texture and/or the procedural map, simply drag and drop it into the *Displace* toggle and to choose to instance it.

In addition, ensure that the *Displace* toggle is disabled to prevent double displacement. Following that, enable the *Show Shaded Material in Viewport* button inside the *Displacement* toggle. ▶**2.62** and **2.63**

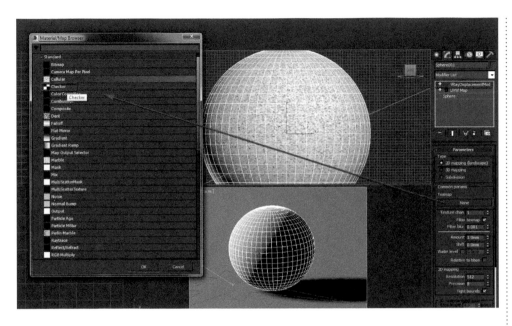

2.61

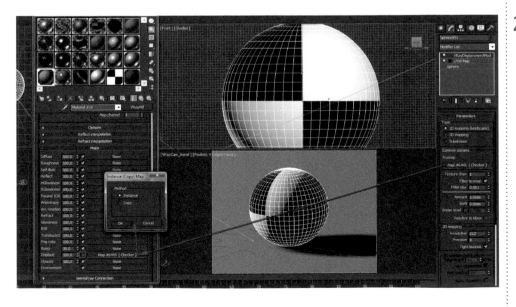

2.62

2.63

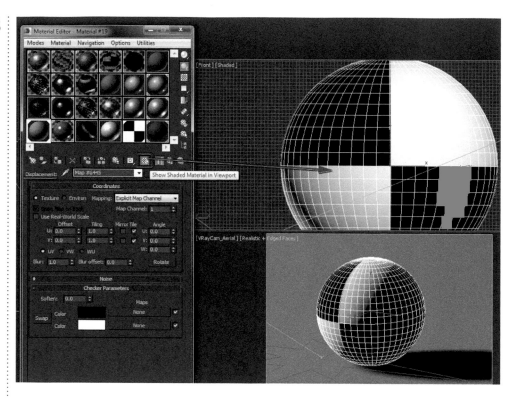

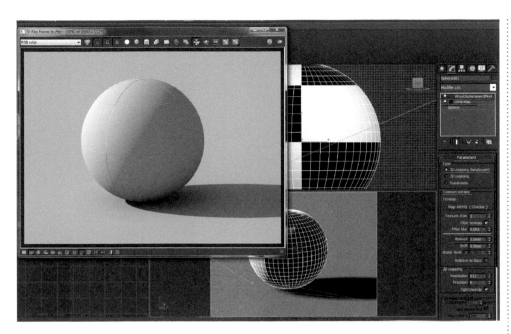

2.64

Furthermore, when using the *VRayDisplacementMod* modifier, the texture/procedural map parameters should always be kept at 1.0 in the Material Editor.

2.65

All texture/procedural map changes such as tiling should occur at the *Modify* level only (e.g. with UVW Mapping and MapScaler). ▶**2.64** and **2.65**

2.7.3 Opacity

This function only works when textures and/or procedural maps are applied to its toggle.

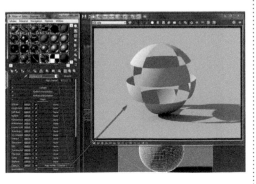

2.66

For best results, use greyscale and/or black and white textures/procedural maps. ▶**2.66**

2.8 More V-Ray Shaders and Procedural Maps

While V-Ray has a host of shaders and procedural maps, the following discussion will focus mainly on those most commonly used by artists and industry professionals.

2.67

2.68

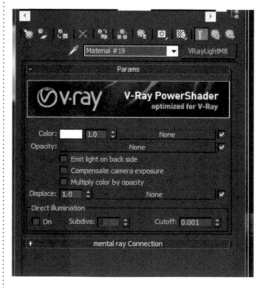

2.9 VRayLightMtl

This shader is primarily used to add self-illumination to objects. It can easily be accessed through the *Material/Map Browser* dialogue, under the *V-Ray* roll-out list. ▶2.67 and 2.68

VRayLightMtl works in exact same way as the V-Ray self-illumination function. In addition, it comes with features given below.

2.9.1 Opacity

This function allows users to apply textures and/or procedural maps to its toggle. As with most opacity toggles, it works best when a greyscale and/or black and white texture/procedural map is used.

2.9.2 Emit Light on Back Side

This function allows the light to be emitted from a side of an object that isn't emitting light. This function is disabled by default.

2.9.3 Compensate Camera Exposure

This function is quite useful for scenes where the exposure controls are causing the self-illumination to be slightly dimmed. Turning this function on will essentially make the self-illumination more visible, by compensating for the exposure. This function is disabled by default.

2.9.4 Multiply Color by Opacity

When turned on, this function increases the colour of the light material, based on the texture/procedural map applied to the *Opacity* toggle. This function is disabled by default.

2.9.5 Displace

This function is enabled when users apply a texture/procedural map to it.

2.69

2.9.6 Direct Illumination

When turned on, it emits light in the same manner as a V-Ray mesh light. As such, it can be time-consuming to render.

To achieve smooth/grainless results, the *Subdivs* value needs to be very high. ▶2.69

2.70

2.10 VRayMtlWrapper

This shader only works if the GI and/or the caustics are enabled in the rendering parameters. It's mainly used to allow certain materials to receive or generate GI and caustics. To access it, simply select an existing material slot and click on the main shader toggle, followed by choosing the *VRayMtlWrapper* shader from the Material/Map Browser list. ▶2.70

2.71

2.72

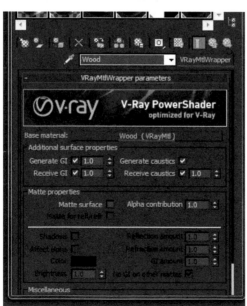

The *Replace Material* dialogue should appear. Choose the option 'Keep old material as sub-material?'. ▶2.71

Its parameters should load up automatically. ▶2.72

2.10.1 Base Material

The sub-material is kept in this toggle.

2.10.2 Generate GI

This function enables users to increase or decrease the quantity of GI being generated by the base material.

2.10.3 Receive GI

This function allows users to increase or decrease the amount of GI being received by the base material. Its value is set to 1.0, by default. This feature is widely used to make shadows/indirectly lit areas darker or brighter. ▶2.73 and 2.74

2.10.4 Generate Caustics

When turned on, it allows caustics to be generated. This option is enabled by default.

2.10.5 Receive Caustics

Users can increase or decrease the amount of caustics being received by the object. Its value is set to 1.0 by default.

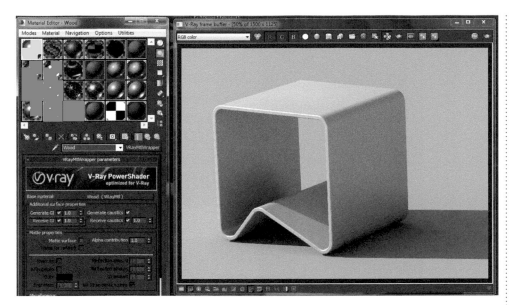

2.73

2.74

2 Materials and Shaders in V-Ray

2.75

2.76

2.77

2.11 VRayOverrideMtl

This shader is mostly used as an override to correct GI 'colour bleeding' artefacts, reflections, refractions and shadows.

It can easily be accessed by clicking on the main shader toggle, followed by choosing *VRayOverrideMtl* from the *Material/Map Browser* dialogue.

Following that, in the *Replace Material* dialogue, choose 'Keep old material as sub-material?'.

The *VRayOverrideMtl* should load up automatically thereafter. ▶2.75, 2.76 and 2.77

2.11.1 Base Material

This is the toggle where the base sub-material can be found.

2.11.2 GI

The toggle allows users to apply a material to be used as a new source of GI reflectance. This toggle is very useful to override the effects of GI colour bleeding on nearby objects.

2.11.3 Reflect Mtl

This function can be used to override its material appearance, when 'seen' on other reflective objects.

2.11.4 Refract Mtl

This toggle works in a similar way to *Reflect mtl*. It can be used to change how its refractions are seen by other reflective surfaces.

2.11.5 Shadow Mtl

This toggle allows users to override the shadow appearance when cast onto its surface.

The examples below depict how colour bleeding and reflection colours were easily changed/corrected, by simply applying different shaders (white floor [*VRayMtl*]) in both the *GI* and *Reflect mtl* toggles. ▶2.78, 2.79, 2.80 and 2.81

2.78

2.79

2.80

2.12 VRay2SidedMtl

This material is mostly used to emulate translucent objects. Its properties are more apparent when there's a strong light hitting its surface internally and/or externally.

To access this shader, simply click on the main *VRayMtl* toggle and choose the *VRay2SidedMtl* shader from the *Material/Map Browser* list.

Following that, choose to keep old material as sub-material in the *Replace Material* dialogue. ▶2.82, 2.83 and 2.84

2.81

2.12.1 Front

This toggle allows users to set up the front material surface. The effect is often more opaque and (preferably) with a slight difference in colour.

2.82

2.12.2 Back Material

The material for this toggle is frequently set up to be less opaque (e.g. more refractive/transparent) and with a slight difference in colour (generally a light yellowish colour).

In addition, being a more refractive material, users normally enable *Affect shadows*.

2.12.3 Translucency

This function allows users to control the transition between the two surfaces (front and back material) with the *Color Selector* or a procedural map through its toggle. If the toggle is being used, the numerical values allow users to blend the toggle content, with the colour selector values. ▶2.85

2.83

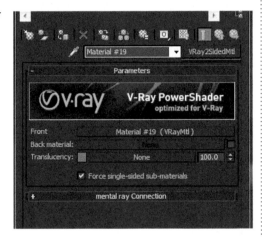

2.84

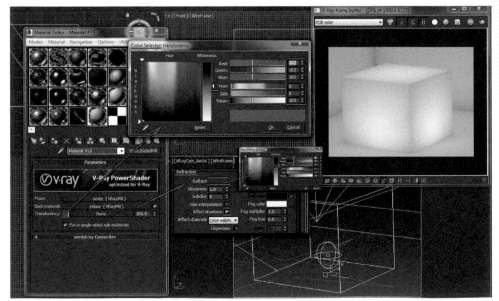

2.85

2.86

2.87

2.88

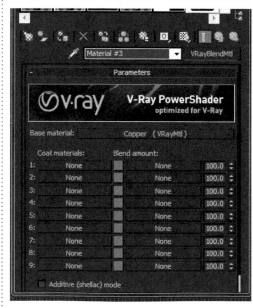

2.13 VRayBlendMtl

This shader is very useful for creating unique and exquisite materials by blending multiple shaders together. Materials can be blended through a toggle or the *Color Selector* dialogue.

To load it, simply click on the main shader toggle and pick *the VRayBlendMtl* from the *Material/Map Browser* dialogue list. Choose to keep old material as sub-material in the *Replace Material* dialogue. ▶2.86, 2.87 and 2.88

2.13.1 Base Material

This toggle is used as the base sub-material.

2.13.2 Coat Materials

This function has nine listed toggles, which can be used to mix shaders with the blend amount.

2.13.3 Blend Amount

This function consists of nine listed toggles, with colour swatches and numerical values to set the blend amount. The adjacent numerical values only work as a blending amount when there's a procedural map/texture inside the toggle. ▶2.89, 2.90 and 2.91

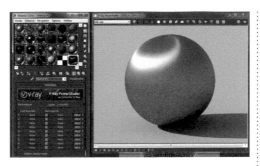

2.89

2.14 VRayCarPaintMtl

As the name suggests, this shader emulates the physical properties of a metallic car paint finish.

Depending on the System Unit Setup being used, a UVW Map modifier might be required in order for the flake layer to be visible.

2.90

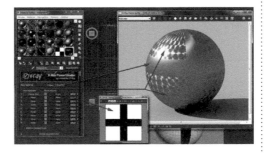

2.91

2.92

To access it, simply click on the main shader toggle and choose the *VRayCarPaintMtl* from the *Material/Map Browser* dialogue. The shader should load up automatically. ▶2.92 and 2.93

2.93

Material #3 ▾ VRayCarPaintMtl

Base layer parameters

base color.......................................
base reflection................................ 0.5
base glossiness............................... 0.6
base trace reflections.......................✓

Flake layer parameters

flake color......................................
flake glossiness............................... 0.8
flake orientation.............................. 0.3
flake density.................................... 0.5
flake scale....................................... 0.01
flake size... 0.5
flake seed....................................... 1
flake filtering................ Directional
flake map size................................. 1024
flake mapping type....... Explicit UVW channel
flake map channel.......................... 1
flake trace reflections......................✓

Coat layer parameters

coat color.......................................
coat strength.................................. 0.05
coat glossiness................................ 1.0
coat trace reflections.......................✓

2.14.1 Base Color

This function determines the main colour of *VRayCarPaintMtl*. ▶2.94 and 2.95

2.14.2 Base Reflection

This function controls the amount of reflectivity, with its numerical values. The default value is 0.5. ▶2.96 and 2.97

2.94

2.95

2.96

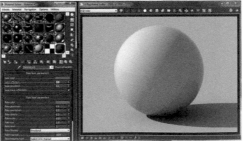

2.97

2.98

2.14.3 Base Glossiness

This function's numerical values determine the amount of glossiness on the surface. The default value is 0.6. ▶2.98 and 2.99

2.14.4 Base Trace Reflections

If enabled, this option allows the reflections to be traced. This option is enabled by default. ▶2.100 and 2.101

2.99

2.14.5 Flake Color

This colour swatch enables users to choose the flake colour, through the *Color Selector* dialogue. The default colour is blue.

2.14.6 Flake Glossiness

2.100

Its numerical values allow the users to control the amount of glossiness on the flake. The default value is 0.8.

2.14.7 Flake Orientation

2.101

This function's numerical values control the orientation of the flake. This option is widely used to randomize the flake rotation. The default value is 0.3.

2.14.8 Flake Density

This function controls the density/number of flakes seen on the surface. The default value is 0.5.

2.14.9 Flake Scale

This option controls the structure of the flakes. The default value is 0.001.
▶2.102 and 2.103

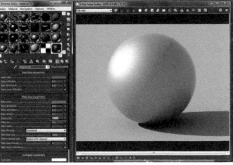

2.102

2.103

2.14.10 Flake Size

This function determines the distance and size of the flakes. The default value is 0.5.

2.14.11 Flake Seed

This option enables users to change the flake pattern. The default value is 1.

2.14.12 Maps

Users can plug procedural maps into the list of toggles seen under the *Maps* roll-out. The procedural maps can be used at 100% value, or blended, by reducing the numerical values.

2.15 VRayEdgesTex

This procedural map is widely used on top of a material or colour, to create edges/wirelines around the surface. It can be applied through the *Diffuse* toggle, or as a render element, to be composed in post-production.

However, it can also be used to emulate chamfered edges on the corners and edges of surfaces, through the *Bump* toggle.

2.104

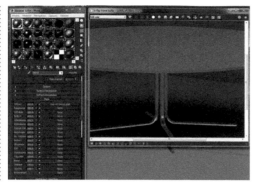

The render below depicts the edge/ corner of a round tabletop, prior to using the *VRayEdgesTex* in its *Bump* toggle. ▶2.104

To add the *VRayEdgesTex* procedural map to the *Bump* toggle, simply scroll down to the *Maps* roll-out and click on the *Bump* toggle.

2.105

The *Material/Map Browser* dialogue should be prompted; under the *V-Ray* roll-out, choose the *VRayEdgesTex* from its list. ▶2.105

2.106

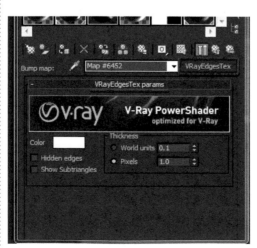

The *VRayEdgesTex* procedural map parameters should load. By default, its thickness is set to pixels. ▶2.106

3D Photorealistic Rendering

To emulate a chamfered edge, it's recommended that the thickness be set to world units instead. Set the appropriate *World units* value depending on the size of the object in question or the scenes' *Unit Setup*. Note that the appropriate *World units* value can be quickly found through quick region renders. ▶2.107

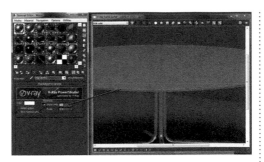

2.107

Alternatively, it is possible to use the *Mix* procedural map in the *Bump* toggle to blend the *VRayEdgesTex* with another texture or procedural map. ▶2.108 and 2.109

2.108

2.109

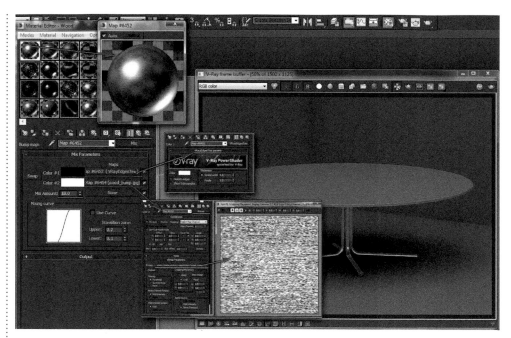

Conclusion

This chapter has introduced users to some of the most popular industry standard V-Ray shaders and procedural maps, followed by guiding them through the process of accessing and using these features. Some of the shaders and procedural map options were discussed in more detail than others, according to their relevance. Other procedural maps are introduced and discussed later, throughout the tutorials ahead.

For more detailed information about the shaders and procedural maps discussed here, as well as others, visit the official V-Ray website:

http://docs.chaosgroup.com/

3

Cameras and Lighting in V-Ray

The following discussion will focus on both V-Ray camera parameters and lights, as the two often go hand in hand.

As mentioned earlier, prior to being able to access any of the V-Ray tools and parameters, the V-Ray renderer needs to be loaded in the 3D scene first.

3 Cameras and Lighting in V-Ray

3.1

3.1 Cameras: VRayPhysicalCamera

This type of camera is the most popular of the two, and it emulates the physical properties of a real camera. To create a VRayPhysicalCamera, go to the *Create* command panel and click on the *Cameras* button. Under the *Cameras* group, select the *Standard* menu and choose *VRay* from its list. ▶3.1

3.2

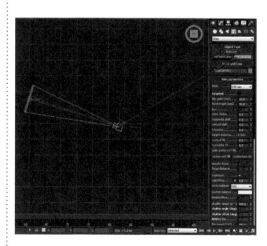

In the *VRay Object Type* group, enable the *VRayPhysicalCamera* and select its target on the top viewport by dragging the cursor across the screen to create the camera target. After creating the camera, right-click to exit and then go to the *Modify* command panel. ▶3.2 and 3.3

Type

This camera function allows users to choose from the following three types of cameras:

Still camera: This camera comes with a host of typical parameters to emulate a still photo camera. The default shutter speed is set to 200.0.

Cinematic camera: This camera type emulates a cinematic camera and comes with similar parameters to a still camera; the default shutter angle is set to 180.0.

Video camera: This type of camera emulates a charge-coupled device (CCD) video camera without shutter speed.

Targeted

When enabled, this function adds a target to the physical camera. The target can be moved by the user to set the camera direction. To move the camera itself, either select both the camera and its target or simply disable the *Targeted* function. This function is enabled by default.

Film Gate (mm)

This function determines the horizontal size of the film gate, in millimetres. Note that the values displayed here are directly connected to the *Units Setup* dialogue. High values have the effect of a camera zooming out, and lower values have the opposite effect. The default value is 36.0.

3.3

Focal Length (mm)

This function emulates the focal length of a real camera lens. High values have the effect of a camera zooming in, and lower values have the opposite effect. The default value is 40.0.

FOV

The fov (field of view) function is an alternative to using the *film gate* and *focal length* functions. This function is disabled by default.

Zoom Factor

This function allows the camera to zoom in and out of the scene. The default value is 1.0.

Horizontal Shift

This function offsets (shifts) the field of view horizontally. High values shift the camera to the right, and low values shift the camera in the opposite direction. The default value is 0.0.

3.4

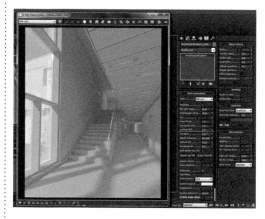

Vertical Shift

It enables users to offset (shift) the camera field of view vertically. High values shift the camera to the right; and low values shift the camera in the opposite direction. The default value is 0.0. ▶3.4 and 3.5

3.5

3D Photorealistic Rendering

F-Number

This function is often used to increase or decrease the render brightness, when the exposure function is turned on. High values decrease the render brightness, and low values yield the opposite result. The default value is 8.0. ▶3.6, 3.7 and 3.8

Target Distance

This function sets the distance of the target camera.

3.6

3.7

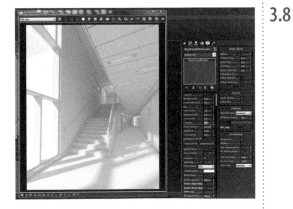

3.8

3.9

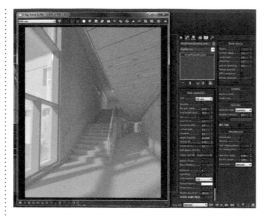

Vertical Tilt

This function is mostly used to correct the verticals of distorted cameras. The default value is 0.0.
►3.9 and 3.10

Horizontal Tilt

This function allows users to correct the camera distortion tilt horizontally. The default value is 0.0.

3.10

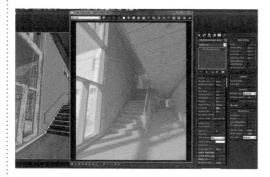

Auto Guess Vert Tilt

When turned on, it maintains the vertical tilt values (if used for tilt correction), when the camera is animated. This function is disabled by default.

Guess Vert Tilt

When this button is clicked, the program tries to automatically correct/guess the camera distortion tilt vertically.

Guess Horiz Tilt

When this button is clicked, the program tries to automatically correct/guess the camera distortion tilt horizontally.

Specify Focus

If enabled, this function uses the focus distance values to specify a different distance value from the camera target.

Focus Distance

Its function value sets a new camera distance (if the specify focus is enabled). The default value is 0.2 m.

Exposure

When turned on, it controls the overall brightness of the render, in conjunction with other functions such as *f-number*, *film speed (ISO)* and *shutter speed*. This function is enabled by default. ▶3.11 and 3.12

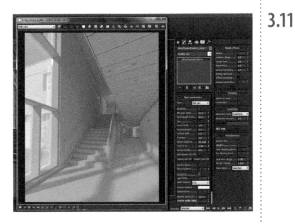

3.11

3.12

3.13

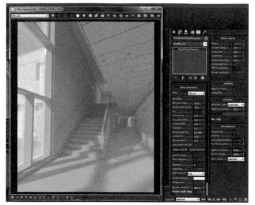

Vignetting

When enabled, this function creates a slightly more contrasting image by darkening the four corners of the render. This real camera effect is known as *vignetting*. This function is enabled by default. ▶3.13, 3.14 and 3.15

3.14

White Balance

As the name suggests, its parameters control the colours that will appear white or whiter in the scene render. It's widely used to balance out overpowering colours in the scene.

In its pull-down menu, there are the following presets: *Custom, Neutral, Daylight, D75, D65, D55, D50* and *Temperature*. The default preset is D65. ▶3.16 and 3.17

3.15

Custom Balance

This colour swatch allows users to pick or sample a custom colour from the *Color Selector* dialogue. The colour displayed here will appear more white in the render. The default colour is bluish.

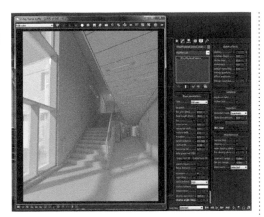

Temperature

This option becomes live when the *Temperature* preset is chosen from the *White Balance* drop-down menu. It allows users to type in a numerical colour temperature value, if selected. For information about colour temperature values, conduct an Internet search on the term 'Kelvin colour chart'.

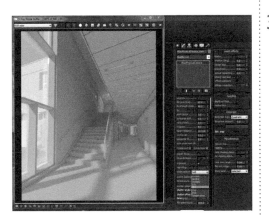

Shutter Speed

This function controls the overall exposure time of the camera. Lower numerical values yield brighter results, and higher values have the opposite effect. The default value is 200.0. ▶3.18 and 3.19

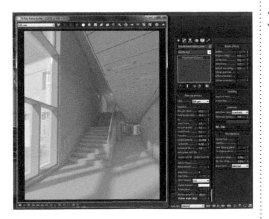

3.19

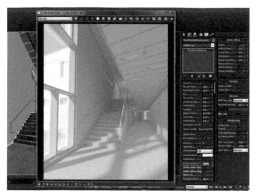

Shutter Angle (deg)
This option determines the shutter angle of the camera, in degrees. It is disabled by default. It becomes live (180.0) when the camera type is set to *Movie Cam*.

Shutter Offset (deg)
This option becomes live simultaneously with the shutter angle, when the camera type is set to *Movie Cam*. Its numerical values determine the shutter offset of the movie camera type.

Latency(s)
This function is only available when the camera type is set to *Video Cam*. It controls the CCD latency of a video camera. The default value is 0.0.

Film Speed (ISO)
This setting controls the camera sensitivity. Lower values darken the image/render, and higher values produce the opposite result. The default value is 200.0.

3.2 Depth of Field, Bokeh Effects, Sampling and Distortion

In a real production environment, depth of field (DOF), Bokeh effects, motion blur, etc. are often applied in post-production.

This post-production technique is discussed in Chapter 5 because these effects are extremely time-consuming to fine-tune/render in 3ds Max, especially when there are quick changes to be addressed.

3D Photorealistic Rendering

3.2.1 Miscellaneous

Horizon Line

When turned on, it draws the exact position of the horizon line in the camera viewport. This tool is quite useful for matching camera views in photomontages or verified views. ▶3.20

3.20

Clipping

When enabled, this option allows the selected camera to clip/slice objects within a specified distance, using the *Near Clipping Plane* and *Far Clipping Plane* options.

The *Clipping* option is widely used in tight/close shots, where objects such as doors and walls are obstructing the camera composition.

Near Clipping Plane

This function controls where the nearest clipping plane from the camera starts.

Far Clipping Plane

This option determines where the farthest clipping plane from the camera starts. ▶3.21 and 3.22

3.21

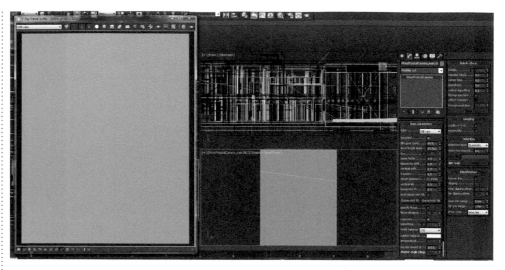

3.22

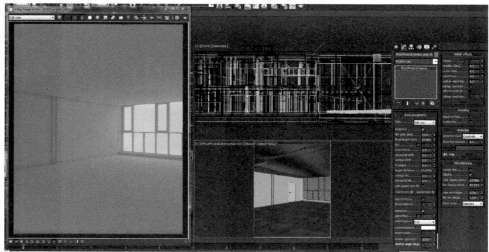

3.3 Lighting in V-Ray

In the discussion that follows we introduce some of the most popular V-Ray lights and take users through the process of using them to light up a scene.

Note that it is common practice to copy/instance lights whenever possible. Instanced lights take substantially less time to render than otherwise.

3.3.1 VRayLight

To create a VRayLight, go to the *Create* command panel and click on the *Lights* button.

Under the *Lights* group, select the *Photometric* menu and choose *VRay* from its drop-down list. ▶3.23

In the *VRay Object Type* group, click on the *VRayLight* button, followed by selecting its target on the top viewport and dragging the cursor across the screen to create the VRayLight object.

3.23

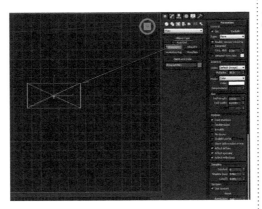

3.24

After the VRayLight object is created, right-click to exit. Go to the *Modify* command panel to see its parameters. ▶3.24 and 3.25

3.25

3.3.2 Plane Light

On

This function allows the light to be turned on or off. It is enabled by default.

Exclude

This toggle allows users to include or exclude scene objects that are being affected by this light. The left and right arrows in the middle allow users to add or remove listed scene objects. To add objects, simply select them from the *Scene Objects* list and click on the button with an arrow pointing towards the right. To remove objects, select them from the *Include* or *Exclude* list, followed by clicking on the button with an arrow pointing towards the left.

By default, the dialogue is set to exclude both illumination and shadow casting.
►3.26

3.26▼

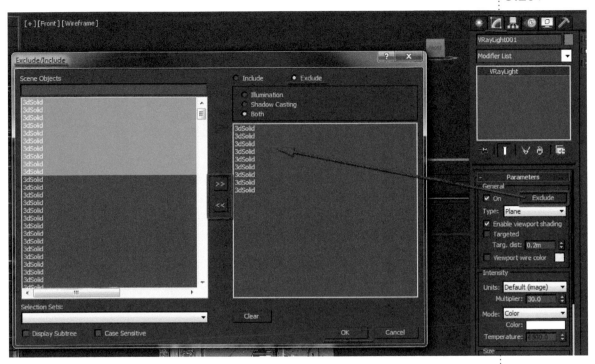

3.27

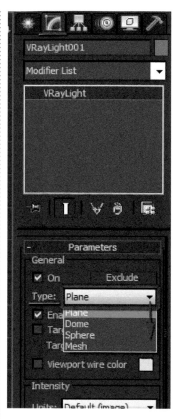

Type
This function allows users to pick from the types of light available: *Plane, Dome, Sphere* and *Mesh*. ▶3.27

Enable Viewport Shading
When turned on, the light effects will be seen in the shaded viewport (not wireframe). This option is enabled by default.

Targeted
When enabled, this feature automatically creates a target direction of the light (only seen in the viewport). The light target helps the user to see and change the direction of the light, if required.

3.3.3 Intensity

This group allows users to control the light intensity through its units or/and multiplier.

3.28

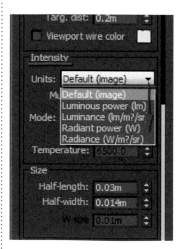

Units
This function menu allows users to choose from a list of well-known light units, to light the scene. ▶3.28

Default (Image)
This intensity unit is based on the colour mode and the multiplier value (30.0 by default). The overall intensity is also dependent on the physical scale/size of the light object.

Luminous Power (lm)
It determines the light power in lumens. This unit acts independently from the physical size of the light object.

Luminance (lm/m²/sr)
This intensity is measured in lumens in square metres per steradian.

Radiant Power (W)
This numerical intensity unit is measured in watts. This unit acts independently from the physical size of the light object.

Radiance (W/m²/sr)
This unit of intensity is measured in watts in square meters per steradian. The overall intensity of this unit is dependent on the physical scale/size of the light object.

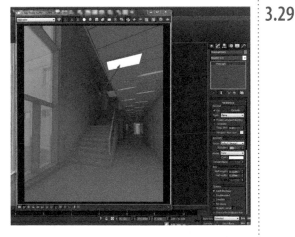

3.29

Multiplier
The default numerical value is based on the type of units chosen.
▶3.29 and 3.30

Mode
This unit determines the colour of the light source.

3.30

Color

This mode allows users to click on the colour swatch to choose or sample a colour from the *Color Selector* dialogue box.

3.31

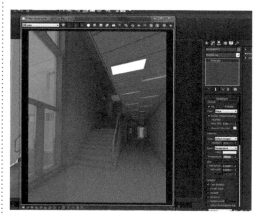

Temperature

If this mode is chosen, users are able to type in a colour temperature value. For information about colour temperature values, conduct an Internet search on the term 'Kelvin colour chart'. ▶3.31 and 3.32

Size

This group is enabled if the light type is *plane*.

3.32

Half-length

This value determines the length of the physical light object.

Half-width

This value controls the width of the physical light object.

The bigger the light size, the softer the shadows will be. This feature is coherent with most V-Ray lights.

Note that plane lights can be scaled independently with the *Select and Uniform Scale* toolbar without affecting the size of other instanced lights in the scene. As mentioned earlier, instanced lights are substantially quicker to render than copies of lights. ▶3.33

3.33

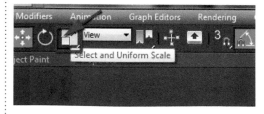

3.3.4 Options

Cast Shadows

If turned on, this function enables the light to cast shadows. This option is enabled by default.

Double-sided

If enabled, this function allows both sides of the plane light to cast light and shadows (if turned on). This option is disabled by default.

▶3.34 and 3.35

3.34

3.35

3.36

Invisible

This function allows the light object to be invisible in the render. This option is disabled by default. ▶3.36 and 3.37

3.37

3.38

No Decay

When turned on, this function allows the light to travel infinitely, without decaying or dimming, from its emitter/source. ▶3.38 and 3.39

Skylight Portal

When on, this function uses the environment intensity to cast light and shadows. This function is disabled by default.

Simple

It livens up when the *Skylight portal* option is enabled. When on, it computes the sky portal lighting much quicker.

Store with Irradiance Map

When enabled, this function caches the light effects and stores them in the irradiance map (if enabled). While this process saves pre-calculation time, the shadows will be less accurate.

3.39

This option is widely used to correct light artefacts from dome or V-Ray mesh light (e.g. graininess and/or splotches). It is disabled by default.

Affect Diffuse

This function allows this light source to affect the diffuse object. It is enabled by default.

Affect Specular

This function enables this light source to affect the specular of objects. It is enabled by default.

This option is often turned off when the light type is dome. It helps to reduce noise artefacts on glossy objects caused by the dome light.

Affect Reflections

This option allows the light object/shape to be visible on reflections. It is enabled by default.

3.40

3.3.5 Sampling

Subdivs

Increasing the value of this function will eradicate any graininess caused by low subdivisions. When using the V-Ray mesh light, the subdivision values need to be very high. High values increase the rendering times drastically.

Before resorting to increasing the values of this function, ensure that the *Probabilistic Lights* function is turned off (in the *V-Ray Global Switches* roll-out), that the image sampler is high and that the reflection subdivisions of the surface are tweaked. ▶3.40

Shadow Bias

This function controls the position of the shadows. Low values are close to objects, and high values detach the shadow from the objects. The default value is 0.0.

Values higher than 5 mm may result in shadow artefacts. This problem is consistent with all types of V-Ray lights.

3.3.6 Texture

Use Texture

This option allows users to apply a texture to the *Use texture* toggle.

Once a texture has been applied to this toggle, it can be edited by simply dragging and dropping it into a Material Editor slot. Choose the *Instance* option from the *Instance (Copy) Map* dialogue box. ▶3.41

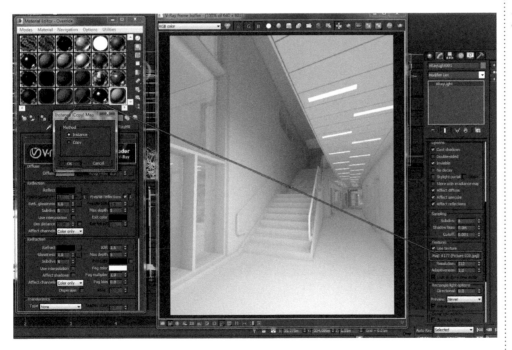

3.41

In the bitmap coordinates, set the mapping type to *Spherical Environment*. Move or rotate the texture with the *Offset* and *Angle* values, if necessary.

Ensure the *Blur* value is set to about 50.0 or higher. Otherwise the texture pattern will be visible on other surfaces, as opposed to its colour hues only. In addition, the *Cropping/Placement* tools can be used to focus on specific areas of an image.

Finally, to have the texture colours more prominent in the render, increase the *Output RGB Level* values and decrease the light's *Multiplier* values. ▶3.42

▼3.42

Vray Sphere Light

This type of light becomes spherical, when chosen. The light is emitted from all sides (spherically). The intensity is based on the size of the sphere's radius and its multiplier value. A bigger sphere radius results in softer shadows. ▶3.43

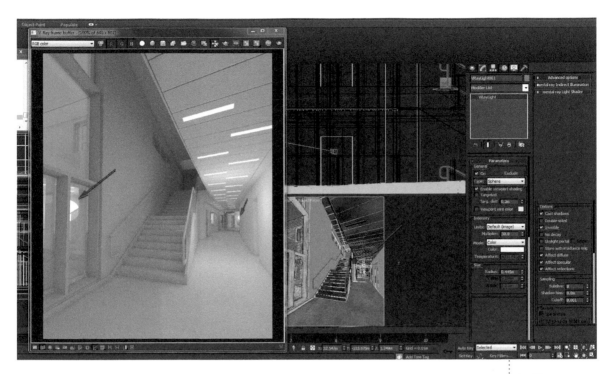

3.43▲

V-Ray Mesh Light

When a mesh light type is chosen, the *Mesh light options* group becomes available.

The *Pick mesh* toggle allows users to pick any mesh/geometry in the scene to be used as a light emitter. Once the mesh/geometry is picked, it is automatically transformed into a physical light source (if the *Replace mesh with light* option is enabled).

3.44

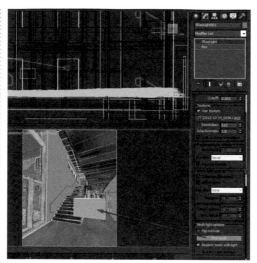

In addition, a VRayLight modifier is automatically added onto the *Modify* stack. ▶3.44 and 3.45

Rendering a scene lit with a mesh light can be extremely time-consuming to render, and it often yields grainy results. Users enable the *Store with irradiance* map function to smooth out the grain and decrease the rendering times. However, this option produces inaccurate shadows. High subdivision values (from the *Sampling* group) is the most accurate method for eradicating the grain caused by the mesh light.

▼3.45

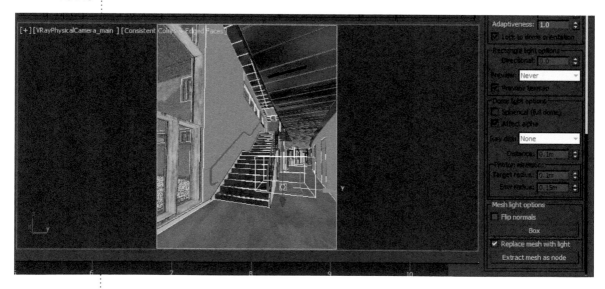

Extract Mesh as Node

This option allows users to extract the original mesh from the mesh light by clicking on its button. ▶3.46

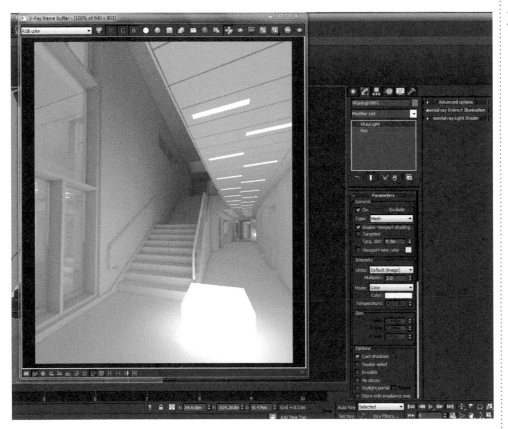

3.46

Dome Light

When chosen, it emulates the effect of an external diffused environment light in the scene. Note that VRaySky has a similar effect. For this reason, when the dome light is chosen the environment light is doubled up, if the VRaySky is being used.

3.47

Spherical Dome

If this option is enabled, the environment light rays are emitted spherically, as opposed to a hemisphere (default).

Ray Dist

This option allows users to specify the maximum distance that V-Ray will trace the shadows to. The distance is set to *None* by default.

Emit Radius

This function sets the radius of the photon emission (seen as a circle in the viewport). It is common practice for users to increase it enough to encapsulate the area seen by the camera. ▶3.47

The *VRayHDRI* procedural map can be applied to the *Texture* toggle.

High dynamic range is a technique to create images that have greater dynamic range of luminosity than normal images. High dynamic range images (HDRIs) are so powerful that they can be used to realistically illuminate 3D scenes. ▶3.48, 3.49 and 3.50

When lighting a scene with an HDRI, it's recommended that users disable the VRaySky in the *Environment Map* toggle (8).

VRaySky has a similar dynamic range as an HDRI map. In addition, the dome light multiplier should be set to 1.0, to prevent overexposure of the scene. In the *Mapping* group, change its type to *Spherical* and change its horizontal rotation, to ensure direct shadows are cast in the direction of the glazed windows in the scene.

Vert. rotation allows users to move the HDRI coordinates vertically.

3.48

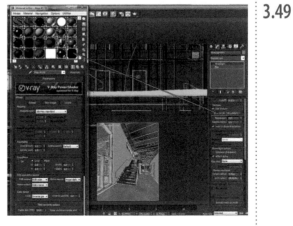

3.49

3.50

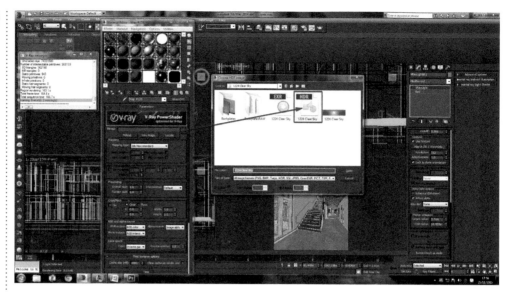

HDRI maps only cast direct shadows if the image is sharp as opposed to blurred (for diffused HDRI shadows). To cast direct shadows, the HDRI needs to have a very bright spot (for a sunlit exterior HDRI) or many bright spots (for an HDRI of an interior scene). ▶3.51 and 3.52

3.51

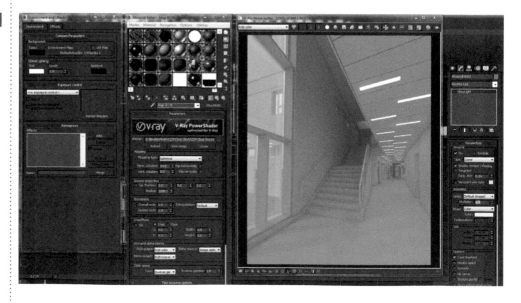

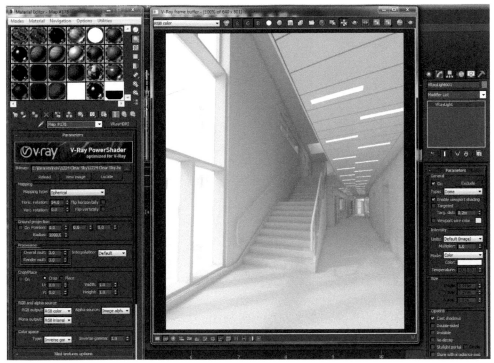

3.3.7 *VRayIES*

To create a VRayIES light, use some of the steps described earlier, followed by selecting the *VRayIES* button, clicking the target cursor on the *Front/Left* viewport and dragging it down to create the VRayIES light facing downwards.

Right-click to exit light creation mode. ▶3.53

3.53

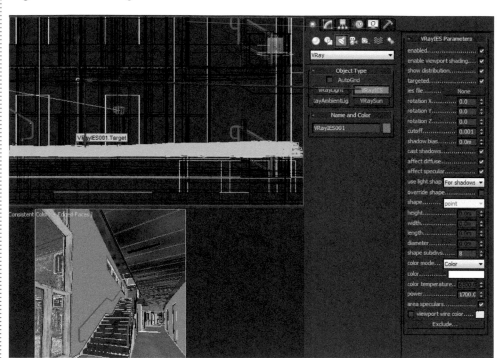

Once the VRayIES light has been created (with its target facing downwards), users often disable the *Targeted* function in order to be able to move the VRayIES light and its target simultaneously.

Most of the VRayIES parameters are self-explanatory. The following discussion focuses on the most important ones. ▶3.54

Enabled
This function turns the light on or off.

Show Distribution
This function shows the distribution of the IES light in the viewport.

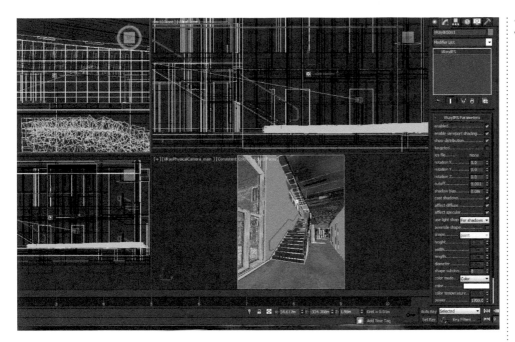

3.54

It only works if the *Realistic* function is enabled (Shift+F3) and the *Illuminate with Scene Lights* option is turned on. To enable this option, right-click on the top right side of the camera viewport/perspective, followed by selecting the relevant option from the drop-down menu. ▶3.55

3.55

3.56

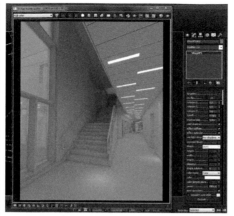

IES File

This toggle is one of the most important. It allows users to locate and plug an IES file into it.

IES web profiles are based on real-world light distribution. IES file 14 is one of the most popular file profiles used, as it leaves patterns of pools of light on the floor and walls. ▶3.56

3.57

Power

This value controls the intensity of the IES light. ▶3.57 and 3.58

Exclude

This option allows users to pick and choose scene objects to be excluded from the effects of this light.

Viewport Wire Color

3.58

If enabled, it allows users to choose a wire colour for the light object by clicking on the yellow colour swatch to bring up the *Color Selector* dialogue box. The default colour is yellow.

3.3.8 VRaySun

The VRaySun emulates the physical properties of real sunlight. When created, it automatically prompts the user to add a VRaySky to the environment map.

The VRaySky works like an HDRI for diffused lighting/shadows.

The VRaySky and VRaySun parameters automatically change according to the sun position. ▶3.59

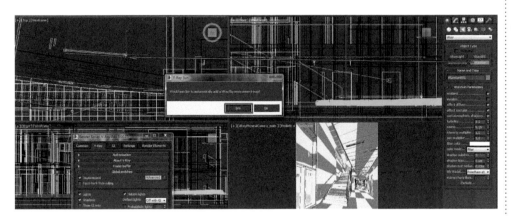

3.59

Enabled
This function turns the VRaySun on or off.

Invisible
This option controls the visibility of the VRaySun.

Affect Diffuse
This function allows the VRaySun to affect the diffuse/surface of objects.

Affect Specular
This function enables the VRaySun to affect the specular of objects.

Cast Atmospheric Shadows

When enabled, this option will cast atmospheric shadows on the scene.

Turbidity

This function controls the colour of the sky and the sun. Lower values yield bluer/ clear skies, while higher values produce slightly yellow/orange skies.

Ozone

This function mainly controls the colour of the sunlight. Higher values yield bluer tones, and lower values produce yellower hues.

Intensity Multiplier

This function determines the intensity of the sun.

Size Multiplier

This option controls the size of the sun in the VRaySky (it's visible in reflections). The bigger the size multiplier, the softer the shadows will be.

Shadow Subdivs

This setting controls the accuracy of the shadow samples cast by the sun.

Shadow Bias

This function controls the position of the shadows. Lower values are close to the objects, and high values detach the shadow from the objects. The default value is 0.0.

Values higher than 5 mm may result in shadow artefacts. This problem is consistent with all types of VRay lights.

Photon Emit Radius

It sets the radius/perimeter of the photon emission area (seen in the viewport). Users often increase it enough to encapsulate the area seen by the camera.

Sky Model

This function allows users to choose a sky model type from its drop-down menu. This sky model is directly connected with the VRaySky.

3.3.9 Daylight System

The VRaySun can also be loaded through the daylight system.

The Daylight System object allows users to pick and choose the correct geographical location, movement and angle of the Sun around the Earth.

To create this option, ensure you have all four viewports on the screen and click on *Create* on the main toolbar. On the drop-down menu, choose *Lights*, followed by clicking on the *Daylight System* option. ▶**3.60**

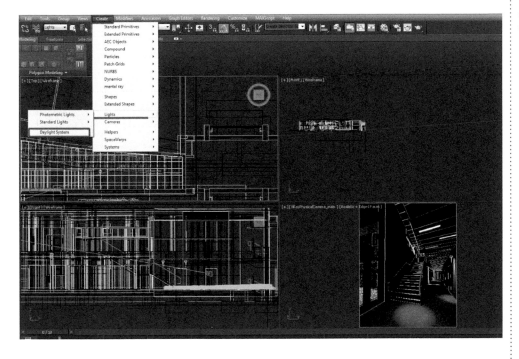

3.60

Following that, click and drag the cursor to create the compass and the sun object. Release the mouse button and drag the mouse to begin setting the distance of the sun's head from the ground.

Right-click to exit creation. ▶3.61

3.61

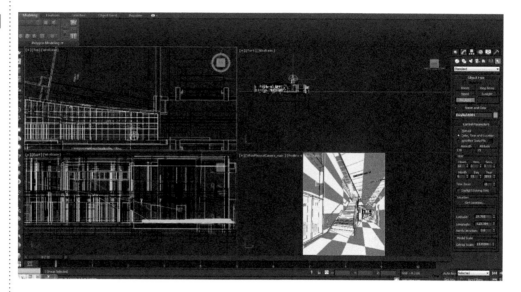

To load the VRaySun, simply open the *Modify* command panel while the daylight object is still selected. In the *Sunlight* option, pick *the VRaySun* from its drop-down menu.

A prompt should appear, asking whether you would like to automatically add a VRaySky to the environment map. Choose the *Yes* option.

In the *Skylight* option, choose the *No Skylight* option. As mentioned earlier it is possible to use a V-Ray dome light object and/or the VRaySky map to emulate a skylight. ▶3.62

To pick a geographic location and set up the time, simply open the *Motion* command panel. The control parameters allow users to set up the year, month, day, hours, minutes and seconds by typing in the relevant numerical values.

To find a geographical location, simply click on the *Location* toggle to bring up its dialogue box.

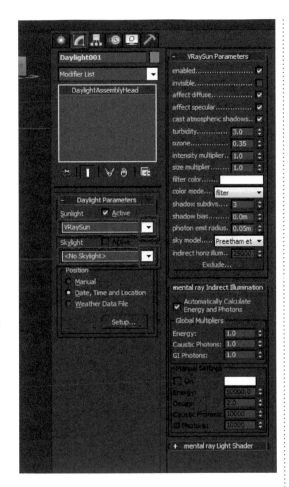

3.62

▼3.63

The *Map* area allows users to pick a location by clicking on it and/or by selecting a continent from the *Map* drop-down menu and choosing a city from its list. ▶3.63

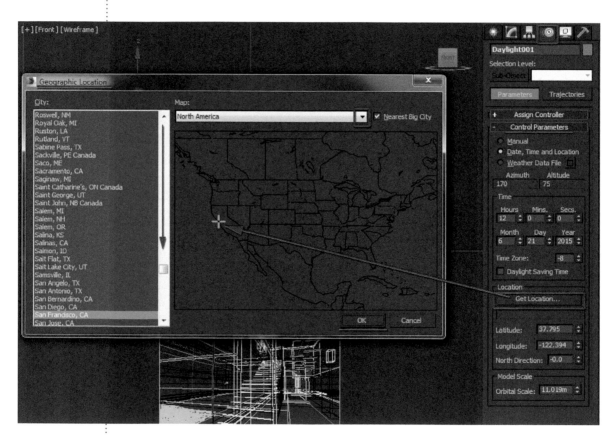

The other parameters should *never* be tweaked or adjusted when using the Daylight System for accuracy in lighting, time, shadows and location.

Conclusion

This chapter has taken users through the process of accessing and using some of the most popular V-Ray lights. Users were also introduced to the Daylight System and shown how to fine-tune some of its common parameters.

For more detailed information about V-Ray lights and other topics discussed here, visit the following V-Ray official website:

http://docs.chaosgroup.com/

4

Rendering in V-Ray

This chapter provides an overview of some of V-Ray's most useful
rendering parameters and shows how to get the best out of them in a
real production environment.

4 Rendering in V-Ray

4.1

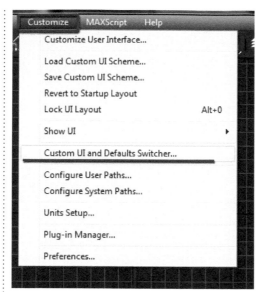

As previously stated, to access V-Ray tools and parameters, the V-Ray renderer needs to be loaded first. To ensure that the V-Ray renderer is automatically loaded at start-up of 3ds Max, click on the *Customize* main toolbar and select the *Custom UI and Defaults Switcher* option from the drop-down list. ▶4.1

In the dialogue box, choose the *MAX.vray* and *DefaultUI* options, then click on the *Set* button.

The *Custom UI and Defaults Switcher* dialogue message should be prompted; click *OK* to accept it. ▶4.2

4.2

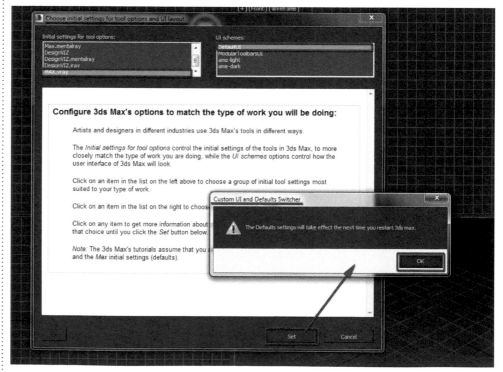

3D Photorealistic Rendering

4.1 Render Set-Up: V-Ray

To open the *Render Setup* dialogue box, press F10 or click on its icon from the main toolbar. ▶4.3

Under the *V-Ray* tab, extend the *Frame buffer* roll-out parameters.

4.1.1 Enable Built-In Frame Buffer

This function uses the V-Ray frame buffer to render the scene. It is enabled by default.

4.1.2 Memory Frame Buffer

When enabled, this option saves/ displays all the rendering data into the memory of the frame buffer. The rendering data is what's viewed in the VRF (e.g. RGB, Alpha) whilst the rendering is taking place and after the rendering is finished. This option is enabled by default.

4.1.3 Show Last VFB

This toggle opens up the V-Ray frame buffer.

4.3

4.2 V-Ray Frame Buffer Parameters

4.2.1 RGB Color/Alpha

The drop-down list displays the render in red, green, blue colour space and the alpha channel. The drop-down menu displays other channels included in the render elements.

4.4

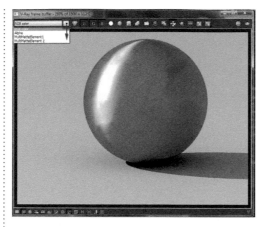

4.5

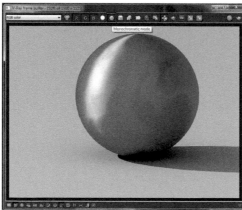

4.6

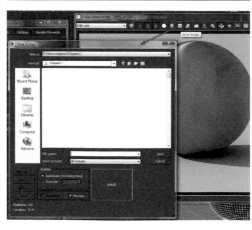

To view any of the listed channels, click and choose from its drop-down menu. ▶4.4

4.2.2 Switch to RGB Channel

This button allows users to switch to the RGB channel colour display (default).

4.2.3 Red/Blue/Blue Channel

These three buttons enable the users to view all render channels (default) or individually by selecting/deselecting each button. These functions are enabled by default.

4.2.4 Switch to Alpha Channel

This button allows users to view the Alpha channel in the frame buffer.

4.2.5 Monochromatic Mode

This button turns the *RGB color* mode into a monochromatic one. This tool is quite useful to assess the overall scene contrast (e.g. visible contrast between dark and bright areas). ▶4.5

4.2.6 Save Image

This button enables users to save the image currently being displayed in the frame buffer. Clicking this button will prompt the *Save Image* dialogue, for users to choose a path location, the file extension type and a filename. ▶4.6

4.2.7 Save All Image Channels

This button automatically saves all image channels listed in the frame buffer drop-down menu list (without having to select them individually).

Clicking the button will prompt its dialogue, for users to type in the filename, choose a location to save files into and the file extension. ▶4.7

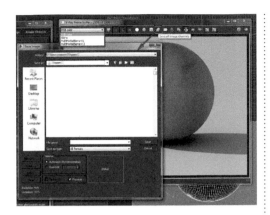

4.7

4.2.8 Load Image

This button allows users to locate and load an image into the VFB. Users can choose to load from any of the listed file types. The default type is V-Ray image file (*.vrimg). ▶4.8

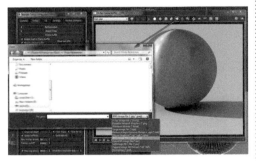

4.8

4.2.9 Clear Image

Clicking this button clears/deletes all channels being displayed in the frame buffer.

4.9

4.2.10 Duplicate to MAX Frame Buffer

This button duplicates the image/render displayed in the frame buffer. ▶4.9

This button/function is also used to check the final gamma output in the render. If the duplicated frame buffer has a different gamma value from main frame buffer (e.g. darker or brighter), it's an indication that the gamma output needs adjustment.

4.10

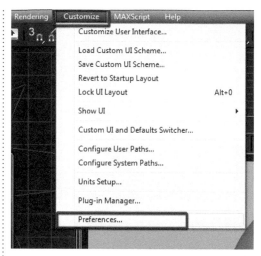

To adjust the gamma output, click on the *Customize* button from the main toolbar and choose the *Preferences* option from the drop-down list. ▶4.10

4.11

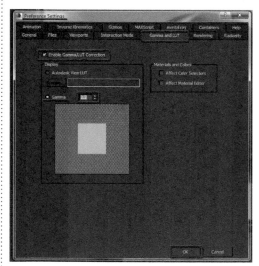

In the *Preference Settings* dialogue, set the gamma value to 2.2. ▶4.11

In addition, when saving the final render output, set the *Gamma* option to *Automatic (Recommended)*. ▶4.12

4.12

4.2.11 Track Mouse while Rendering

When selected, this function allows users to use the mouse to control the areas of the frame buffer the buckets should render. Essentially, the rendering buckets follow the mouse (as they finish computing the last bucket) on the frame buffer. ▶4.13

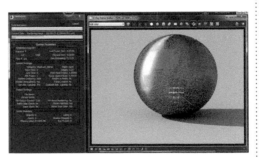
4.13

4.2.12 Region Render

This function allows users to draw a region to render, on the frame buffer. It works best when there's already a previous render in the frame buffer.

This V-Ray function overrides the region render from 3Ds Max (*Common* tab). ▶4.14

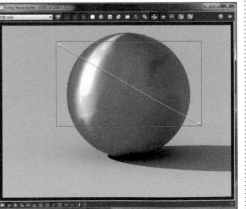
4.14

NOTE

Ensure to disable this function when sending the full render.

4.15

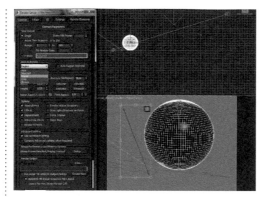

The region render function from 3Ds Max allows users to draw a region to render in the actual viewport. ▶4.15

4.2.13 Stop

When enabled it abruptly stops the rendering process.

4.2.14 Render Last

It re-renders the area that was rendered last.

4.16

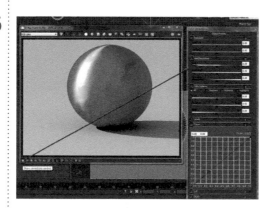

4.2.15 Show Corrections Control

This button opens up the *Color corrections* dialogue.

When enabled, users can adjust/correct many aspects of the image using Photoshop tools such as *Exposure, Hue/Saturation, Color Balance, Levels and Curve.*

These Photoshop tools are used in the same manner as depicted in Chapters 9, 12, 16 and 19. ▶4.16

4.17

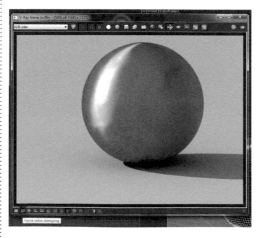

4.2.16 Force Color Clamping

When enabled, it forces the colour clamping in the frame buffer. Clicking and holding this button will give users the option to see the clamped colour in the frame buffer.

This function is enabled by default. ▶4.17 and 4.18

4.2.17 Display Colors in sRGB Space

When enabled, it displays the render in sRGB colour space. Users can click and hold its button to select ICC colour space.

This function is enabled by default.
▶4.19 and 4.20

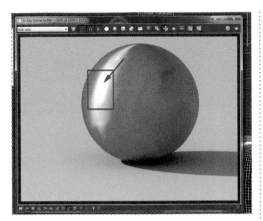

4.18

4.19

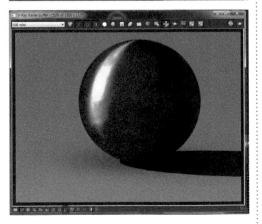

4.20

4.21

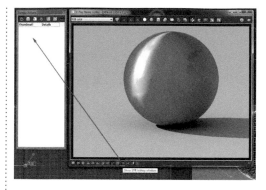

4.2.18 Show VFB History Window

Clicking this button opens up the *Render history* dialogue. The dialogue allows users to show the history of all renders, save them, remove them, etc. ▶4.21

To begin saving the images into the *Render history* dialogue, first click on the *Historysettings* button, to bring up the *Render history settings* dialogue.

4.22

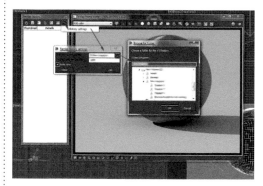

Enable the *Auto save* function and click on the *VFB history temp path* toggle, to bring up the *Browse for Folder* dialogue.

Choose the path location and click *OK* to close the dialogue. ▶4.22 and 4.23

4.2.19 Stereo Red/Cyan

4.23

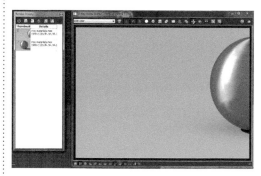

When enabled, it allows users to see the stereoscopic preview. Clicking and holding its button enables switching between other stereoscopic modes.

4.2.20 Open Lens Effects Settings

Clicking this button opens up the *Lens Effects* dialogue

Parameters such as *Bloom Effect*, *Intensity*, etc., need to be turned on prior to sending a render, in order to utilize many of its interactive parameters. This function is disabled by default. ▶4.24

4.24

4.2.21 Get Resolution from Max

This option uses the *Output Size* values from the *Common* tab, to render the frame. If disabled, the greyed out parameters will become live and allow users to manually type in the image aspect values, pixel aspect, etc. This function is enabled by default.

4.2.22 V-Ray Raw Image File

When enabled, this option renders the raw image format directly into the disk (bucket by bucket as the render progresses). This feature is quite useful when rendering extremely high resolution images that may cause the VFB to crash during the rendering process.

Disabling the *Memory frame buffer* function whilst using this option will render the high resolution images.

The *Generate preview* function allows users to have a small preview of the render in progress.

4.25

The browse toggle allows users to find a location to save the VRIMG file. Alternatively, users can choose other file formats, such as EXR, etc. EXR file formats save the render elements into the final output file automatically. ▶4.25

4.26

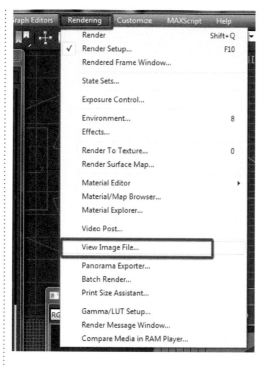

The V-ray raw image file can only be opened inside 3ds Max. To do so, go to the *Rendering* main toolbar and choose the *View Image File* option from the drop-down list. Then open the desired image. ▶4.26

Once the V-ray raw image file is open in 3ds Max, users can save it as a different file format.

4.27

The EXR files can be opened in Photoshop. ▶4.27

Alternatively, you can open the EXR main render and its elements in 3ds Max, one at a time, and then save them in a different file format. ▶4.28

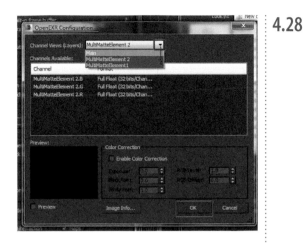

4.2.23 Separate Render Channels

When enabled, it determines the path/location of the ticked render channels, after being rendered. This function also saves the channels added in the Render Elements list. ▶4.29

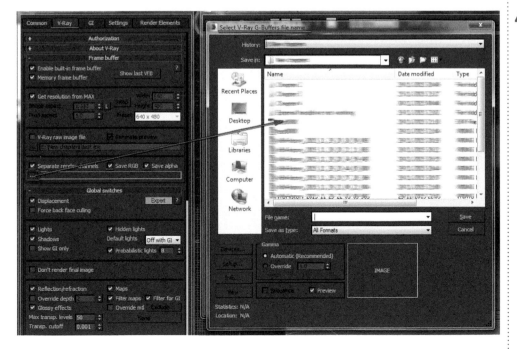

4 Rendering in V-Ray

4.30

4.3 Global Switches

To see more global switches functions, click on the *Basic* button twice to get to *Expert* mode. ▶4.30

4.3.1 Displacement

When on, it renders the displacement effects applied on materials. This feature is enabled by default.

4.3.2 Lights

When on, it renders the light effects in the scene. This feature is enabled by default.

4.3.3 Shadows

If turned on, it renders the shadows. This feature is enabled by default.

4.3.4 Hidden Lights

When on, it renders the effects of hidden/isolated lights. This feature is enabled by default.

4.3.5 Probabilistic Lights

This function is quite useful for computing the light effects very quickly in test renders.

However, when sending the final high resolution renders, it needs to be disabled at all costs, as it will cause the renders to be extremely grainy. This function is enabled by default.

4.3.6 Don't Render Final Image

When on, it computes the pre-pass without rendering. It's quite useful for saving the GI pre-calculation. This function is disabled by default.

4.3.7 Reflection/Refraction

It computes the reflection/refraction of objects in the scene, if enabled. This function is enabled by default.

4.3.8 Glossy Effects

It calculates the glossy effects on reflections and refractions. Otherwise, glossy effects on reflections will be mirror-like (non-diffused). This function is enabled by default.

4.3.9 Override Mtl

This toggle allows users to use it on a material/shader, as an override for the entire scene.

This function is quite useful for chalk renders or light studies, whereby the entire scene has one basic white/grey material, with the lights turned on.

The *Exclude* toggle allows users to pick and choose which objects in the scene to exclude from the override material.

4.4 Image Sampler (Antialiasing)

This roll-out controls the quality of the final quality of the renders.

4.31

4.4.1 Type

This function allows users to choose from a list of different image samplers. This chapter focuses on the *Adaptive* type and some of its parameters. ▶4.31

4.4.2 Render Mask

This function does not work well with region renders. It allows users to choose from a list of different types of areas/masks to render: Texture, Selected, Include/Exclude list and Layers.

This tool is quite useful for final renders that require one or two object surfaces to be changed. Instead of having to re-render the entire scene, users can select the objects in question and re-render them solely.

The default selection is *None*.

4.4.3 Image Filter

This group allows users to choose from a long list of image filters. Each filter has its own distinctive effect (e.g. Mitchell-Netravali yields very sharp results). ▶4.32

4.5 Adaptive Image Sampler

4.5.1 Min Subdivs

It controls the minimum number of samples necessary to compute each rendered pixel.

The value is often sufficient.

4.32

4.5.2 Max Subdivs

It controls the maximum number of samples necessary to compute each rendered pixel. This value is always multiplied by 4 (e.g. if a value of 6 is entered, it will produce 24 samples).

For high resolution renders, this value needs to be at least 6.

4.5.3 Color Threshold

This option determines the final quality of the render. Low values yield better quality; high values produce draft results.

4.5.4 Use DMC Sampler Thresh

If enabled, this function will automatically ignore the *Color threshold* values and use the DMC noise threshold instead. This function is disabled by default.

4.33

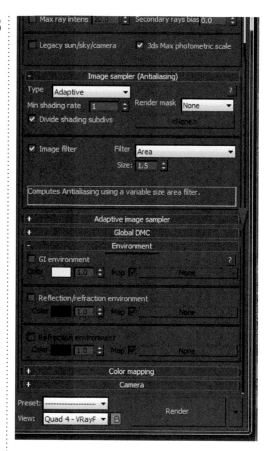

The DMC noise threshold works like the colour threshold: Low values yield better quality; high values produce draft results.

4.6 Environment

When used, the *Environment* parameters will override the *Environment map* toggle. ▶4.33

4.6.1 GI Environment

If turned on, this option controls the environment/background *Global Illumination* parameters.

Color

This function allows users to pick a colour from its colour swatch and control its intensity with its values.

This value rarely has any big impact on the overall scene.

Map

Users can apply a *VRayHDRI* procedural map to produce more accurate environment lighting. A high dynamic range image (HDRI) makes a huge impact on the environment GI.

4.6.2 Reflection/Refraction Environment

If turned on, this function controls the global reflection/refraction of the environment.

Map

A *VRayHDRI* procedural map can be plugged in here to produce the environment's reflection/refraction.

4.7 Color Mapping ▶4.34

4.7.1 Type

This function allows users to choose a color mapping type from its long drop-down list. One of the most popular ones is *Linear multiply*.

4.7.2 Gamma

This function controls the gamma value. The most accurate value is 2.2.

4.34

4.7.3 Dark Multiplier

This function controls the intensity of the dark multiplier in the render. The default value is 1.0. This tool is quite useful to help integrate photomontages or verified views.

4.7.4 Bright Multiplier

This option determines the intensity of the bright multiplier in the render. The default value is 1.0.

This tool is quite useful to help integrate photomontages or verified views. In addition, it can be used to help reduce overly exposed bright areas.

4.7.5 Sub-Pixel Mapping

This function applies color mapping to individual sub-pixel samples. It also helps to remove artefacts such as overly bright pixel dots in the render. This function is enabled by default.

4.7.6 Affect Background

When this function is on, the colour mapping is applied to the *Environment* map. For photomontages, users often disable this option to avoid doubling up the gamma. This function is enabled by default.

4.7.7 Clamp Output

If turned on, colours will be clamped out after colour mapping.

4.35

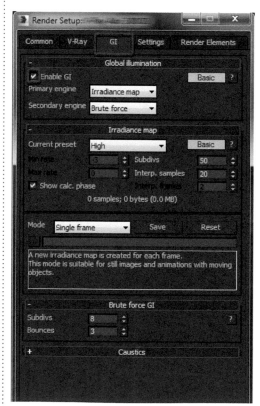

4.8 Global Illumination

4.8.1 Enable GI

This function is disabled by default. It activates indirect illumination.

4.8.2 Primary Engine

This option computes the GI primary bounces. Its drop-down menu allows users to choose from a list of other prime engines. *Irradiance map* is often the best choice. ▶4.35

4.8.3 Secondary Engine

This option computes the GI secondary bounces. *Brute force* is the default secondary engine.

While this GI engine is more accurate, it does take a considerable amount of time to render. For this reason, *Light cache* is often chosen instead.

Light cache GI approximation is less accurate than brute force. However, it produces similar results, much faster.

4.8.4 Multiplier

For both primary and secondary engine, this function helps to reinvigorate or diminish their influence in the GI calculation. The default value is 1.0.

4.8.5 Refractive GI Caustics

When enabled, this option allows the GI caustics to be computed on refractive (transparent) surfaces. It is enabled by default.

However, it only works when the *Caustics* roll-out parameters are enabled. These parameters are disabled by default.

4.8.6 Saturation

This option controls the colour saturation of the GI effect. Higher values cause the GI to produce more saturated colours.

The default value is 1.0.

4.8.7 Contrast

This function controls the overall contrast of the GI. Higher values increase the GI contrast.

The default value is 1.0.

4.8.8 Contrast Base

This option controls the base contrast values. The default value is 0.5.

4.8.9 Amb. Occlusion

When on, this function enables connecting shadows on indirectly lit areas. It is disabled by default.

4.8.10 Radius

This option controls the propagation of the connecting shadows from its starting point. The default value is 10 mm.

4.8.11 Subdivs

This option controls the smoothness of the connecting shadows. Higher values yield smoother results.

The default value is 8. ▶4.36 and 4.37

4.36

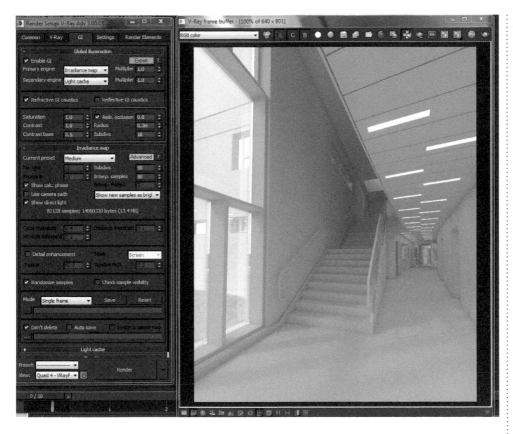

4.37

4.9 Irradiance Map

4.9.1 Current Preset

This option controls the quality of the irradiance map, by choosing from the following presets.

Custom
This function allows users to manually control the min and rate values.

Very Low

This option computes the irradiance process with very low values. While quick to process, the results can be draft quality.

Medium

This function computes the irradiance map with medium values.

High (default)

This function calculates the irradiance map with high values. While the irradiance map will be high, its pre-calculation will be relatively slow.

4.9.2 Use Camera Path

When enabled, the irradiance map is computed from the entire camera path (animated cameras), as opposed to view only. This function is disabled by default.

4.9.3 Show Calc. Phase

This option allows users to preview the pre-calculation phase in the frame buffer. It is enabled by default.

4.9.4 Show Direct Light

This function allows users to preview, in the frame buffer, the direct light (sunlight) during the pre-calculation process.

4.9.5 Subdivs

This function controls the quality of each irradiance map sample (e.g. ray). The default value is 50.

4.9.6 Interpolation Samples

This option determines the smoothness of the irradiance map on indirectly lit areas, by adding interpolation samples.

The higher the interpolation sample values, the smoother the results. There are extreme cases when users may need to increase these values to 120 or higher.

Increasing these values may take away some of the scene's depth. However, adding ambient occlusion will help rectify this problem.

The default value is 20.

4.9.7 Detail Enhancement

When enabled, this function adds extra shadow details to the scene, while using parameters such as *Radius* and *Subdivs mult* values.

It's disabled by default, as it increases the rendering times excessively.

4.9.8 Mode

This option allows users to choose from a number of different calculation modes seen in the pull-down list.

The default mode is single frame. Single frame mode calculates the irradiance map for a single frame only.

4.9.9 Switch to Saved Map

When turned on, this function automatically uploads an irradiance map file that was previously saved.

To save and re-use the irradiance map, first enable the *Switch to saved map* function and click on its browse toggle.

The *Auto save irradiance map* dialogue should appear; name and save the file to close the dialogue.

To save the irradiance map, it is necessary to process the pre-calculation first. ▶4.38

Users tend to enable the *Don't render final image* option whilst saving the irradiance map file. Having this function enabled will allow users to save the irradiance pre-calculation file without having to render the image.

4.38

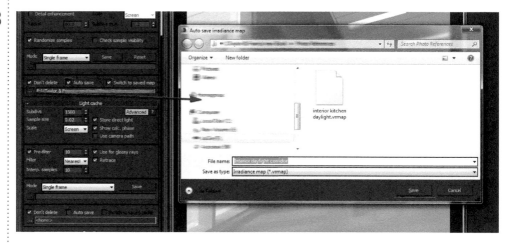

Once the pre-calculation of the irradiance map is finished saving, the file will be automatically loaded and ready to be reused for rendering.

Ensure that the *Don't render final image* option is turned off prior to sending the final render.

4.10 Brute Force GI

This GI approximation method is the most accurate one, and more time-consuming. However, the rendering results are often grainy. Increasing the *Subdivs* values will help reduce the grain, but the rendering times will increase substantially.

When selected (rarely), *Brute force* is often used as a secondary engine only.

4.10.1 Subdivs

This function controls the number of samples required to compute the brute force GI. The default value is 8.

4.10.2 Bounces

This function determines the number of light bounces. More light bounces yield a better GI.

4.11 Light Cache ▶4.39

This GI approximation is a much quicker alternative to brute force. However, while extremely good for most high resolution renders, the results are not as accurate as brute force.

Like brute force, the light cache is often used as a secondary engine.

4.39

4.11.1 Subdivs

This function determines the accuracy of the light cache calculation. High values produce results closer to brute force.

High values are considered to be between 1000 and 3000. The default value is 1000.

Sample size is 0.02.

4.11.2 Pre-filter

This function allows the light cache samples to be computed during the pre-calculation, as opposed to during the rendering time.

This option is faster and reduces the noise in the render by blurring the light cache.

4.11.3 Use for Glossy Rays

When enabled, this option uses the light cache to compute the glossy rays (from glossy materials in the scene). Having this option enabled can speed up rendering times considerably.

4.40

4.12 Settings ▶4.40

4.13 System

4.13.1 Bucket Width

This option sets the size of the buckets in the render. All renders are performed in small buckets. The default size is 48.

4.13.2 Dynamic Splitting

This function automatically splits the bucket rendering size according to the bucket width value. In addition, it occasionally decides whether to reduce or increase the bucket size depending on the area being rendered and the overall render output size.

It is enabled by default.

4.13.3 Sequence

This function determines the sequence/movement of the bucket rendering. The default sequence is *Triangulation*.

4.13.4 Reverse Sequence

This function reverses whatever sequence is chosen. For instance, if the sequence was Top->Bottom, this option would reverse it to Bottom->Top.

4.13.5 Dyn Mem Limit, mb

This option sets the memory limit to compute a render. This function is quite useful to increase or decrease the rendering power, depending on the available resources.

4.13.6 Max. Tree Depth

It determines the maximum depth of the geometry tree. High values use more memory, for quicker rendering times.

4.13.7 Use Embree

When enabled, it uses the Intel Embree raycaster.

4.13.8 Frame Stamp

When enabled, the bottom part of the V-Ray frame buffer will display key render information such as V-Ray version (e.g. V-Ray %vrayversion) and filename (e.g. file: %filename).

This option is disabled by default.

4.13.9 Distributed Rendering

When enabled, this option uses the distributed rendering system to allocate assigned computers to the rendering calculation.

Computers are assigned/allocated through the *Settings* toggle.

The more assigned computers there are, the faster the renders will be. Distributed rendering only works in conjunction with V-Ray Spawner.

For more information about V-Ray Spawner, visit http://docs.chaosgroup.com/.

Distributed rendering is disabled, by default.

4.13.10 Settings

This toggle allows users to add/allocate computers to the distributed rendering process.

By clicking on this toggle, the *V-Ray distributed rendering settings* dialogue will be prompted with the following functions.

Add Server

This function allows users to type in the machine/server name or IP address. ►4.41

4.41

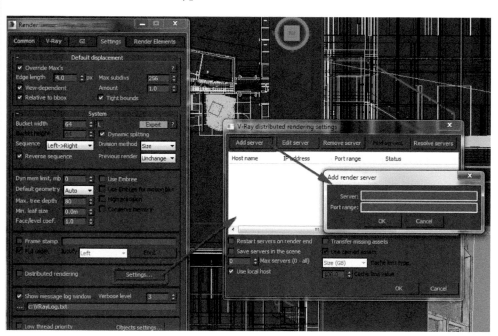

Edit Server

This feature allows users to edit an existing machine/server name or IP address. To do so, select the listed host name, then click on the *Edit server* function.

Remove Server

This feature enables users to select and remove existing servers from the list.

Resolve Servers

This function allows V-Ray to automatically resolve incorrect server names or IP addresses listed in the dialogue.

4.14 Render Elements

Render elements are extremely useful to help enhance key physical properties of materials and improve the overall render.

To add a render element, click on the *Add* button, then select one or more of the listed elements in the dialogue and click *OK*.

Chapters 8, 9, 12, 16 and 19 take users through the process of using most of these render elements.

Conclusion

This chapter has introduced and navigated users through some of the key V-Ray rendering parameters.

For more detailed information about V-Ray rendering parameters, visit the official V-Ray website

http://docs.chaosgroup.com/

5

Tips and Tricks

Always select *Adopt the File's Unit Scale* when opening a new file. This will prevent scenes from being rescaled and looking inaccurate. There are only a handful of times when it might be necessary to choose the *Rescale the File Objects to the System Unit Scale* option. It only happens when the incoming file is not accurate and requires rescaling.

Use the same approach for incoming gamma settings. ▶5.1

5.1

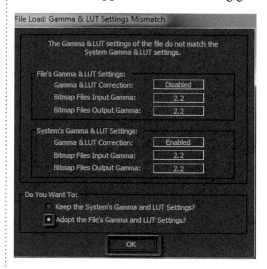

Before importing 2D drawings (DWG files) into 3ds Max, it's important to do the following:

- Ensure that the original 2D drawing is completely 'cleaned/stripped' from AutoCAD or MicroStation (e.g. omit unnecessary text and other layers). This action will reduce the incoming file size when it is imported into 3ds Max.

- Drawings are often created far away from the 0.0.0 point; thus 3ds Max and most 3D applications will have difficulty in displaying/representing lines or objects accurately at such distances.

    Therefore, it is imperative to reposition the drawings as close to the 0.0.0 point as possible prior to importing them into 3ds Max.

- One of the most popular techniques to reposition the drawings is to first create a dummy/point/line at the 0.0.0 point.

    Select the drawing layers from the file and move or snap them onto the previously created dummy/point/line (i.e. at the 0.0.0 point).

- Once the drawings are close to or at the 0.0.0 point, it is important to save the file out under a different name, to prevent overwriting the original file.

Prior to importing the CAD file into 3ds Max, ensure that all files are bound in AutoCAD.

To bind xreferenced files, simply type in 'xref' to enable its dialogue box.

Next, in the dialogue box, select the relevant file(s) and right-click to enable its pop-up list. The pop-up list should give the user the option to click on the 'bind' function, if desired.

In some cases it may be necessary to explode objects in AutoCAD in order to ensure that specific objects/lines are imported, without artefacts. ▶5.2

5.2

There are occasions when drawings come with multiple elevations and sections and are therefore unwise to be imported as a whole in 3ds Max.

The common approach is to first use the rectangular selection tool (click and drag to select a specific region); press Ctrl+C to copy the selection. Create a new document by pressing Ctrl+N. Paste the copied drawing to its original position in the new document by pressing Paste+O, hitting Enter and double-clicking the middle mouse button anywhere in the viewport.

- In MicroStation, professionals often select the fence tool, draw around the desired area and type in 'FF=', to save out the drawing under a different name.

    Note that MicroStation is set to automatically save the file every time a change is made to the drawing. For this reason, it is necessary to 'Fence save' first, prior to moving/snapping the drawings to the dummy line/point/object.

5.3

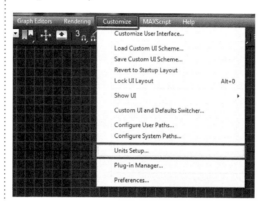

It's worth mentioning that the DGN (i.e. MicroStation) file has to be saved as a DWG file first, prior to being imported into 3ds Max.

- It is also important to have the metric system set up (e.g. millimetres, meters), as opposed to keeping the default system of *Generic Units*. ▶5.3 and 5.4

5.4

It is also necessary to set the system to *Respect System Units in Files*. These two functions will prove vital in ensuring that incoming files are not disproportionate in size and/or automatically rescaled. ▶5.5

5.5

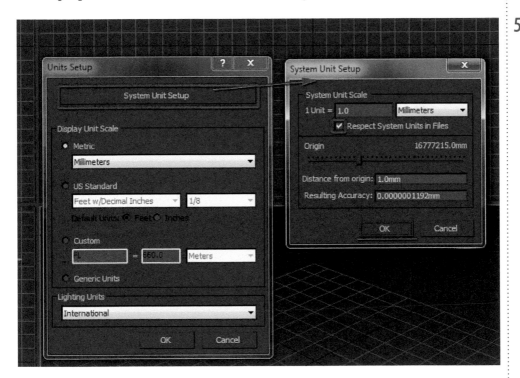

Furthermore, pay extra attention to the 'model scale' group, in the *AutoCAD DWG/DFX Import Options* dialogue box. The *Incoming file units* function should be left untouched.

Simply enable or disable the *Rescale* function, depending on the total value of the *Resulting model size* function. The rule of thumb is to *always* choose the smaller metric value displayed on the *Resulting model size* text field.

5.6

In addition, the *Curve steps* values should be increased if the smooth curves of the incoming drawings are not accurate in the main 3D software. This function will essentially increase the number of vertices in such areas. ▶5.6 and 5.7

Once the drawing is imported into the scene, it's common practice to quickly check the dimensions of walls, stairs, chairs, etc., with the *Tape* helper. This precautionary measure is to ensure that the scale of the imported file is correct.

5.7

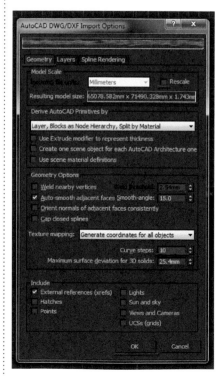

Doors are often 2.2 m in height, chairs 400/600 mm in width, etc. Some professionals find it easier to continuously switch the metric display unit scale between metres, millimetres, centimetres, etc., depending on the value for input (e.g. millimetres for small values, metres for large values). ▶5.8

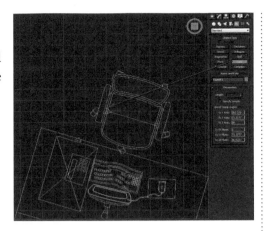

5.8

- Once the drawing is in the scene, select it in its entirety by first pressing the H to open the *Select From Scene* dialogue box, followed by clicking on the *Select All* button and *OK* to close the dialogue box.

    With all objects in the scene selected, it is then possible to group it.

    It is common practice to name the group in accordance with its original name (e.g. 2D_DWG_ Level 1). ▶5.9

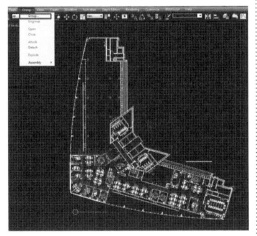

5.9

Some users also choose to create a layer under a similar name. However, the only drawback is the fact that all the drawing content will be culminated into one single colour. To prevent this artefact, simply place the script under the name of 'color layer' in the following folder:

C:\Program Files\Autodesk\3ds Max 2014\scripts\Startup

To create the new layer, simply select the relevant objects in the scene. Then open the layer dialogue box, click the *Create New Layer* button and rename it, if necessary.

5.10

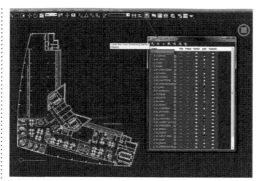

When renaming the layer(s) of objects, names should have the form '#3D_DWG_Ceiling...', etc. This is to ensure that the layers of relevance always stay on top of the list, as they can easily be overlooked or lost among the other named layers. ▶5.10

To edit, move or delete a layer or folder, select it from the dialogue list first (e.g. highlighted). To rename a layer or folder from the list, double-click it and type in the name.

Some studios find it easier to work with layers mainly due to its ease of use and its flexibility to provide control over the contents in the scene.

When selecting an object in the scene and creating a new layer, the dialogue box adds or moves the object selected in the list into the newly created layer. It works almost like a folder that can be selected as a group or have individual objects selected from its content list, be turned on/off, be frozen, etc.

When a layer or folder is created and the objects are automatically moved into this newly created layer or folder, the main *Layer* dialogue box list will still retain the unused copies of the object's name(s) in the list. These unused names and layers can be found in the root of the dialogue box or inside another layer/folder.

5.11

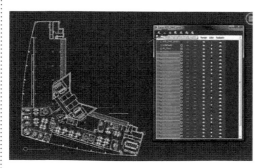

It is also common practice to delete all unused layers and objects from the list in order to tidy up the dialogue box.

The layer under the name of '0(default)' is the default layer, which is created automatically. It *cannot* and *should not* be deleted. ▶5.11

3D Photorealistic Rendering

If a new layer or folder isn't manually created, most objects created in the scene will be automatically added or moved into this default layer or folder.

Although it is possible to select and move the contents of this default layer or folder (e.g. '0(default)'), it cannot be deleted, even when empty.

As with all new layers or folders created by the user, it is possible to select and move its content into a different layer or folder and to delete the empty layer or folder thereafter. ▶5.12

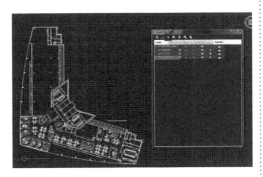

5.12

Before beginning to trace the drawing to create 3D objects, it is imperative to do the following:

- Set up the snap tool parameters and set the toggle to 2.5 (2D).

  Because the drawings are in 2D (e.g. sfplines), professionals usually change the snaps toggle from the default 3 to 2.5, by clicking and holding down on the tool's icon in the main toolbar. ▶5.13

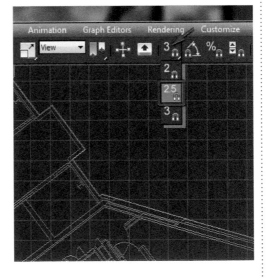

5.13

5 Tips and Tricks

5.14

To quickly snap the splines while tracing the drawing, it is necessary to change some key parameters: right-click on the snaps toggle icon in the main toolbar. A dialogue box should pop up. Enable the *Vertex* and *Endpoint* functions. ►5.14

5.15

In addition, in the *Options* tab, enable the *Snap to frozen objects* function. This step will ensure that even frozen drawings/splines can be traced and snapped onto. ►5.15

You may be wondering why not simply extrude the 2D drawing lines in 3ds Max.

Most drawings' vertices are not welded (e.g. opened) and are often *not* drawn on the same plane/level; they are therefore difficult to extrude as a whole, even when welding vertices globally with a target distance value.

Welding the drawings manually often takes much longer than tracing them.

DWG plans are always more accurate than the elevations or sections.

3D Photorealistic Rendering

To ensure the elevations and sections line up with the plan(s), trace/draw the simplest area of the drawing plan that is relevant to the section or elevation first. Extrude it thereafter.

Next, position the elevation or section to match this newly created object. Use the same procedure to position the following elevations and sections.

There are times when it's difficult to trace and create objects from rotated DWG drawings.

To make this process easier, it is often necessary to create a grid helper from the rotated DWG drawing and use it as the basis to trace and create objects from a specific angle.

- The next step is to use the *Auto grid pivot point* script to automatically create and align a grid to any particular spline or object angle. Start by selecting the relevant spline in the *Viewport*, then click on the *MAXScript* main toolbar and choose the *Run Script* option. ▶5.16

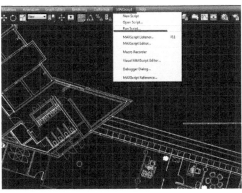

5.16

Next, locate and open the *Auto grid pivot point* script. ▶5.17

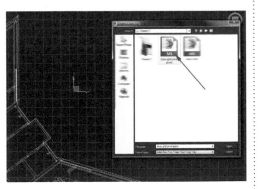

5.17

The grid should appear and activate automatically. If it is too small, modify its parameters to increase it. ▶5.18

5.18

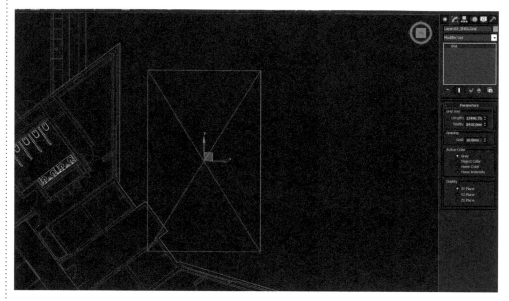

5.19

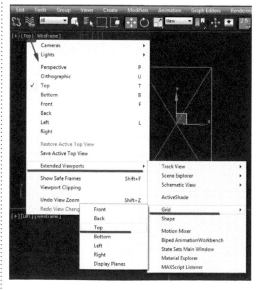

From this point, it is possible to begin tracing and creating shapes and geometry from the grid angle/position.

To view the rotated drawing plan in a straight angle, do the following: right-click on the *Top* viewport text and select the *Extended Viewports* function. Next, choose the *Grid* option, followed by the *Top* view. ▶5.19

The drawing should automatically rotate and position itself correctly. The *Grid* tool is the ideal solution when working with rotated drawings. This way it is *not* necessary to rotate drawings individually.

The grid helper can also be very useful when setting 3ds Max to automatically create objects at a certain height level (i.e. 2.5 m) without having to manually move the objects from the 0.0.0 point. To do so, simply move the grid to the desired height level on the left or right viewport.

Before moving/rotating the grid, be sure to *deactivate* it and set the view to the normal viewport first (e.g. *not* grid view). Once finished moving and rotating the grid helper, simply activate it again.

If you wish to start tracing lines in the front viewport, simply create a grid in the front viewport.

As drawings are produced in plans, elevations and sections, professionals often have to work with a variety of grid helpers, at different height levels and in different viewports.

One good technique for tracing and creating a spline continuously without having to exit creation is to occasionally press the *I* and *Z* keys on the keyboard.

It is also important to set a keyboard shortcut to freeze selected objects. This step ensures that even objects from opened groups can be frozen, without the need to close the group first. Professionals often resort to this keyboard shortcut to have better selection control of objects when working in dense and complex scenes.

To access this dialogue click on the *Customize* menu and choose the *Customize User Interface* option from the list. Its dialogue should open. In the *Action* list, scroll down to select the *Freeze Selection* option. Click inside the *Hotkey* box, press Ctrl+F on the keyboard and click *Assign* to apply this setting. ▶5.20 and 5.21

5.20

5.21

5.22

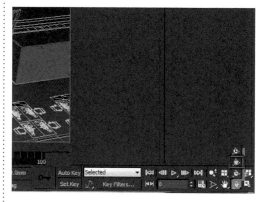

It's also important to set the viewport *Orbit selected* tool to rotate around the selected object. This function makes it possible to rotate the viewport around the axis of the selected object. ▶5.22

Furthermore, set 3ds Max to show the most commonly used modify buttons such as *Extrude* and *UVW map*. Doing this will save time by *not* having to constantly pick through drop-down list menus for commonly used modifiers.

To customize and display the modifier buttons, click and hold the *Configure Modifier Sets* button and choose the same from the pop up list. ▶5.23

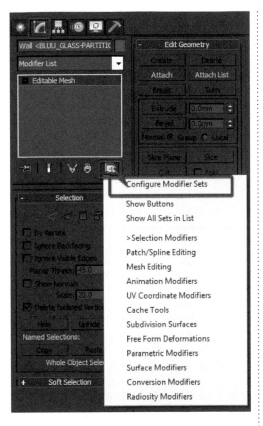

5.23

In the dialogue box, drag-drop the desired commonly used modifiers from the list onto the *Modifiers* group buttons (e.g. add and replace). Scroll down the list to pick other useful modifiers. ▶5.24

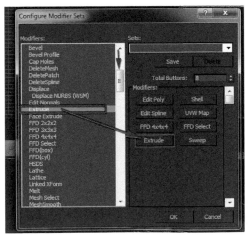

5.24

5.25

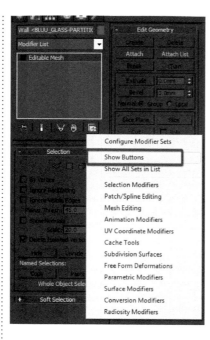

Once finished, close the dialogue and set the *Configure Modifier Sets* to *Show Buttons*. ▶5.25 and 5.26

While it's important to use photo references and drawings to help create convincing 3D models, it is important to concentrate mainly on detailing objects that are closer to the camera. Objects in the distance often look acceptable with a realistic texture and a good shader applied.

Furthermore, it is crucial to pay extra attention to scale relationships between objects by using 2D drawings, photos and your surroundings as reference points, as our eyes can inexplicably pinpoint scale discrepancies!

5.26

Finally, when creating and detailing models, it is worth finding an efficient way of navigating in the viewport by occasionally displaying the less relevant objects as boxes (i.e. box display mode) and/or hiding them when necessary. This technique will help speed up the viewport performance whilst navigating and creating geometry the 3D scene.

Although not always necessary, creating proxies is also a great technique for working and rendering efficiently. VRay proxies can reduce the MAX file size and rendering times by a great deal.

3D Photorealistic Rendering

To create a proxy, select the object in question and right-click to bring up the quad menu. Choose the *V-Ray mesh export* option to open its dialogue. ▶5.27

The *Folder* field allows users to choose the location where the proxy mesh will be saved into. The *File* field allows users to name or rename the VRMESH file. The file name should be kept as simple as possible (e.g. sphere. vrmesh).

To prevent unexpected proxy artefacts, always choose the option *Export each selected object in a separate file*.

Finally, always choose the *Automatically create proxies* option. ▶5.28

To control the display and other aspects of the VRayproxy, open the *Modify* panel.

The *Scale* function allows users to control the size of the proxy in the scene. A value of 1.0 is often correspondent to the original size of the object.

The *Display* group controls the preview of the proxy object in the viewport. It is common to choose the *bounding box* display type for very dense objects such as trees, grass and hairs.

5.27

5.28

The *Import as mesh* function allows users to retrieve the original mesh. Complex geometry may take a considerable amount of time to retrieve. In some cases it may even crash the system. ▶5.29

5.29

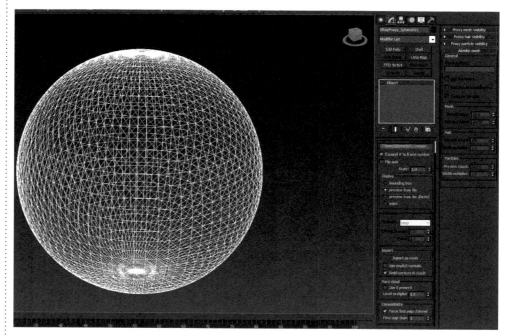

Producing realistic textures is another important part of the production process

When textures are applied in a competent manner, the ideal 3D scene should look convincing or close to it even before the lights and the indirect illumination have been implemented.

It's a common mistake of users to take high resolution photos of a smaller area of an object or surface, as opposed to high resolution photos of the entire object or surface. The former approach often leads to users having to resort to Photoshop to build the entire texture of an object or surface by tiling it. This methodology subsequently causes the final texture to look artificially tiled and have a lack of important details that frequently make a texture look convincing and realistic.

A widely used technique to prevent such problems from occurring is to take a high resolution photo of the entire object or surface desired or of an extensive area of the relevant object or surface. This approach captures all the important details of the entire surface (i.e. scratches, dust, AO, subtle discrepancies, etc.) without having to resort Photoshop to tile the surface.

Script for Verified Views

In architectural visualisation, typing in individual survey point values in 3ds Max can be very time-consuming, especially when working with multiple camera views for verified views. Most verified views come with at least 10 individual survey points per camera.

Below is an example of a typical survey data spreadsheet, provided by the surveyor. ▶5.30

5.30

The *View* name or number often refers to the camera. The *Easting* value is the equivalent of the *X* position in 3ds Max. The *Northing* value is the equivalent of the *Y* position in 3ds Max. The *Level* value is the equivalent of the *Z* position in 3ds Max.

5.31

The script, SurveyPointImporter, will help create and position each survey value automatically/accurately in 3ds Max, as instanced point helpers. The great advantage of having survey points in 3ds Max as instanced point helpers is that their sizes in the camera viewport can be set to have a constant screen size. ▶5.31

Note that the first line of code of this script is set to go to the root of the C drive and extract/open a CSV file type (spreadsheet) under the name of surveypoints.csv (e.g. **f = openFile "c:/surveypoints.csv" mode:"rt"**).

This means that every time this script is run, it will automatically look for a file under the above-mentioned name (i.e. surveypoints.csv), the file extension/type (i.e. CSV) and the specified location, as described above (c:/).

However, you can change the location and the file name as you see fit (although not the file extension, CVC).

Example: **f = openFile"F:/scene tests/Wembley Stadiumsurveypoints.csv" mode:"rt"**

5.32

Once satisfied, simply name and save the script as a MAXScript file type. ▶5.32 and 5.33

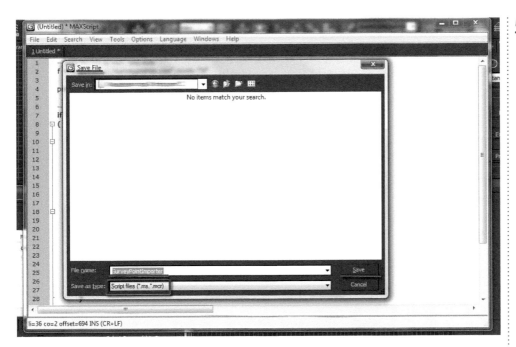

5.33

Once saved, close the dialogue box. ▶5.34

To run the script, click on the MAXScript toolbar and choose *Run Script*.

5.34

All survey points should be created automatically. ►5.35

5.35

At times it may seem that there's only survey point in the scene, due to its gigantic size in the viewport. If the survey points are too big, reduce their size manually.

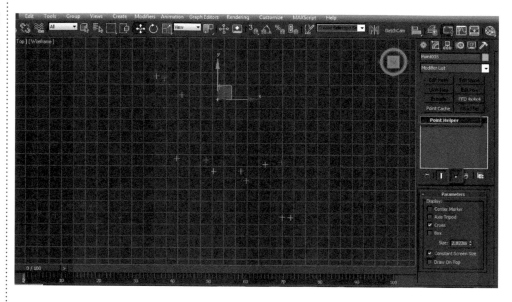

5.36

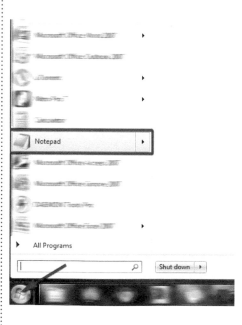

Note that the last three or four digits of the survey values might be slightly off. This is *not* a script error: 3ds Max has difficulty with accuracy when working or displaying numbers/units that are too far away from 0.0.0.

If by chance there is a script error reading the spreadsheet file, open the spreadsheet file in a simple text editor such as *Notepad* and resave it as a CVC file. ►5.36

The next step is to create and position the 3D cameras according to the values (X, Y, Z) depicted in the CVC file. In addition, you can also begin camera-matching each view according to the camera info and the photography provided. ▶5.37

5.37

While camera matching, it is possible to use tools such as 2D Pan Zoom Mode to zoom into a camera position, without affecting the camera itself. To begin zooming in, simply right-click on the plus sign at the top left corner of the camera viewport and choose *2D Pan Zoom Mode*. ▶5.38

To return to the original camera position, simply right-click on the text *2D Pan Zoom* and choose *Exit 2D Pan Zoom Mode*. ▶5.39

5.38

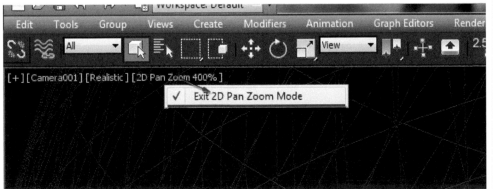

5.39

5.40

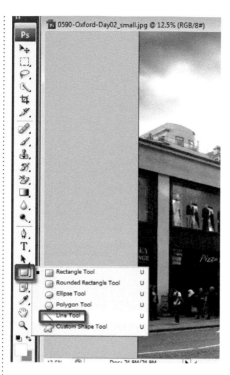

Using the vanishing line to correct camera shifts for verified views

Users are often required to create vanishing lines in Photoshop in order to correct camera shifts from photos taken for verified views or photomontages. To create the vanishing lines, go to the *Tools* sidebar and choose *Line Tool* from the list. ▶5.40

To create the vanishing line, set the line weight to a visible size (i.e. 5 pixels) and begin creating it by clicking and dragging it. ▶5.41

5.41

Once the vanishing lines are created, duplicate the background layer (Ctrl+J) and enable the canvas ruler (Ctrl+R). It's imperative to duplicate the layer prior to using the Crop tool in a non-destructive way.

Next, click on the top part of the ruler and drag it down to create a guide. Ensure the guide is positioned exactly where the vanishing lines meet. ▶5.42

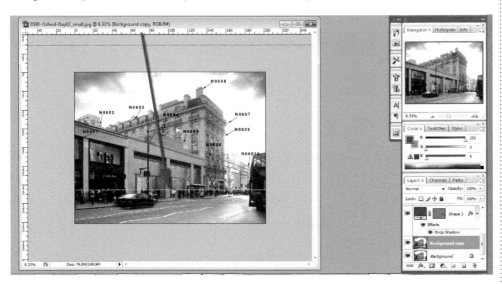

5.42

To correct the camera shift, the vanishing line (guide) needs to divide canvas into two equal sides. This exercise will require extending the canvas.

To crop, extend the canvas in a non-destructive way; first zoom out of the canvas and enable the crop tool (C). Next, drag down the crop tool until its midpoint is positioned at the centre of the guide (vanishing line). Before cropping, ensure that the *Hide* option is enabled, as opposed to *Delete*. Once satisfied, press Enter to crop extend the document/canvas. ▶5.43 and 5.44

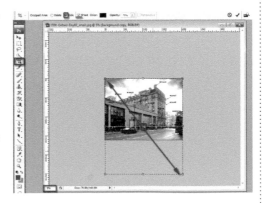

5.43

5.44

Following that, create a rectangular selection around the extended area with the marquee tool. Create a new layer (Ctrl+Shift+Alt+N), fill the selection with the paint bucket tool (G) and save the document as a PSD file.

In addition, save another version in JPEG format. ▶5.45 and 5.46

5.45

5.46

Once the document is saved as a PSD file, you'll be able to go backwards and forwards between the original and cropped versions at any point in the future. ▶5.47

The JPEG format should later be used as a background image in the camera viewport, for camera matching purposes only. The image to be used as background in 3ds Max needs to be reduced in size for camera matching purposes only.

Very large images used in the 3ds Max viewport tend to slow down the graphics card. ▶5.48

In 3ds Max, to insert the resized background image, first set and lock its width and height output size to match the resized incoming background image (e.g. 1500×1872). ▶5.49

5.47

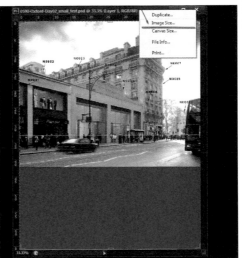

5.48

5.49

Next, go to the camera viewport and right-click on the viewport display type (e.g. wireframe, realistic, shaded, etc.). On the drop-down quad menu, choose *Viewport Background*, followed by selecting the *Configure Viewport Background* option (Alt+B). ▶5.50

5.50

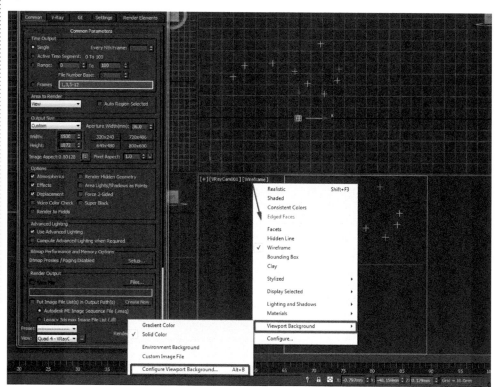

In the *Configure Viewport Background* dialogue, open the *Background* tab and choose the *Use Files* option.

In the *Setup* dialogue, choose the *Match Rendering Output* option, followed by clicking on the *Files* toggle to select and open the background image.

3D Photorealistic Rendering

Use Shift+F to enable the *Show Safe Frames* option. ▶5.51 and 5.52

After camera matching the view, it is then possible to resize the final output size to high resolution (e.g. 6000×7488).

5.53

To transfer some of the camera data (e.g. *ISO speed, F-stop, Exposure Time, Day, Time*) into the VRayPhysicalCamera, select and right-click on the raw photo. Next, select the *Properties* option and open its *Details* tab. ▶5.53

In architectural visualisation/verified views, it's common for users to have an AutoCAD drawing with the survey reference. Architectural companies often use this drawing (in conjunction with the cameras and point helpers) to help with the alignment against the existing context model.

5.54

To align the matched survey and cameras with the context model, it is necessary to first save the working scene containing the survey points, cameras and the AutoCAD drawing (if available).

5.55

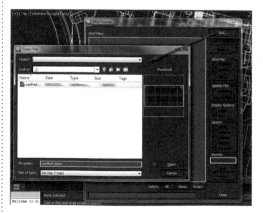

Next, open the main scene containing the context model, building and lights.

Following that, open the *XRef Scene* dialogue and *Add* the scene containing the matched survey data with cameras. ▶5.54, 5.55 and 5.56

3D Photorealistic Rendering

5.56

It's common for the matched survey points and cameras to be miles away from the 0.0.0 point and the main scene. ▶5.57

5.57

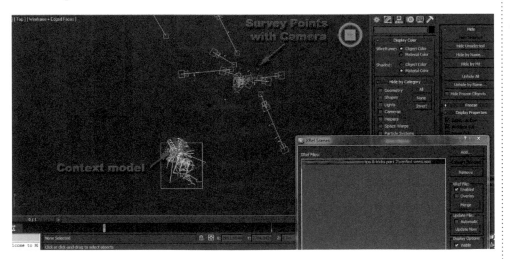

To line up the XRef survey points with the main scene, create a dummy object and bind it to the XRef scene. ▶5.58 and 5.59

5.58

5.59

Following that, move and/or rotate the dummy object in order to line it up perfectly with the main scene. ▶5.60

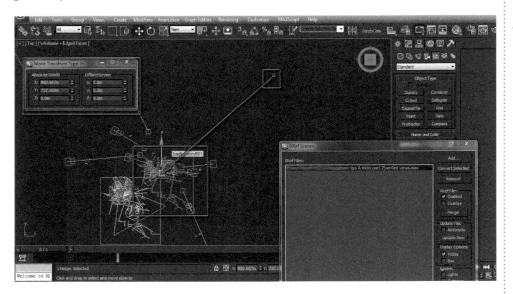

5.60

An XRef and a dummy object were used to ensure the original survey point values remained intact from their original scene location.

Camera matching without survey data

Before beginning the process of camera matching a photo, it's imperative to be aware of the following:

1. Have an almost accurate dimension of a relevant object in the photo (e.g. at least one object in the photo).

2. Be aware that photos are usually taken at eye level (e.g. 1.65 m), unless stated otherwise.

3. The average height of most people in photos is between 1.70 and 1.75 m, unless there's an exception.

4. The average door height is around 2.2 m, unless there's an exception.

5. The average height of a chair is about 0.4 m, unless there's an exception.

5.61

Start by setting up the output size to match the incoming background photo to be camera matched. ▶5.61 and 5.62

Next, load the background photo in the perspective viewport and use Shift+F to enable the *Show Safe Frames* option. ▶5.63

5.62

While the perspective viewport is still selected, click on *Tools* in the main toolbar, followed by choosing the *Perspective Match* option. ▶5.64

Perspective Match should be prompted automatically from the *Utilities* command panel. Click on the *Hide Vanishing Lines* button to make it visible in the viewport. ▶5.65

The two blue vanishing lines are usually moved to line up closely with two key horizontal lines of the photo. The two green vanishing lines are often moved to line up closely with two key perspective lines of the photo (e.g. bottom/ foreground and a top perspective line). The two red vanishing lines are often moved to line up closely with two key horizontal lines of the photo.

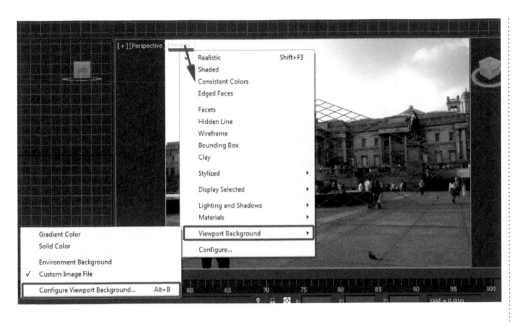

5.63

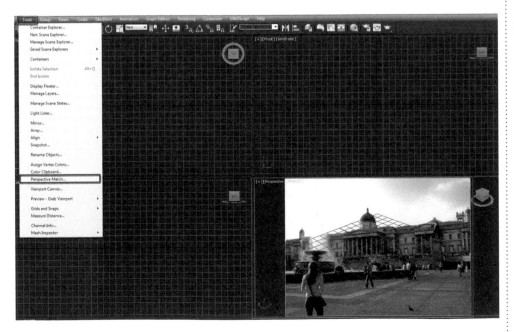

5.64

5.65

To move a vanishing line as a whole, click on its middle point and move it. To move parts of the vanishing line, click on one of its handles and move it accordingly.

The rule of thumb is to keep the top vanishing lines (e.g. red and green) on the upper areas of the photo and the lower vanishing lines (e.g. red and green) on the lower areas of the photo.

After much pulling and moving the vanishing lines around, the result should look similar to the figure depicted below. ▶5.66

5.66

Once satisfied with the position of the vanishing lines, click on *Create Camera From View* (or use the shortcut Ctrl+C). ▶5.67

As mentioned earlier, because cameras are often at eye level (e.g. 1.65 m), it is possible to create a surface (e.g. box – geometry standard primitive) 1.65 m below the camera, and increase its width and length to fit the dimensions of the photo reference. ▶5.68

5.68

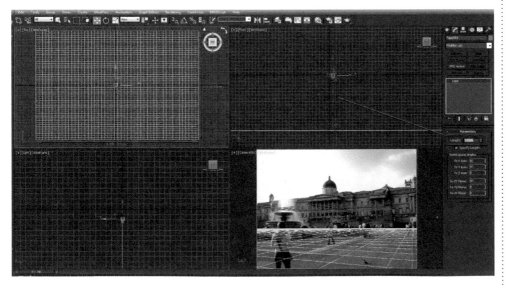

From this point onwards, it is possible to create other reference points such as people and other objects in the scene.

Because a standard 3ds Max camera is currently being used in the scene, it is possible to recreate a similar *VRayPhysicalCamera* manually or via a script camera converter. Alternatively, simply keep the current standard 3ds Max camera and open the *Environment and Effects* dialogue (8).

5.69

In the *Exposure Control* roll-out parameters, load the *VRay Exposure Control* option from its drop-down list. ▶5.69

Use the background photo property details to enter more accurate camera detail parameters such as *Focal Length, F-Stop* and *ISO speed*. The *Origin* info from the property details can be used in the *Daylight System* parameters (Chapter 3) to enter the time, day and location of the photo taken.

3D Photorealistic Rendering

Also refer to Chapters 9, 12, 16 and 19 to match the overall colour and feel of the render with the background photo in post-production. ▶5.70

For aerial shots looking down, the previously described methodology might not work. Instead it might be necessary to eyeball the correct camera perspective by constantly rotating, moving and tilting the camera accordingly. It often takes a bit of practice to camera match aerial shots accurately.

5.70

Integrating shots in 3ds max
Prior to starting, ensure the background photo is applied to the *Environment Map* toggle and that its *Mapping* coordinates are set to *Screen* type. ▶5.71

5.71

5.72

In the *Color mapping* roll-out parameters, ensure the *Affect background* function is disabled.

This function will prevent the environment background photo from being affected by the GI and the *VRayPhysicalCamera* settings (e.g. prevent it from being washed out and overexposed). ▶5.72

Next, ensure the *Enable GI* option is turned on. ▶5.73

If the 3D surface/ground in the scene is to be used as a matte object to cast shadows, do the following:

Select the surface in the scene and right-click on it to bring up its quad menu. Select the *V-Ray properties* option, to open its dialogue box. ▶5.74

In the *Matte* properties group, enable the *Matte* object option and set the *Alpha* contribution to –1.0. The value of –1.0 will ensure the 3D surface is not included in the alpha channel.

To have shadows cast onto its matte surface, enable the *Shadows* option in the *Direct light* group and close the dialogue. ▶5.75

5.73

5.74

After closing the dialogue, apply a V-Ray material similar to the ground surface seen in the background photo.

If it's a daylight shot, ensure that a *Daylight System* object is created and that the date and time information is accurately entered in its parameters, as previously covered in Chapter 3.

5.75

It's utterly imperative to enable the *Daylight Saving Time* option.

5.76

In addition, the daylight compass should be placed on the same level as the ground. ▶5.76 and 5.77

To prevent the 3D orange cone in the scene from colour-bleeding onto the matte object surface, a *VRayOverrideMtl* needs to be applied onto the original material.

5.77

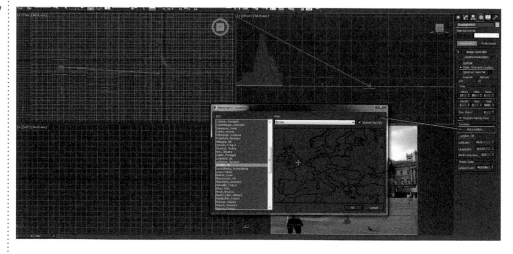

A V-Ray black material (or similar) should be applied to its GI toggle. For more information about this procedural map, refer to Chapter 2. ▶**5.78**

5.78

In addition, to make its indirectly lit areas slightly darker, open its *VRay object properties* dialogue and set its *Receive GI* value to about 0.1. ▶**5.79**

Next, create a V-Ray dome light and increase its *Intensity* value until the shadow colour is matched with the background photo. Tweak its colour temperature or sample it from the background photo in the viewport. Alternatively, plug a high dynamic range image (HDRI) into the dome light as depicted in Chapter 3. ▶**5.80** and **5.81**

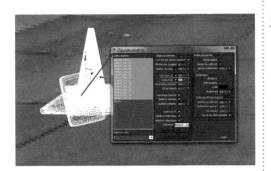

5.79

5.80

If it's a night shot, the daylight system object needs to be deleted or disabled.

By default the 2D reflections/refractions in the scene come from the *Environment Map* toggle. To override this, simply open the *Environment* roll-out from the *Render Setup* dialogue and enable the *Reflection/refraction environment* option.

Following that, apply a different bitmap or an HDRI (spherical mapping coordinates type) to its toggle. Refer to Chapter 3 to see how an HDRI can be used.

5 Tips and Tricks

To seamlessly match the bright highlights of the render with the background photo, go to the *Color mapping* roll-out parameters and increase the *Bright multiplier* value to 1.8 or higher. ▶5.82 and 5.83

5.83

Useful render elements

In addition to some of the render elements to be covered in later chapters, the following ones are also worth paying attention to:

VRayExtraTex

This render element is often used to add extra details/depth to renders in post, especially in exterior scenes. To add it, simply open the *Render Elements* tab and add *VRayExtraTex* from the *Render Elements* dialogue box. ▶5.84

5.84

5.85

Once loaded, the *VRayExtraTex* element can be renamed in the *Name* text field (e.g. type in the text and hit Enter). The next step is to add the *VRayDirt* to the *texture* toggle. ▶5.85

To edit the *VRayDirt* settings, drag it from the *texture* toggle and drop it onto a material slot as an instanced copy. Test render its default parameters. ▶5.86

5.86

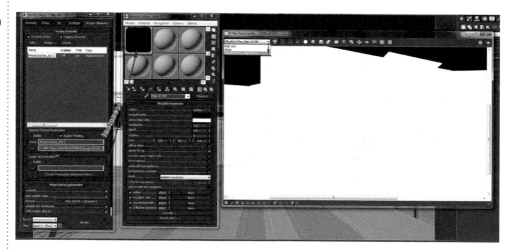

Most of the *VRayDirt* parameters are self-explanatory. The darker areas represent the occluded colour, and the white areas represent the unoccluded colour.

The *radius* parameter determines the occluded colour radius. The *subdivs* parameter controls the smoothness of the occluded colour. The default value is 8 (very grainy). Try different values to see what works best. ▶5.87

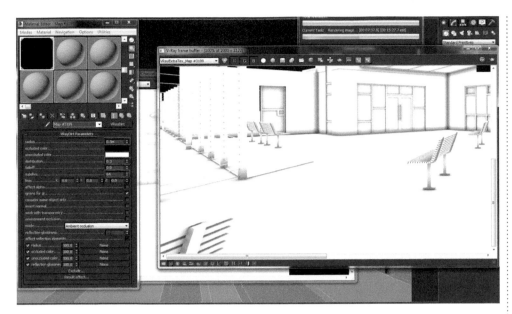

5.87

5.88

Sometimes users also create a second *VRayExtraTex* element (renamed) with the *invert normal* enabled.

The standard ambient occlusion/dirt adds shadows to cornices. The *invert normal* function allows corners (facing outwards) to also have shadows applied onto them. This effect can sometimes add detail to 'flat' areas of an image. ▶5.88

It's widely recommended that the VRayExtraTex element be used in a separate 3ds Max file, as it may contribute to drastic increases in the rendering times.

5.89

Refer to some of the techniques covered in Chapters 9, 12, 16 and 19 to help blend and tweak this V-Ray element with the original render in post-production. ▶5.89

For more realistic and complex weathering effects, use a V-Ray plug-in called *enRichPro*. While film/production companies make discrepancies very prominent in their shots, professional 3D visualizers tend to make them as subtle as possible, as clients often expect their buildings to appear relatively new (e.g.

5.90

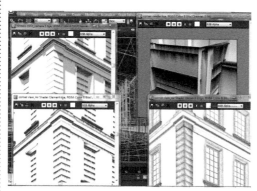

architects and developers). To make exterior renders more realistic, this unique and particularly useful plug-in can be subtly overlaid in post-production as multiple render passes. For more information about it, visit: ▶5.90

http://www.enrichpro.com/en/richdirt/index.html

VRayLightSelect

This render element is quite useful to help control the intensity and colour of specific lights in post-production. Note that this element only works with V-Ray lights. To use it, simply select and add it to the *Render Elements* list. ▶5.91

5.91

Following that, in the *Lights* group, click on the *Add* button to select the light(s) in the scene. ▶5.92

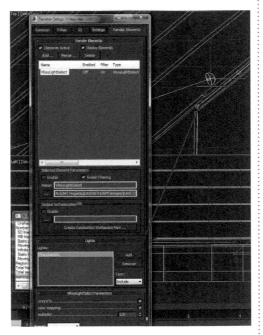

5.92

5.93

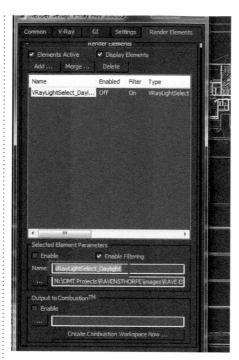

If you intend to have different sets of *VRayLightSelect* elements in the list, rename the element and press Enter. ▶5.93 and 5.94

5.94

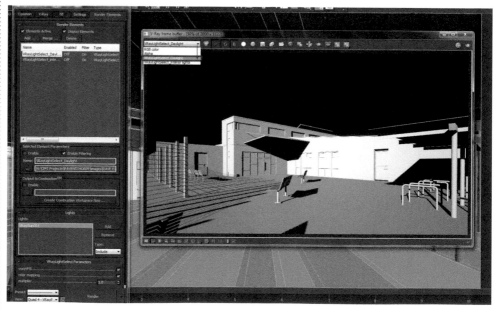

To tweak the rendered *VRayLightSelect* element in post-production, use some of the techniques covered in Chapters 9, 12, 16 and 19 to help blend, tweak and change the colour of the *VRayLightSelect* element. ▶5.95 and 5.96

5.95

VRaySampleRate

Users often add this element to closely monitor how V-Ray is handling the rendering process throughout the scene.

5.96

The blue colours depict areas of the scene where few or no render samples are being used.

The green colours highlight areas of the scene where some render samples are being used. These areas often take little or no time to process the render.

The red colours depict areas of the scene where a substantial or large number of render samples are being used.

These areas normally take an exceptionally long time to process the render. The red areas seen in the frame buffer often contain high levels of glossiness/reflectivity, high mesh density, displacement, smooth shadows, etc. ▶5.97

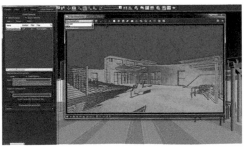

5.97

VRayZDepth

This render element allows users to set the Z-depth of a scene. The render channel can later be used in post-production to create effects such as depth of field (DOF) and fog.

The *zdepth min* value determines the minimum camera/view value where the Z-depth should start. The default value is often 0.0.

The *zdepth max* value determines the maximum camera/view value where the Z-depth should stop (gradient). The value of 9.0 is often used to cover some of the foreground areas of the view/camera.

The Z-depth channel works best when there's a clear gradient between bright and very dark areas. ▶5.98

5.98

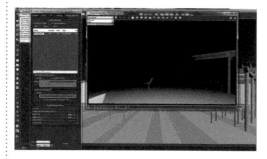

One of the most common ways to use it in Photoshop is to emulate the DOF. To do so, open the *VRayZDepth* and its *Channels* palette, then hold down the Ctrl key and click on its RGB channel to enable the gradient selection. ▶5.99

5.99

While the selection is still active, save it by clicking on *Select* on the main toolbar and choosing the *Save Selection* option from the drop-down list. The *Save Selection* dialogue should appear. Choose the document destination to save it, then rename it and click *OK* to close the dialogue.

This new saved selection should be added to the *Channels* palette of the document destination chosen.

Note that selections can only be saved to a different document when both documents share the same pixel size (same proportions). ▶5.100 and 5.101

5.100

5.101

5.102

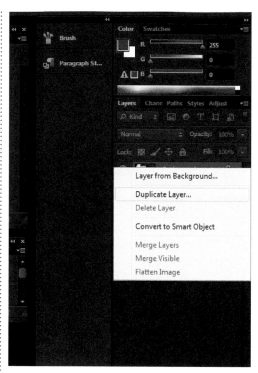

Before applying the Lens Blur filter to emulate the DOF effect, duplicate the main layer first by right-clicking on the layer and choosing the *Duplicate Layer* option. This precautionary measure will make it possible to revert back to the original layer, if required. ▶5.102

5.103

Next, click on the *Filter* main toolbar and choose the *Lens Blur* option from its drop-down list. ▶5.103

The *Lens Blur* dialogue should appear. To begin using this filter, choose the *Depth Map* selection previously saved in this document (e.g. *z*-depth).

Enable the *Invert* function if necessary and begin playing with functions such as *Blur Focal Distance, Radius, Shape* and *Noise*. ▶5.104

5.104

For more professional high-end results in Photoshop, use plug-ins such as DOFPRO (http://www.dofpro.com/index.htm).

VRayDRBucket

This render element is quite useful to display the machines being used to render each bucket. In addition, it can also be used to identify render buckets generating artefacts. ▶5.105

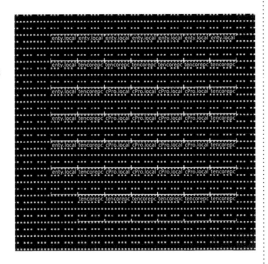

5.105

6

Interior Daylight

Pre-production

6 Pre-production

6.1 Client Brief

For this project, the main brief from the client was to have a daylight shot, with the camera emphasis on the corridor area.

Furthermore, there was an additional request to 'tell a story', by having people utilizing the main features of the space such as the staircase, corridor and window.

6.2 Photo References and Mood Board

To help convey their ideas and aspirations, the designers/architects supplied the visualizers with reference images. In addition, the studio/artists also chose the photo references for the overall lighting and 'feel' of the image.

Note that most designers/architects supply the studio/artists with their own design mood board(s) depicting their furniture and materials.

Finally, whatever furniture the client and/or the artist/studio chooses, it has to be a highly detailed model with photorealistic textures and shaders applied onto it. Design Connected (http://www.designconnected.com/) is amongst the most popular websites to find such types of models.

6.1

Camera and lighting suggestions

Camera/colours

Lighting

Alternatively, you can create your own photorealistic models and shaders, if the requested furniture is bespoke. ▶6.1 and 6.2

Material and finishes suggestions

Windows

Glass

Floor

Handrails

Conclusion

The pre-production process is vital to sign off on key camera angles and the scene composition as a whole. The studio/artist also often uses this stage to iron out the art direction, furniture, materials, colours, etc., prior to entering the production phase.

7

Interior Daylight

Creating Materials

This chapter will help users understand the process of loading the V-Ray renderer in the scene, setting up the 3ds Max file, creating shaders, applying textures and tweaking the overall material realistically.

Furthermore, materials such as metal, floor, glass and walls are explored in detail throughout the chapter.

Tip: https://www.arroway-textures.ch/ is a good resource to find seamless and realistic textures.

Creating Materials

7.1 Creating Materials

Let's start by opening the MAX file under the name of 'SMESTOW_Interior_ Start'. You should be prompted with the warning 'File Load: Gamma & LUT Settings Mismatch'.

7.1

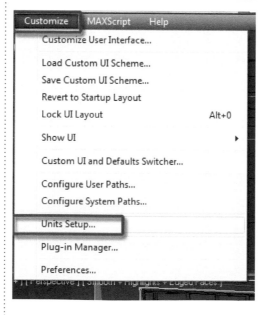

Accept the option *Adopt the File's Gamma and LUT Settings?* and click *OK* to close the dialogue. ▶7.1

Next, to ensure that we work within the right system units, set it up accordingly. It's vital to work within the correct units display and correct model scale to achieve realistic results.

Click on the *Customize* main toolbar and choose the *Units Setup* option from the drop-down list. ▶7.2

7.2

In the *Units Setup* dialogue, choose the *Metric* option, from the *Display Unit Scale* group. Note that this function only affects the metric display in the viewport (for measuring purposes only). Choose *Millimetres* from the drop-down list or another metric system that you're more accustomed to working with.

Users often switch between millimetres and meters, depending on what they're trying to measure. ▶7.3

To check or tweak the physical scale of objects in the scene, click on the *System Unit Setup* button to bring up its dialogue box.

7.3

Note that changing any of the values displayed in this dialogue will affect the physical scale of all objects in the scene. Click *OK* to close the *System Unit Setup* dialogue and *OK* again to close the *Units Setup* dialogue. ▶7.4

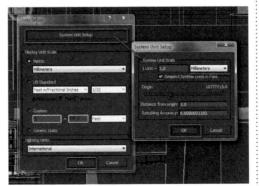

7.4

To ensure objects in the scene are at the correct scale, users often measure basic items such as doors and other common objects that we can easily reference for real scale.

Open the *Select From Scene* dialogue by pressing the *H* key on your keyboard. In the *Find* field, type in the letter *D*, then click on the *Name* tab.

7.5

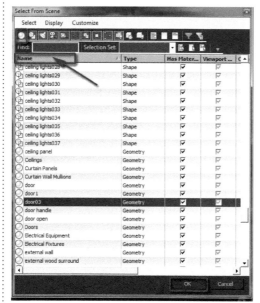

By clicking on the *Name* tab, 3ds Max will automatically find all listed objects starting with the letter *D* alphabetically. From the list, select the object under the name 'door03' and click *OK* to select it in the scene. ▶7.5

Next, isolate the object by pressing Alt+Q on the keyboard. Next, open the *Create* command panel and select the *Helper* button. Then click on the *Tape* tool.

To measure, click and drag its target on the viewport. ▶7.6

7.6

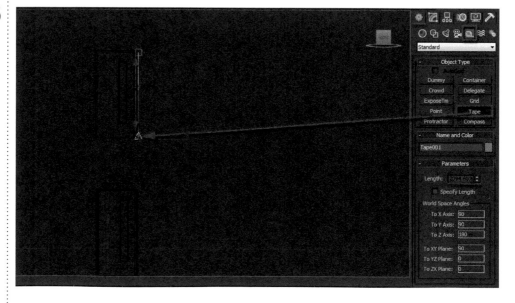

3D Photorealistic Rendering

If you are not accustomed to seeing units being displayed in millimetres, change the display units as described earlier.
▶7.7 and 7.8

The door scale seems correct. However, feel free to measure other objects in the scene.

Exit Isolation Mode by clicking its button.

Next, choose and load the rendering engine. Open the render setup dialogue by pressing F10. In the *Common* tab, scroll down and open/extend the *Assign Renderer* parameters.

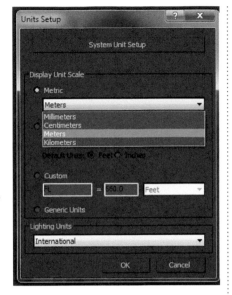

7.7

7.8

7.9

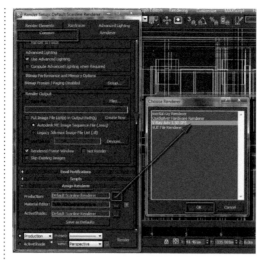

To choose and assign a renderer, click on the *Production* toggle. The *Choose Renderer* dialogue box should pop up. Choose the V-Ray renderer from the list and click *OK* to close the dialogue box. ▶7.9 and 7.10

Alternatively, it is possible to set up 3ds Max to automatically load a specific renderer when starting a fresh 3ds Max scene.

7.10

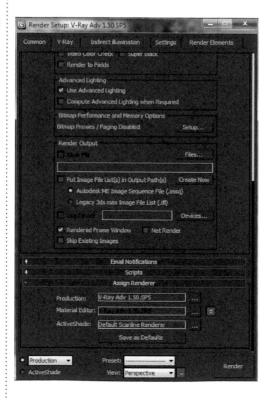

To do so, go to the *Customize* main toolbar and choose *Custom UI and Defaults Switcher* from the drop-down list. In its dialogue, pick your preferred rendering engine and click *Set*. Also click *OK* to the dialogue warning you about the next time you restart 3ds Max. ▶7.11, 7.12 and 7.13

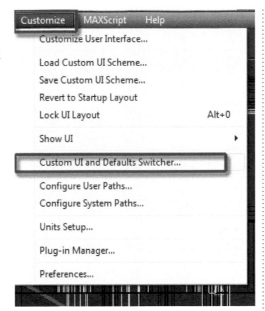

7.11

7.12

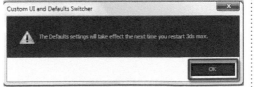

7.13

7 Creating Materials

7.14

T--I--P

To move a
targeted
camera freely,
users often
disable its
camera target
first, then
move the
camera. Once
satisfied with
the camera
location, its
camera target
can then be
re-enabled and
moved/set, if
necessary.

7.15

Prior to beginning creation of
materials, we need to set up the
camera first. This will ensure that we
only work on areas within the camera
range.

In the *Create* command panel, click
on the camera button and choose
VRay from the drop-down list
(which appears after clicking on
Standard). ▶7.14

Select the top viewport first. Back in the V-Ray *Object Type* group, click on the
VRayPhysicalCamera button, followed by clicking the cursor target on the top
viewport and dragging it to the left, to set its camera target. ▶7.15

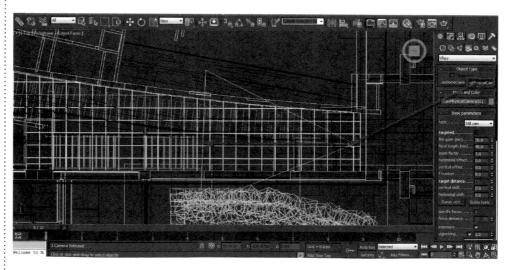

3D Photorealistic Rendering

Accept the default V-ray physical camera settings to start with, followed by moving the camera to eye level (e.g. 1.65/1.70 m) from the floor. Rename the camera as 'VRayPhysicalCamera_main'.

In addition, choose a specific location in the scene: Corridor area.

For this project, the camera location chosen was as follows: $X = 36.819$; $Y = -334.252$; $Z = 0.877$; Dolly = 22.155. ▶7.16

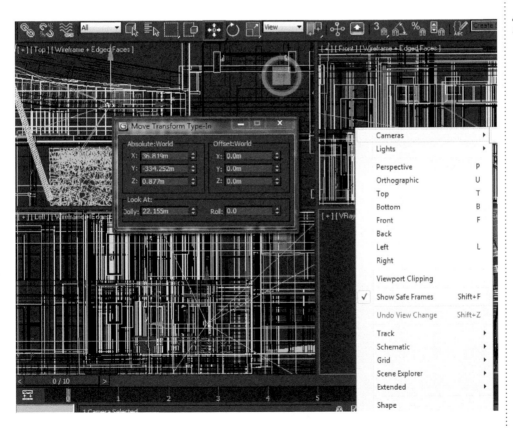

7.16

Its rotational position was as follows: $X = -80.371$; $Y = -180.0$; $Z = -71.665$; Dolly = 22.155. ▶7.17

7.17

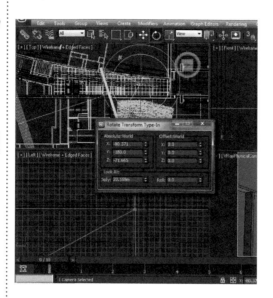

T--I--P

It's always helpful to have all four viewports (top, left, front and camera) visible when positioning a camera.

The camera target position was as follows: $X = 16.085$; $Y = -341.123$; $Z = 4.583$. ▶7.18

7.18

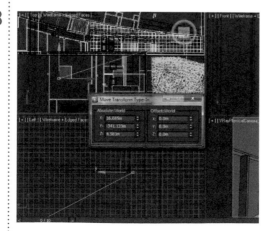

The subsequent step is to set up the film gate and vertical shift values to capture the desired area. Increase the film gate value to about 65.0 and decrease the vertical shift to about 0.13. The remaining values have not been changed. ▶7.19 and 7.20

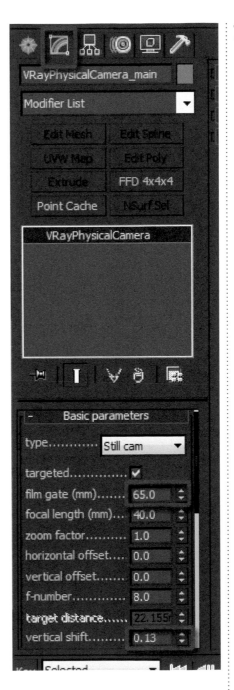

7.19

7.20

Although the above positions and values have worked well for this project, please feel free to try different values and positions, if desired.

To capture more of the foreground, we're going to tinker with the scene's common output size values.

Open the *Render Setup* dialogue as previously done (press F10).

In the *Common* tab, under the *Output Size* group, increase the *Height* value to about 800.

7.21

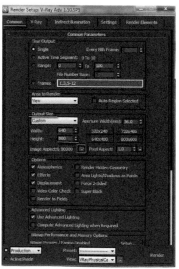

The *Image Aspect* ratio should automatically change to 0.8. Lock it by clicking on its padlock button. This will enable you to tweak the width and height values proportionally. ▶7.21

If this camera were to be part of an animation, to be later exported as a movie/video; then the *Output Size* would have had to be one of the listed drop-down presets (e.g. HDTV video). ▶7.22

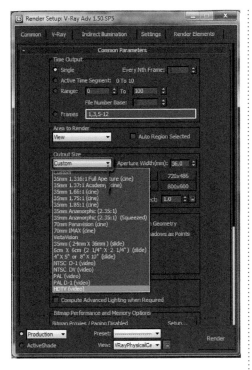

7.22

7.2 Glass Material

Prior to creating the glass material, let's start by viewing its photo references as previously discussed.

Click on the *Rendering* main toolbar and choose *View Image File* from its drop-down menu. In the resource files, pick the photo named 'reference 5.jpg'. ▶7.23 and 7.24

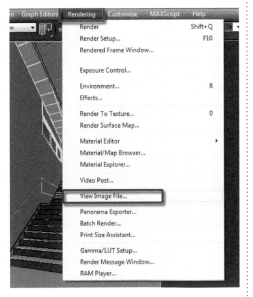

7.23

7.24

In addition, also open the photo named 'reference 6.jpg'. There are now two good references of a glass material in the viewport.

One of the references depicts a clear/transparent glass with a similar camera angle, reflecting and refracting its surroundings.

The second reference depicts a slightly tinted (green) and reflective glass. ▶7.25

7.25

The subsequent step is to try to emulate some of the glass properties depicted in both photo references.

Click on an empty space/area of the main toolbar and press *M* to open the Material Editor. Select an empty material slot and click on the *Standard* toggle to bring up the *Material/Map Browser* dialogue.

In the *Material/Map Browser* dialogue, expand the *V-Ray Adv 1.50.SP5* roll-out and double click on *VRayMtl* to load this shader. ▶7.26 and 7.27

7.26

7.27

Next, select the object under the name of *Curtain Panels* in the scene (using the *select by name* dialogue (H) or by selecting it directly from the viewport). Assign it to the empty material slot previously selected.

Rename the material (by typing the name) as 'glass external'. ▶7.28

7.28

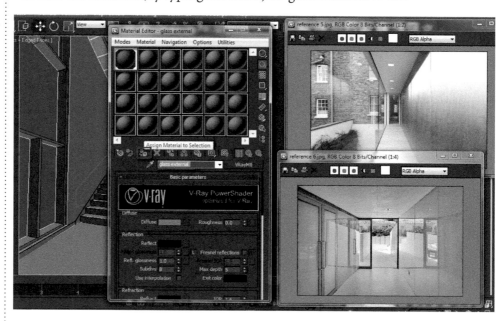

First, we will set the opacity of the glass as per one of the photo references. In V-ray, the opacity is determined by the refraction colour: very dark = opaque; very bright = transparent. Scroll down to the *Refraction* group. Click on the *Refract* colour swatch and hold down the mouse button.

The *Color Selector* dialogue should pop up. To make the glass material more transparent, slide down the *Whiteness* arrow to almost white or enter 215 for the red, green and blue values. Click on *OK* to close the dialogue.

In addition, enable the *Background* button in the *Material Editor*. This function will help visualize any changes of the material in the editor. ▶7.29

3D Photorealistic Rendering

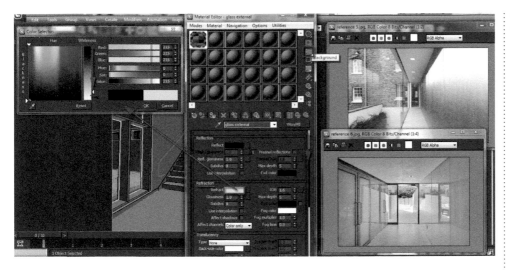

By default the IOR is set to 1.6, which is slightly too high when compared to the photo reference. To adjust this to be closer to the photo reference, type 1.1 in the IOR field. Note how its material thumbnail changes simultaneously.

Next, we will change the glass tint. Open the diffuse *Color Selector* dialogue. Click on its *sample screen color* tool and pick the green tone of the photo reference. Note how its diffuse colour is automatically changed. Click *OK* to close the dialogue box. ▶7.30

Next, we will finalize the glass properties.

First, increase the default reflectivity of the glass. Open the *Reflection* group and click on the *Reflect* colour swatch to open the *Color Selector* dialogue. Decrease its whiteness arrow to almost white (e.g. R, G, B = 176) to make the glass more reflective. Note that the *Material Editor* thumbnail changes simultaneously.

To add a bit of sharp shine as per the photo reference, decrease its *Refl. Glossiness* value to about 0.9. Notice the shine appearing in the *Material Editor* thumbnail. Also increase its *Subdivs* values to about 12.

This will help eliminate potential glossy artefacts when rendering. At times, these values may require increasing to 30 or higher.

The rule of thumb is: lower *Refl. Glossiness* values = higher *Subdivs* values.

To ensure shadows are cast through the transparent glass/material, go to the *Refraction* group and enable the *Affect shadows* function.

Furthermore, in *Affect channels*, choose the '*Color+alpha*' option from the drop-down list. This option is quite useful when editing the alpha channels in post-production, especially when dealing with reflections. ▶7.31

7.31

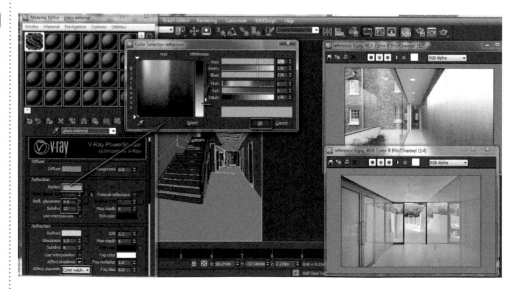

Finally, while the object under the name of 'Curtain Panels' is still selected in the scene, right-click and choose *Object Properties* from the quad menu. ▶7.32

The *Object Properties* dialogue should pop up. Open its general parameters.

In the *Rendering Control* group, click on the *By Object* button to enable the group (grey by default).

In the *G-Buffer* group, change the *Object ID* to 1 and click *OK* to close the dialogue. The G-Buffer Object ID number will later play a crucial part when setting up the render elements for post-production. The following objects in the scene (that are relevant) can be numbered incrementally.

Also apply this glass material to other glass objects in the scene and close the glass photo references. Please refer to the final scene.

Note that no test renders are carried out until the lights are created. This stage is mainly to create the basic material parameters with the help of the Material Editor and the viewport. Once the lights are created, the materials will be tweaked further to react realistically to the lights and *vice versa*. ▶7.33

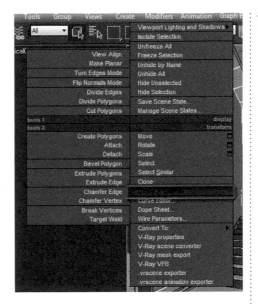

7.32

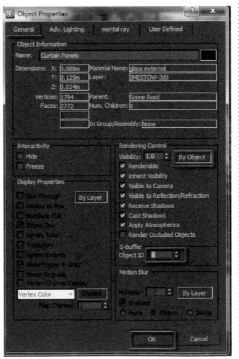

7.33

7.3 Metal Material

As previously done, we'll start by loading photo references of the relevant material in the viewport. Open the following photo references using some of the techniques described earlier: 'reference 9.jpg' and 'reference 16.jpg'. ▶7.34

The photo references depict some of the key physical properties of the metal surface, such as the overall shine, glint on corners and the reflectiveness across its dark surface. In addition, some subtle surface discrepancies such as scratches are visible.

To start, select a new material slot and load VRayMtl as previously done. Rename the new material slot 'metal'. ▶7.35

3D Photorealistic Rendering

In the scene, select the object under the name of 'Curtain Wall Mullions' and assign the 'metal' material slot to it. Change its diffuse colour by opening the *Color Selector* and using the *Sample Screen Color* tool to pick the colour depicted in 'reference 16.jpg' (*R* = 69; *G* = 74; *B* = 78). Use some techniques highlighted earlier. ▶7.36

7.36

7.37

Next, change its reflectivity to match the photo reference. In the *Reflection* group, open the *Reflect Color Selector* dialogue and decrease its *Whiteness* value to about mid-grey (R, G, B = 36). Notice the changes in the *Material Editor* thumbnail. ▶7.37

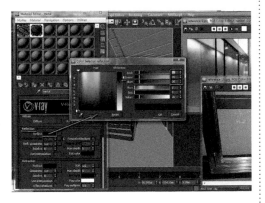

To emulate the metallic shine and the subtle discrepancies that break its surface uniformity, apply a pre-created grey material to its *Refl. glossiness* toggle.

Click on the *Refl. glossiness* toggle. In the *Material/Map Browser* dialogue, pick the *Bitmap* procedural material, under the *Standard* roll-out.

In the *Select Bitmap Image File* dialogue, choose the 'paint grey.jpg' texture and click *Open* to load it. ▶7.38

7.38

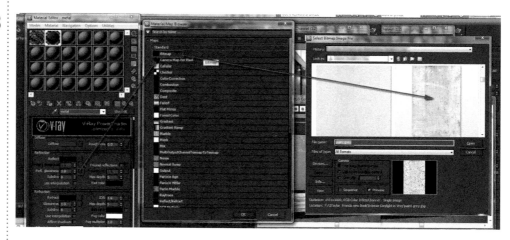

7.39

A very good resource to find seamless high resolution textures is, www.arroway-textures.com

The bitmap parameters should load automatically. To view the texture in the viewport, click on the button *Show Standard Map in Viewport*. ▶7.39

The texture doesn't seem to be displaying properly in the viewport. To rectify this, go to the *Create* command panel and open the *Modify* tab.

Click on the *Modify list* button and select the *UVW Map* modifier from the drop-down list. Use the slider to scroll down.

Also choose the *Box* mapping type.
▶7.40 and 7.41

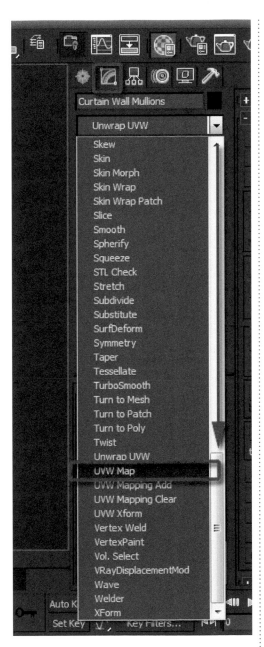

7.40

7.41

7.42

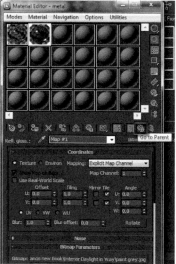

Back in the *Material Editor,* go to the main *Diffuse* parameters by clicking on the *Go to Parent* button. ▶7.42

With the new grey texture applied onto the *Refl. glossiness* toggle it may be necessary to reduce the reflectivity slightly. Open the *Reflect Color Selector* and set the RGB whiteness to about 35.

For a better preview of the material changes, double-click on its *Material Editor* thumbnail to maximize it.

Furthermore, increase the *Subdivs* value to about 12. It's worth noting again that all values applied at this stage are preliminary. ▶7.43

7.43

Assign this material to other objects in the scene such as the window upstairs (detach objects if necessary) and door frames.

Finally, change its G-Buffer *Object ID* value to 2, using some of the steps described earlier. Other material effects such as VRayEdgesTex will be introduced once the lights have been created.

7.4 Hand Rails

First, load the photo reference under the name of 'reference 17.jpg' using some of the steps covered earlier.

Some of the main characteristics of this type of metallic finish are the direction of its reflection (e.g. horizontal), its shine and its slightly dark grey colour.

To begin emulating this material, select the object under the name of 'hand rails' in the scene.

In the *Material Editor,* select the previous metal material thumbnail, followed by left-clicking, holding down the mouse button and dragging it to the next available thumbnail.

This technique will help progress this process much faster.

Next, rename this new material as 'metal handrail' and assign it to the selected object in the scene. ▶7.44

7.44

3D Photorealistic Rendering

To emulate the intensity of its reflection, go to the *Reflect* group and increase the *Reflect* brightness (R, G, B = 205). ▶7.45

To change the direction of its reflection, scroll down to the *BRDF* roll-out and decrease its Anisotropy (–1…1) spinner to about –0.8. Note the changes taking place in the *Material Editor* thumbnail.

7.46

The values can be tweaked later once the lights are incorporated in the scene. ▶7.46

Next, scroll back to the *Reflection* group and clear the current material (M) from the *Refl. glossiness* toggle by right-clicking on its toggle and choosing *Clear* from the pop-up list.

In addition, change its value to about 0.87. ▶7.47

7.47

Apply this material to the other handrail in the scene and change both objects' G-Buffer object ID number to 3, using some of the steps described earlier.

7.5 Floor

Select a new *Material Editor* and load the VRayMtl shader into it. Rename it as 'Floor'.

Prior to begin working on the floor material open the photo references under the names of 'reference 10.jpg' and 'reference 11.jpg'.

Note how the concrete surface is slightly uneven and reflective. In addition, its rough texture is quite apparent. ▶7.48

7.48▼

In the *Diffuse* group, click on its toggle and choose the texture under the name of 'Cimento 01 CLARO.jpeg', using some of the steps covered earlier. ▶7.49

7.49

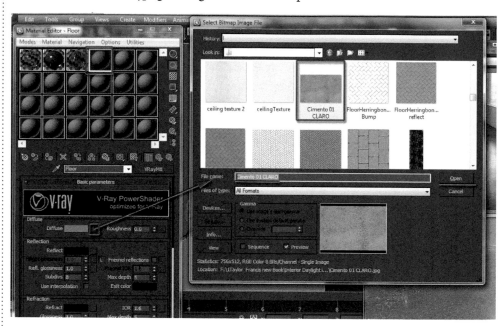

7.50

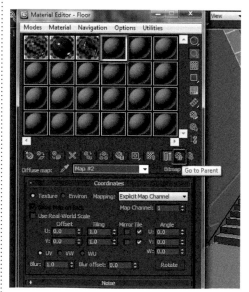

Once the texture is loaded, click on the *Go to Parent* button, to go back to the main material parameters. ▶7.50

In the scene, select the object under the name of 'Floor' and assign the floor material to it. In addition, go inside its *Diffuse* toggle and enable *Show Standard Map in Viewport*, followed by applying a UVW mapping to it.

To make its texture tiling similar to the photo references, set the *U Tile* value to about 5.0 and the *V Tile* value to 3.0. Feel free to try different values, if desired. ▶7.51

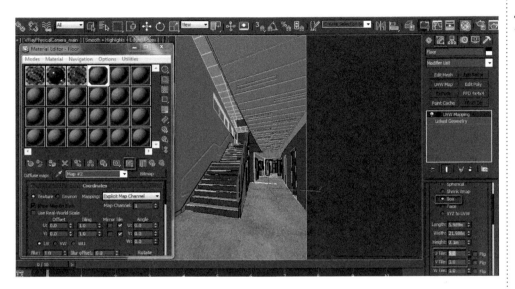

7.51

As with most surfaces, they reflect different amounts of energy throughout. To emulate this physical property, apply a greyscale texture to its *Reflect* toggle.

Note that a greyscale version of the diffuse texture has already been created. The more contrast the greyscale texture has, the sharper/more defined will be the results.

For this exercise we'll use a greyscale texture with no contrast, in order to achieve a more diffused/smoother result.

Locate and apply the texture under the name of 'Cimento 01 CLARO_gloss.jpeg' to the *Reflect* toggle. Keep the *Fresnel reflections* function enabled.

To control its shine, enable the *Hilight glossiness* function by deselecting its *L* padlock.

Next, decrease its value to about 0.71. Set its *Refl.glossiness* value to about 0.88 and double its *Subdivs* to 16.

7 Creating Materials

7.52

Note again that these values are preliminary and will be tweaked later once the lights are incorporated in the scene. ►7.52

The final step is to emulate the surface undulation as seen in one of the photo references.

Start by scrolling down to the *Maps* roll-out and expanding it. Click on its *Bump* toggle and choose the texture under the name of 'noise.jpeg'. ►7.53

7.53

3D Photorealistic Rendering

Once the texture is loaded and made visible in the viewport, tweak its *Coordinates* parameters in order to make it fit realistically on the surface.

Begin by rotating its *W Angle* to about 90 degrees. Also set its *U Tiling* value to 0.1 and *V Tiling* value to about 0.3.

These values worked adequately for this exercise. However, feel free to try different values, if desired. ▶7.54

7.54

Finally, assign this material to the stairs. Change the G-Buffer *Object ID* number of all objects with this material to 4.

7.6 Ceiling Panels

Start by opening the photo reference of a ceiling panel in 3ds Max. Use some of the steps described earlier to open the file named 'Picture 003.jpg'. ▶7.55

7.55

Note the subtle and 'Fresnel-like' reflectivity displayed in the ceiling panel. To recreate this effect in 3ds Max, first create a new V-Ray material slot and name it 'ceiling panels'.

7.56

Use some of the steps highlighted earlier. ▶7.56

Next, select in scene the object under the name of 'Ceiling panels' and assign the newly created material slot to it.

In its *Diffuse* group, open the *Diffuse Color Selector* by double-clicking on its colour slot. In the *Color Selector* dialogue, set its base colour to off-white, by dragging down its *Whiteness* slider.

Alternatively, enter the value of 226 in the *Value* colour swatch. Click *OK* to close the dialogue. ▶7.57

7.57

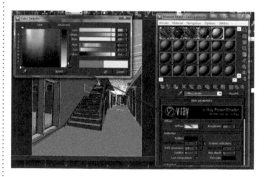

To emulate the Fresnel reflections as depicted in the photo reference, disable the V-Ray Fresnel reflections function and use the falloff procedural material instead. This will allow better control of the Fresnel reflectivity.

3D Photorealistic Rendering

However, first enable the *Hilight glossiness* function by deselecting its *L* padlock and click on its *Reflect* toggle.

In the *Material/Map Browser* dialogue, pick the *Falloff* procedural map and click *OK* to close the dialogue. ▶7.58

7.58

The *Falloff* parameters should load up. The falloff is broken down into two colour swatches, black and white. The first colour swatch represents the middle part of a surface, and the second swatch represents the fringe areas of a surface.

To start with, set the middle part of the surface to be slightly reflective, as opposed to not reflective at all (i.e. black).

To increase its reflectivity, set its colour value to about 37. Note that most values might require tweaking further once lights are added to the scene. ▶7.59

7.59

Next, decrease the fringe reflectivity of the surface, by setting its white colour (i.e. fully reflective) to a greyish tone (e.g. 189).

In addition, enable the *Background* button in the *Material Editor*. This function will help visualize any changes of the material in the editor. ▶7.60

7.60

Next, click on the *Go to Parent* button to go back to the main diffuse parameters.

To closely monitor the material changes, double click on the *Ceiling panels* material slot to maximize it.

To spread out the ceiling panel highlights as seen in the photo reference, decrease its *Hilight glossiness* value to about 0.43. Blur the reflections slightly by decreasing the *Refl. glossiness* to about 0.84. Note the changes taking place in the material slot.

7.61

Furthermore, set the *Subdivs* value to about 16. The default value of 8 is often too low to smooth out reflection graininess. ▶**7.61**

Since the base Diffuse has no texture, it is possible to make it more interesting by also applying the falloff procedural map to its *Diffuse* toggle.

7.62

Next, set its first colour swatch to a darker white (i.e. *Value*: 195); and the second colour swatch to a slightly darker white (i.e. *Value*: 221). In addition, set the *Falloff Type* to *Fresnel*. ▶**7.62**

This falloff type will yield the effect of a rim light on a surface, depending on the camera angle. ▶7.63

To 'break up' the ceiling panel surface slightly, plug in the same noise texture applied earlier to the *Bump* toggle.

To rotate the texture as previously done, in the coordinates parameters, set the W angle to 90.0 degrees.

7.63

To tile the texture, apply a *UVW Mapping* modifier to it. In the *Mapping* group, set the *Tiling* type to *Box* and tile it until the texture looks correct in the viewport.

For this scene, the following values worked well to start with: *U Tile*, 4.0; *V Tile*, 2.0.

As mentioned earlier, some of these values/parameters may require fine-tuning further once the lights are added to the scene. ▶7.64

7.64

Finally, assign this material to another object in the scene, named 'ceiling'. Change the G-Buffer *Object ID* number of all objects with this material to 5.

7.7 Ceiling Lights

For this specific material, create a basic VRayLightMtl and plug a texture into its *Map* toggle.

To load the VRayLightMtl shader, create a new V-Ray material slot and name it as 'ceiling lights'.

Following that, click on its *VRayMtl* toggle to access the *Material/Map Browser* dialogue.

In the *Material/Map Browser* dialogue, pick the *VRayLightMtl*, under the *Standard* material roll-out.

7.65

In more recent versions of 3ds Max, this procedural material will be under the V-Ray material roll-out and/or directly included into the *VRayMtl* parameters/functions. ▶**7.65**

Once the *VRayLightMtl* is loaded, apply a texture to its colour by clicking on its toggle and picking the texture under the name of 'uplight_03_w copy.jpg'. ▶**7.66**

7.66

Once the texture is loaded, assign it to the object under the name of 'ceiling lights034' and make the texture visible in the viewport.

To do so, click on the button *Show Standard Map in Viewport*. Rotate the texture coordinates by 90.0 degrees. ▶7.67

Next, isolate the relevant object (Alt+Q) to closely work on the texture.

7.67

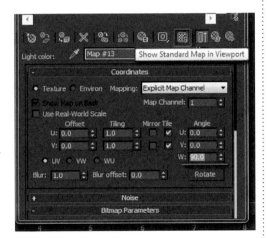

In the top viewport, the texture display seems slightly whitewashed. To correct it, go back to the main *VRayLightMtl* parameters and double-click on its colour swatch to bring up the *Color Selector* dialogue.

In the *Color Selector* dialogue, change its value to black by typing in the value of 0. Note how the texture is less washed out in the viewport now.

To correct the bitmap tiling on the object's surface, apply the *UVW Mapping* modifier and set the *Mapping* type to *Box*.

The *Make Unique* button directly below the modifier list indicates that the object is an instance. As such, all changes made to this object will affect other equal instanced objects, unless you click on the *Make Unique* button to collapse it.

Back on the *UVW Mapping* modifier, click on it once to highlight its UVW gizmo in the viewport and enable the *Rotate* button from the main toolbar.

With the UVW gizmo enabled in the viewport (yellow), begin rotating the bitmap to match the object's angle. ▶7.68

7.68

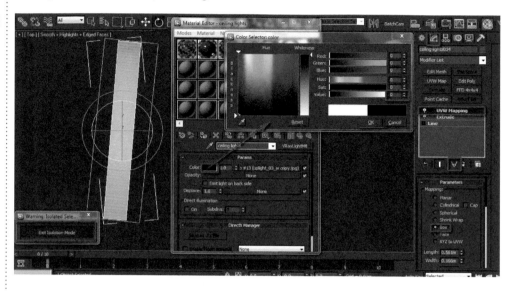

Once the bitmap's angle on the surface is correct, scroll down to the *Alignment* group and click on the *Fit* button. If necessary, rotate and fit the bitmap multiple times until the bitmap is aligned more perfectly. ▶7.69

7.69

Click on *Exit Isolation Mode* and switch to the camera viewport.

Finally, apply this material to all ceiling lights in the scene. Change the G-Buffer object ID of these objects to 6.

7.8 Walls

Because this specific material is quite basic, no photo reference will be required.

Start by creating a new V-Ray material slot, naming it 'Wall' and assigning it to the object under the name of 'Wall'. ►7.70

Next, apply the bitmap under the name of 'Stucco.jpg' to its *Diffuse* toggle. ►7.71

Once the bitmap is loaded, make it visible in the viewport and decrease its *Blur* value to 0.01.

Due to the bitmap size being relatively small, reducing the *Blur* values and enabling the *Filtering* type to *Summed area* will sharpen the bitmap. However, it will also increase the rendering time slightly.

In addition, apply the *UVW Mapping* modifier to the 'wall' object.

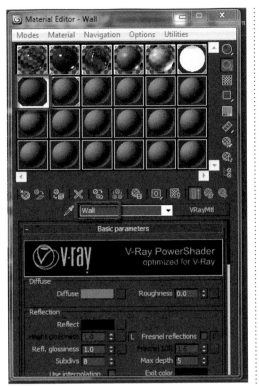

7.70

7.71

7 Creating Materials

Set the *Mapping type* to *Box* and tile the texture realistically. The following values worked well for this scene: *U tile*, 19.0; *V Tile*, 1.0.

7.72

While these values worked well, feel free to experiment with different values/parameters, if desired. ▶7.72

Back in the main *Diffuse* parameters, scroll down to the *Bump* toggle, and apply the 'noise.jpg' bitmap.

Tile and move it realistically on the wall surface. After few tweaks, the following values worked well as a starting point: Offset, *U* = –0.7; *V* = 1.44; *Tiling*, *U* = 0.3; *V* = 0.1. ▶7.73

7.73

Finally, apply this material to all Wall objects in the scene. Change the G-Buffer object ID number of these objects to 7.

The remaining materials in the scene were created using the same techniques described earlier.

Conclusion

Materials/shaders play a vital role when achieving photorealistic results. While this stage of the process might be considered preliminary, it is still quite important to diligently set up key material parameters such as the following:

- Realistic texture tiling.
- The correct amount of glossiness, reflectivity and highlights.
- Create, tweak and plug multiple textures into a variety of different toggles such as *Bump*, *Reflect*, *Hilight glossiness* and *Refl. Glossiness*.

8

Interior Daylight

Lighting and Rendering

Lighting and rendering a scene is one of the most crucial parts of the entire production process.

As such, the following tutorial will take users through the intricacies of creating, setting up and rendering the final image realistically, while implementing some of the best techniques used by professional production houses.

Lighting and Rendering

8.1

8.2

8.1 Getting Started

Start by opening the MAX file under the name of 'SMESTOW_Interior Lighting_Start.max'.

If prompted with the 'File Load: Gamma & LUT Settings Mismatch' warning, accept the *Adopt the File's Gamma and LUT Settings?* option and *OK* to close the dialogue. ▶8.1

Next, set the gamma to 2.2, to ensure the light and material colours are displayed accurately.

To do this, click on the *Rendering* button from the main toolbar and choose the *Gamma/LUT Setup* option from the drop-down list. ▶8.2

In the *Preference Settings* dialogue, open the *Gamma and LUT* tab, and check the *Enable Gamma/LUT Correction* option.

3D Photorealistic Rendering

In the *Display* and *Bitmap Files* groups, set all gamma values to 2.2. ▶8.3

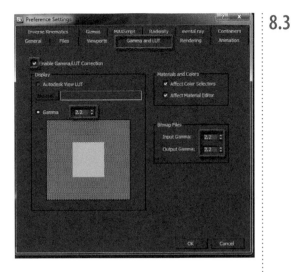

8.3

To quickly set up the lights, start by creating basic V-Ray parameters with a simple override material.

Once the preliminary lighting has been signed off on, we'll disable the override material and begin fine-tuning both the lights and materials to coexist realistically in the scene.

First, open the *Render Setup* dialogue (press F10). In the *Indirect illumination* tab, turn on the *V-Ray:: Indirect illumination (GI)* function. ▶8.4

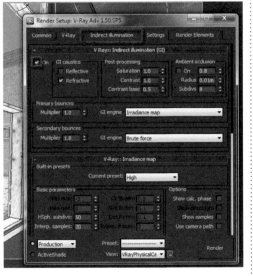

8.4

Next, we are going to tweak some of its default settings for quick and satisfactory results.

In the *Ambient Occlusion* group, set the *Radius* value to about 0.3 (the units display is in meters) and the *Subdivs* value to about 16.

The value of 16 may take slightly longer to render, but the ambient occlusion results will be much smoother and more realistic.

In the *Secondary bounces* group, choose the *Light cache GI engine* by clicking and choosing it from the drop-down list.

While brute force is more unbiased and accurate, light cache can also produce excellent results at a much quicker rendering pace.

8.5

In the *V-Ray:: Irradiance map* roll-out, choose the *Low* built-in preset from the drop-down list next to *Current preset*. When setting up the lights for the first drafts, it's common practice to start with low presets and build from there.

In addition, during the rendering precalculation phase, it's prudent to turn on the *Show calc. phase* and *Show direct light* functions. These two functions allow users to visualize the direction of the lights in the scene and the overall GI before the rendering process begins.

Being able to visualize the precalculation phase provides the user with the option to either let the process continue or abort it before the rendering is initiated. ▶8.5

8.6

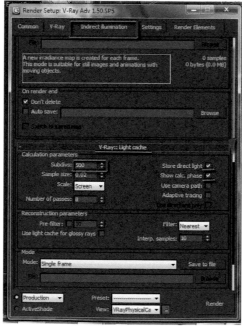

The subsequent step is to expand the *V-Ray:: Light cache* roll-out and decrease its *Subdivs* values to about 500.

The value of 500 is neither too low nor too high to get the first draft renders. In addition, enable *Store direct light* and *Show cal. phase*.

This option will help speed up the light cache calculation, especially when there too many lights in the scene. ▶8.6

Next, we're going to set up the image sample and the colour mapping parameters.

Open the *V-Ray* tab and scroll down to the *V-Ray:: Image sampler (Antialiasing)* roll-out parameters. In the *Image sampler* group, change the type to *Adaptive DMC*.

While this image sampler works consistently well and fast with most scenes, you can try a different image sampler, if desired.

In the *V-Ray:: Adaptive DMC image sampler* roll-out, disable *Use DMC sampler thresh.* to control the image quality from the *Clr thresh* values as opposed to *Settings* parameters. Note how the *Clr thresh* field goes from inactive to live.

Controlling the image noise/sharpness from the *Clr thresh* values yields better and faster results.

In the *V-Ray:: Color mapping* roll-out, change the default *Linear multiply* gamma value to 2.2 and enable the *Sub-pixel mapping* function.

Turning on this specific function corrects rendering artefacts related to white dots in the render. ▶8.7

The following step is to enable the *Override mtl* function, for quick rendering feedback while creating and test-rendering lights in the scene.

Scroll up to the *V-Ray:: Global switches* roll-out and enable the *Override mtl* function from the *Materials* group.

The next step is to create and apply a white base material to the *Override mtl* toggle

Open the *Material Editor* dialogue and create a new *VRayMtl* slot. Name it 'Override' and set its base *Diffuse* colour swatch to whitish (e.g. *Color Selector Value*: 196).

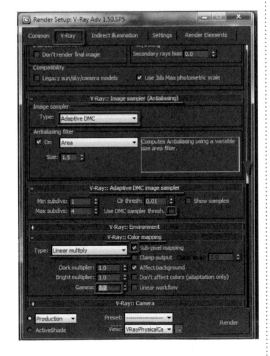

8.7

8   Lighting and Rendering

8.8

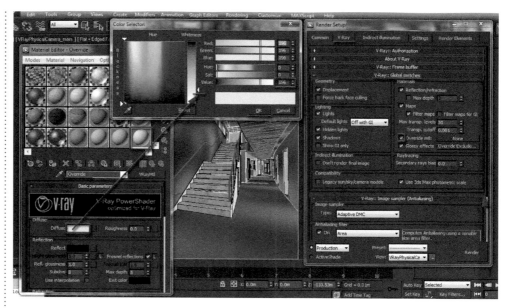

8.9

White colour is often used as a base material to tweak/match light colours. ▶8.8

To use this new material as an override, drag it from the Material Editor slot onto the *Override mtl* toggle. The *Instance (Copy) Material* dialogue should be prompted. Choose the *Instance* method and click *OK* to close it. ▶8.9

With the material override set up, the subsequent step is to exclude scene objects such as glass and the ceiling lights. The glass material needs to be excluded from the *Override mtl* in order to let the sunlight through the glass window.

The ceiling light material is often excluded from the *Override mtl* so users/clients can see where the light fixtures/sources are positioned. In addition, it also adds character/style to the chalk renders.

To exclude scene objects from the *Override mtl* click on its toggle to bring up the *Exclude/Include* dialogue.

One of the main reasons why it's important to name objects correctly is for instances such as this and when merging objects. In the *Scene objects* name field, begin to type the relevant object(s) you require excluding.

The dialogue should automatically list the names matching your keyword(s). Click on the button with an arrow pointing outwards to bring in selected objects from the list. ▶8.10

8.10

Alternatively, select a material slot from the *Material Editor* containing the glass material, followed by clicking on the *Select by Material* button to bring up the *Select Objects* dialogue.

All the relevant objects with the glass material should be automatically selected. Click to choose them, then click *Select* and *Isolate* them (Alt+Q) thereafter. ▶8.11 and 8.12

8.11

8.12

8.13

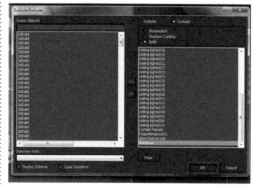

From this point you can select the objects in the scene and type in/paste their respective names in the *Exclude/Include* dialogue. ►8.13

8.14

8.2 Lighting

Before we begin creating lights, inside 3ds Max open the photo reference previously chosen during the pre-production phase. Use some of the steps described earlier to open the photo reference under the name of '48.jpeg'. ►8.14

3D Photorealistic Rendering

The first light we are going to start with is the slight blue ambient light seen directly behind the window. This type of ambient light can usually be achieved with a V-Ray dome light object.

- First maximize the viewport toggle (Alt+W).
- To create a light, expand the *Create* command panel.
- In the *Light* group, select the *VRay* type from the drop-down list. ▶8.15

8.15▼

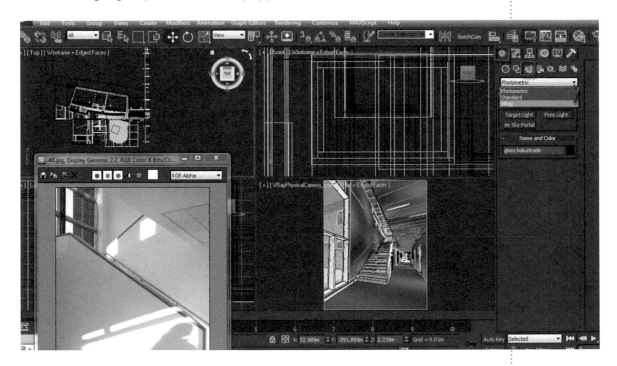

▼8.16

Under the *VRay Object Type* group, select the *VRayLight* button and click anywhere in the top viewport to create it. Once the light is created, right-click to exit creation. ▶8.16

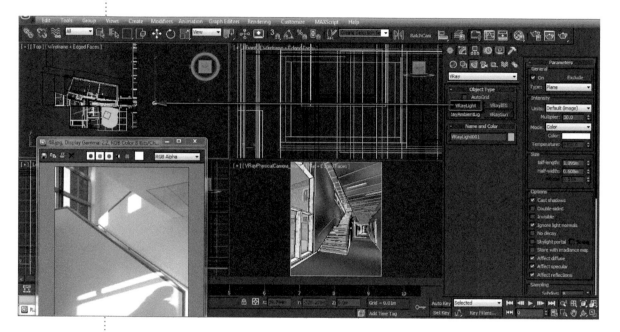

To begin editing some of the light parameters, open the *Modify* command panel while the light is still selected.

3D Photorealistic Rendering

In its *Parameters* roll-out, in the *General* group choose the *Dome* type. ▶8.17

Do a quick test render (Shift+Q) to see the results. Note that the camera viewport has already been padlocked. This is to avoid rendering the wrong selected viewport.

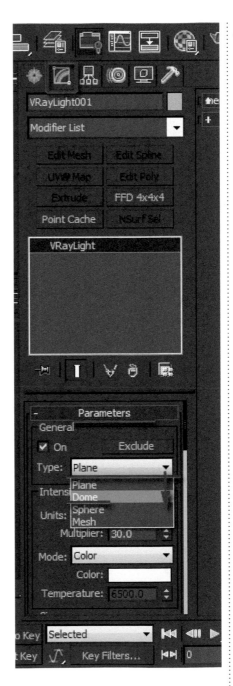

8.17

By default 3ds Max renders the selected viewport (highlighted), when the padlock is not selected. ►8.18

8.18

As evident from the draft render, the first results are nowhere near the photo reference yet.

Start by enabling the V-Ray frame buffer. In the *Render Setup* dialogue, open the *V-Ray* tab and expand the *V-Ray:: Frame buffer* roll-out.

All parameters are greyed out by default. Turn on the *Enable built-in Frame Buffer* function to switch on all parameters and click on the *Show last VFB* toggle.

The *V-Ray frame buffer* dialogue should appear. Enable the *Display colors in sRGB space* button to display the correct colours. ►8.19

8.19

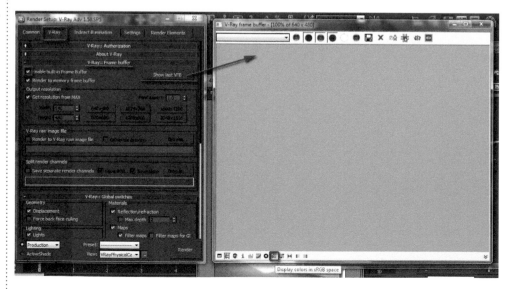

3D Photorealistic Rendering

Back in the scene, select the dome light and rename it 'VRayLight_Dome'.

Next, open the *Modify* command panel and add a slight blue tint to its colour swatch. The following values worked well: *Hue* = 155; *Sat* = 118; *Value* = 147. ▶8.20

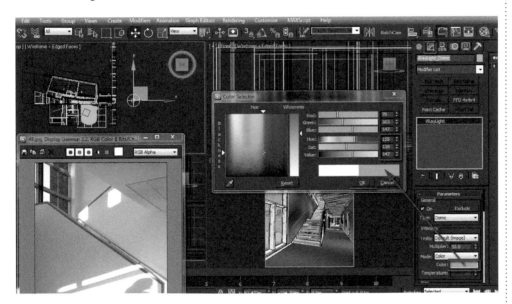

8.20

In addition, scroll down to the *Options* group and enable the *Invisible* option. This option will make the dome light object not visible in the render, even though it's fully active.

Also disable the *Affect specular* and *Affect reflections* options. Dome lights often yield grainy results/ artefacts on the secularity and reflectivity of objects. Having these two options unticked will help improve your renders. ▶8.21

Next, create some direct shadows to help make the scene more interesting.

Open the VRay light group following some of the steps described earlier and choose the *VRaySun*,

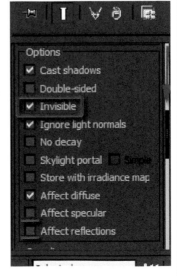

8.21

8 Lighting and Rendering

8.22

then click and drag it into the front viewport.

The *V-Ray Sun* dialogue should be prompted; click *Yes* to automatically add a *VRaySky* environment map. ▶8.22

To create an interesting image, it's often common to have the sunlight cast long shadows through the window and fall over key objects in the scene. To achieve this, it is necessary to move around the sun object and its target to the appropriate position in the scene.

For quick viewport feedback on the direction of the shadows, turn on *Enable Hardware Shading* (Shift+F3).

Following that, right-click on the top part of the camera viewport to bring up the viewport menu.

From the pop-up menu, select the *Lighting and Shadows* option,

Next, select *Enable Ambient Occlusion* to disable it and turn on the *Illuminate with Scene Lights* option. ▶8.23

8.23

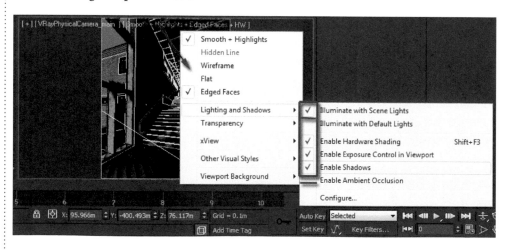

To place the sunlight and its target in a good position, start by moving its target.

Select the sunlight target and place it in the following position, using the *Move* tool: $X = 24.696$; $Y = -331.07$; $Z = 0.0$. ►8.24

8.24▼

Next, select the sunlight and place it in the following position: $X=95.966$; $Y = -400.493$; $Z = 76.117$. ►8.25

8.25▼

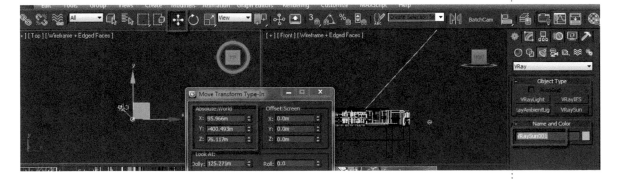

Test render the scene to double-check the recent changes. ▶8.26

8.26

The next step is to create the effect of a diffused light coming through the main window and the roof light upstairs.

8.27

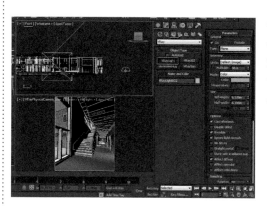

Create a *VRayLight* plane by clicking and dragging it into the front viewport. Use some of the techniques covered earlier to do so. ▶8.27

While the new *VRaylight* plane is still selected, rename it as 'VRayLight_Window' and open the *Modify* command panel.

In the *Intensity* group, change the multiplier to about 7.0.

In the *Size* group, change the *Half-length* value to about 2.02 and the *Half-width* to about 2.964.

In addition, with the *Move* tool, place the light closer to the window next to the camera view: $X = 36.462$; $Y = -337.006$; $Z = 2.635$. ▶8.28

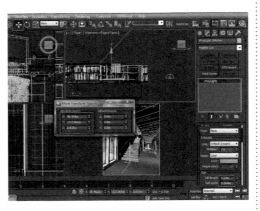

8.28

Before the next test render, change the window light colour to: *Hue* = 155; *Sat* = 150; *Value* = 133. ▶8.29

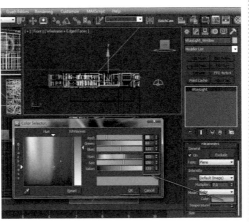

8.29

8.30

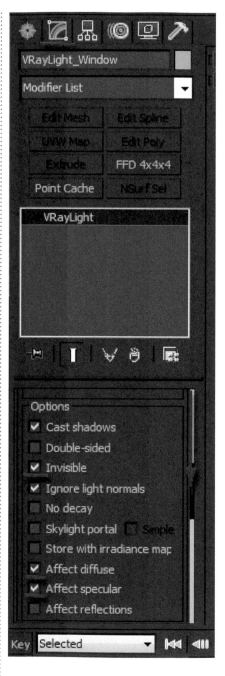

Finally, in the *Options* group, enable the *Invisible* option, as well as *Affect diffuse* and *Affect specular*. ▶8.30

The next step is to create and place another V-Ray plane light directly above the roof light area upstairs, to emulate a light coming from it.

With the *Move* tool, place it in the following position: $X = 24.817$; $Y = -334.944$; $Z = 5.589$.

Rename this new light as 'VRayLight_Roof light' and change its intensity multiplier to about 3.0. It's worth noting that most of the light settings and positions suggested in this exercise were only achieved after trial and error. ▶8.31

8.31

The final lights to be created are the ceiling lights.

Start by creating a V-Ray plane light in the top viewport, using some of the techniques covered earlier. Creating this specific light in the top viewport will ensure that it's pointing downwards.

Place it directly below the ceiling panels in the following position: $X = 34.568$; $Y = -333.557$; $Z = 2.1$.

While selected, open the *Modify* command panel and change its *Multiplier* value to 10.0; change its colour temperature values to the following: *Hue* = 13; *Sat* = 237; *Value* = 235.

Also change its dimension as follows: *Half-length* = 0.086; *Half-width* = 0.336. The V-Ray light dimensions are slightly bigger than the model, for reflection purposes and to cast softer shadows.

The wider the light planes, the softer the shadows will be. ▶8.32

8.32

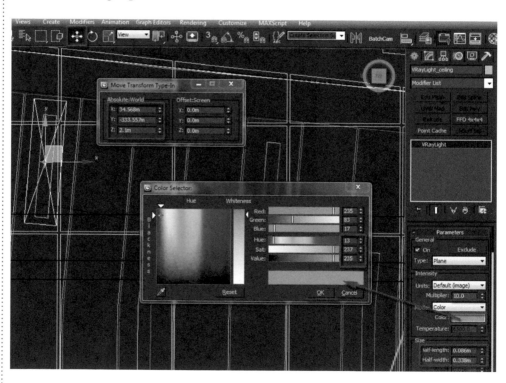

To finalize the light settings, scroll down to the *Options* group and enable the *Affect reflections* function, in addition to turning on all the previously discussed options. ▶8.33

Next, we are going to copy/instance multiple lights along the ceiling panel areas.

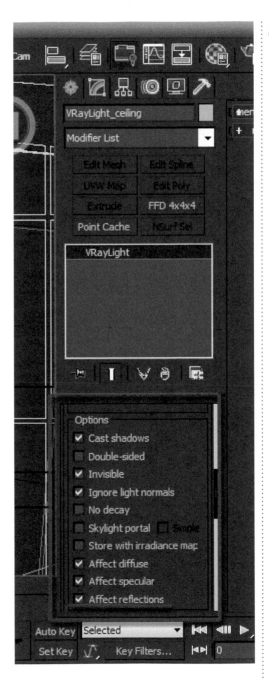

8.33

8.34

To prevent selecting any geometry accidentally, filter the selection to *Lights*, from the main toolbar. ▶8.34

Create a total of 32 instanced lights along the ceiling panels. To create them, select a light, then hold down the Shift key and move the light.

When the *Clone Options* dialogue is prompted, choose the *Instance* method and click *OK* to close it. It is also possible to enter the number of copies to be cloned (default = 1). ▶8.35 and 8.36

8.35

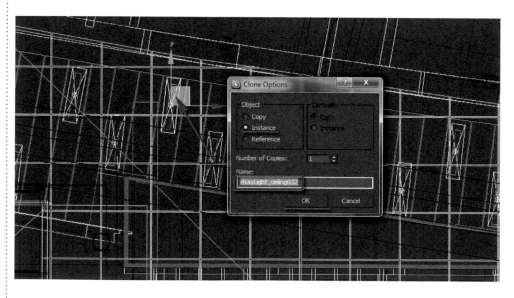

3D Photorealistic Rendering

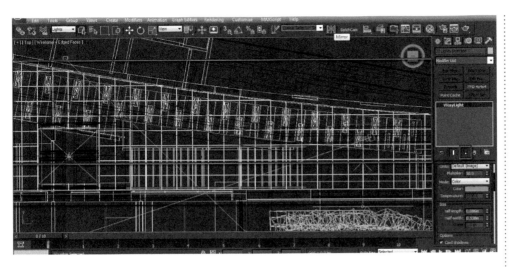

8.36

NOTE

It's worth creating instanced lights whenever possible, as they are quicker to compute during the render time.

Test render the scene with the new added lights.

The following step is to fine-tune the lights and the materials in order to complement each other realistically.

Disable the *Override mtl* and test render the scene to assess it. ▶8.37

8.37

8 Lighting and Rendering

8.3 Fine-Tuning Materials

While the overall lighting is looking acceptable, some materials require attention.

Start with the big window frame in the foreground (i.e. Curtain Wall Mullions). The first test render shows that the *Refl. glossiness* texture tiling is too large and too intense. To correct this, first select the metal material slot and change its *Refl. glossiness* value to about 0.88.

While its *Material* toggle has a texture, the current value of 0.88 will have no effect.

However, once its texture percentage is reduced, V-Ray will blend both the *Refl. glossiness* value and the texture percentage.

To change the texture percentage, scroll down to the *Maps* roll-out and change the *Refl. glossiness* percentage value from 100% to about 25%. In addition, rotate the texture by 90 degrees.
▶8.38 and 8.39

8.39

8.40

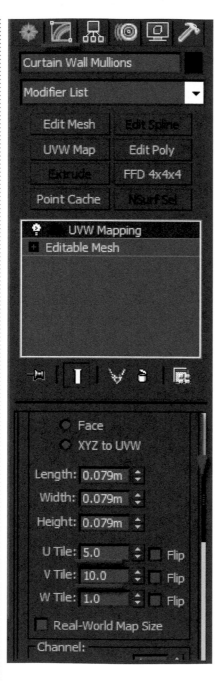

To correct the texture tiling realistically, open the *Modify* command panel and change its *U Tile* value to 5.0 and *V Tile* to 10.0. ▶8.40

Before test rendering the new changes, duplicate the current V-Ray frame buffer by clicking on the *Duplicate to MAX frame buffer*.

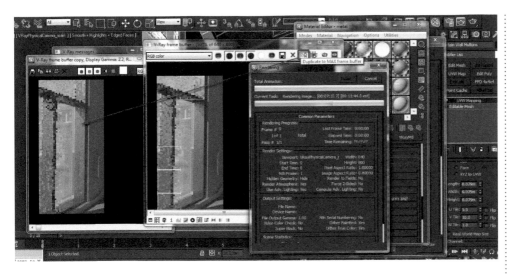

This action will allow you to compare changes between renders. In addition, do a region render of the area in question. To region render, click on its button in the frame buffer and draw the region directly in the frame buffer. ▶8.41 and 8.42

Alternatively, in the *Render Setup/ Common* tab dialogue, choose the *Region* method in the *Area to Render* group. A square region render should appear in the viewport.

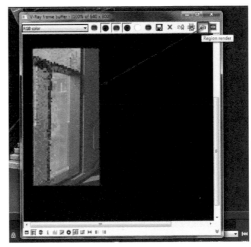

8.43

To adjust the region size, move its point handles around the square region. ▶8.43

To deselect the region, enable the *Select and Move* tool from the main toolbar. To reselect it, return to the *Common* tab dialogue and choose the *Region* method as previously done.

Textures such as the floor require sharpening and adjusting the contrast slightly. To do so, open its *Diffuse* map toggle and reduce the *Blur* value to about 0.01.

8.44

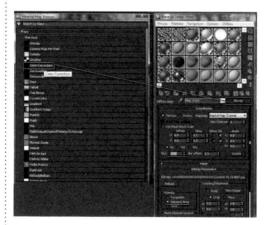

Also change its *Filtering* type to *Summed Area*. These two changes will sharpen the texture, although they will also increase the rendering times slightly, as mentioned earlier.

To adjust the texture contrast, add the *Color Correction* procedural map. To do so, start by clicking on the *Bitmap* toggle and choosing the *Color Correction* map from the *Material/ Map Browser* list of standard maps.

In the Replace Map dialogue, choose Keep old map as sub-map. ▶8.44, **8.45** and **8.46**

8.45

To add contrast to the texture, scroll down to the *Lightness* roll-out parameters and choose the *Advanced* options.

Decrease the *Gamma/Contrast* RGB value to about 0.5. While these parameters worked well here, feel free to try different values/parameters, if necessary. ▶8.47

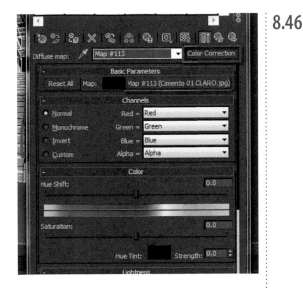

8.46

8.47

8.48

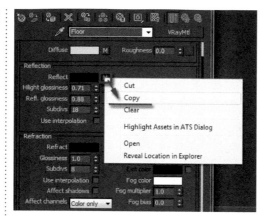

8.49

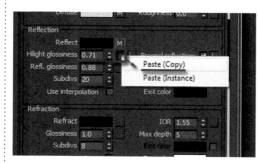

8.50

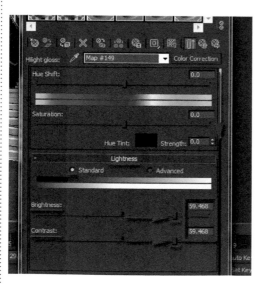

The subsequent step is to add a bit of interesting specularity to the *Hilight glossiness* toggle. To achieve this, we're going to copy the greyscale texture previously applied to the *Reflect* toggle, and paste it into the *Hilight glossiness* toggle. ▶8.48 and 8.49

To increase the specular contrast of the greyscale texture, add the *Color Correction* procedural map to it. In the *Lightness* roll-out, increase the brightness and the contrast to about 59.468.

Note the glaring difference of the glossiness appearance in the material slot. ▶8.50 and 8.51

While the colour contrast and sharpness of the texture have improved, some of its glossy highlights are still looking grainy in the render.

To correct this, first change the global rendering settings to ensure the overall pixilation is smoother.

Open the render *Setup* dialogue. Under the *V-Ray* tab, scroll down to the *V-Ray:: Adaptive DMC image sampler* roll-out and reduce the *Clr thresh* value to 0.003.

Lower values yield smother overall results. ▶8.52

To completely remove the graininess caused by the glossy highlights, increase the material *Subdivs* value to about 50.

This value was achieved by gradually increasing the *Subdivs* values and repeatedly test rendering until the graininess was completely removed.

8.51

8.52

▼8.53 The tests were carried out as region renders. ▶8.53

Chamfering the edges of an object often contributes to the overall realism of an image. Users can do this manually through the sub-object level or *via* a material.

To add this effect *via* a material, scroll down to the *Maps* roll-out and open its *Bump* toggle. In the *Material/Map Browser* dialogue, choose the *VRayEdgesTex* from the list.

This procedural map can be found under the *Standard* or *V-Ray* roll-out list. ▶8.54

Once loaded, in the *Thickness* group set its *World units* to about 0.05. Again, this value was achieved by test rendering multiple times, with different values. Try different values, if desired.

The white colour determines the direction of the bump (i.e. white sets the bump upwards and black downwards). ▶8.55

8.55

The remaining materials in the scene were tweaked by using most of the techniques described earlier. In addition, some of the bump values were also increased or decreased accordingly, to react realistically to the lights.

8.4 Setting Up for the Final Render

Prior to sending out the high resolution render, make some final tweaks.

Select the *VRaySun* and increase its shadow *Subdivs* value to about 13 and the size multiplier to 5.0. Increasing the size multiplier value will help produce feathered edges on direct shadows.

Increase the *photon emit radius* value enough to encapsulate the relevant areas of the render (i.e. 23.324 m).

Next, select the *VRayLight_Dome* and increase its *Sampling* group *Subdivs* value to about 20. This value may take slightly longer to compute but will help cast more defined shadows.

Also increase its multiplier to about 100, to allow more of its light into the scene. ▶8.56, 8.57 and 8.58

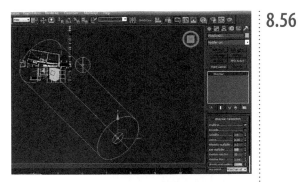

8.56

8.57

8.58

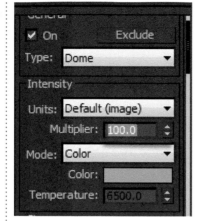

8.59

Following that, increase the sampling *Subdivs* of the *VRayLight_Window* and *VRayLight_Roof* lights to 20. In addition, increase their multiplier value to about 15.0. ▶8.59

The next step is to increase the render output size to 3500×4379. While most post-production companies often render to 6000 pixels or above, 3500 pixels is good enough for the purpose of this tutorial.

3D Photorealistic Rendering

Ensure the *Vray Region* button is turned off in the frame buffer. ▶**8.60**

While still in the *Render Setup* dialogue, open the *V-Ray* tab and enable the *Split render channels* function.

To name the final high resolution output file, click on the *Browse* toggle. The *Select V-Ray G-Buffers filename* dialogue should open up.

8.60▼

Name the file 'Interior DayLightVray' and save the file type as a *Targa Image File* (TGA). The *Setup* toggle should bring you to the *Targa Image Control* dialogue. ▶8.61

8.61

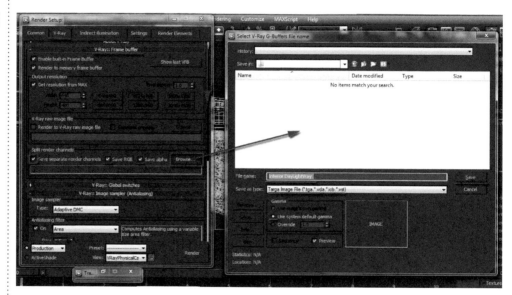

8.62

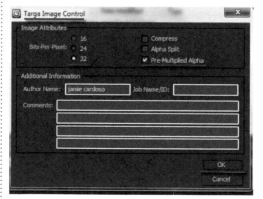

Set the *Image Attributes* to 32 *Bits-Per-Pixel*, with *Pre-Multiplied Alpha* enabled. ▶8.62

Alternatively, you can choose the TIFF file format, with *16-bit Color* and *No Compression* selected. ▶8.63

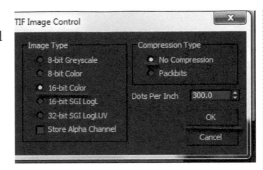

8.63

Also, open the Global switches rollout parameters, and disable the Probabilistic lights function.

While this function is great to decrease the lights' rendering time; it also yields grainy results. ▶8.64

In the *Indirect illumination* tab, scroll down to the *V-Ray:: Irradiance map* roll-out and change the *Current preset* to *Medium*. For this specific scene, the *Medium* preset was acceptable.

However, some interiors may require going to presets such as *High* or *Very High*.

In the *Basic parameters* group, increase the *Interp. samples* value to about 70. This value is good enough to eliminate the current artefacts seen in the test render.

8.64

Note that higher values may reduce the appearance of shadows in the scene. Therefore these values should be increased with caution. ▶8.65

8.65

8.66

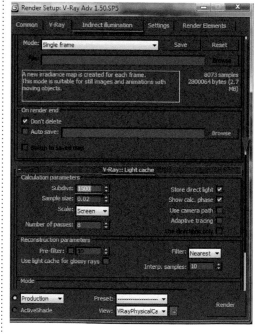

Next, scroll further down to the *V-Ray:: Light cache* roll-out parameters and increase the *Subdivs* value in the *Calculation parameters* group to about 1500. There are scenes where it may be necessary to go as high as 2000–2500.

The rule of thumb is to start with lower values and gradually increase as necessary. ▶8.66

To finalize the render tweaks prior to sending out the final render, add a few render elements.

Render elements are one of the most important parts of the render, as they will help fine-tune shader settings in post-production, without the need to resend the renders.

The *Elements Active* and *Display Elements* functions can be turned on or off as required.

The *Add* toggle allows users to add elements to the *Name* list below. The *Merge* toggle allows users to pick one or a host of elements from a different 3ds Max scene. The *Delete* toggle allows users to select and delete elements from the *Name* list below.

Start by opening the *Render Elements* tab and clicking on the *Add* toggle to bring up its dialogue. Choose the *MultiMatteElement* from the list and click on *OK* to close the dialogue. *MultiMatteElement* is currently the best render element to select colours in post-production.

Each *MultiMatteElement* can take up to three different colours. Each colour is a true representation of red, green and blue, which are very easy to select in post-production.

The default numbers being displayed are ID numbers representing object IDs or material IDs (when ticked on). The numbers can be manually changed, if required. ▶8.67 and 8.68

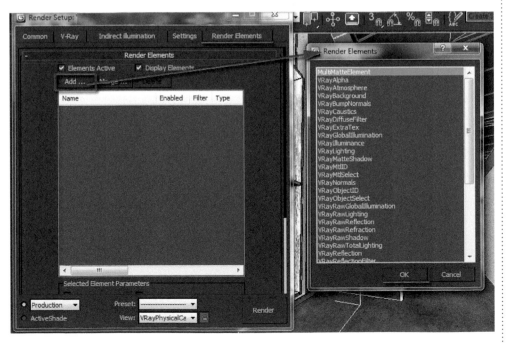

8.67

8.68

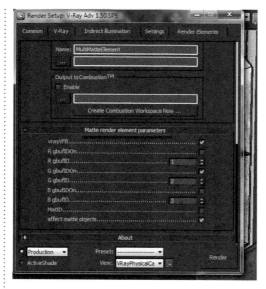

For this exercise we will only use object IDs, because the Material Editor ID numbers are restricted to 15 only.

By default, the R and B colours are disabled. To enable all three colours, select the element from the name list and turn each colour function on.

Because there are numerous objects in the scene with different object ID numbers, we are going to create multiple layers of *MultiMatteElement*.

8.69

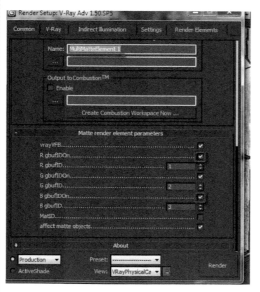

Start by renaming this element 'MultiMatteElement 1'. ▶8.69

Create the next *MultiMatteElement* and rename it 'MultiMatteElement 2'. It's important to rename elements with similar names, to avoid being overridden.

Also change these new RGB ID numbers to 4, 5, 6 and so forth. ▶8.70 and 8.71

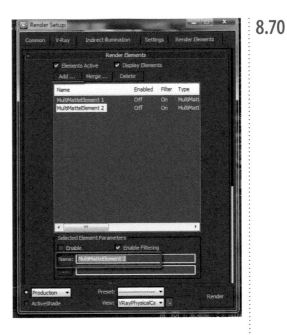

8.70

Repeat the previous steps to create more *MultiMatteElement* objects, to represent all object ID numbers previously created.

Once all the *MultiMatteElement* objects are created, add the following elements:

- VRayBumpNormals
- VRayDiffuseFilter
- VRayGlobalIllumination
- VRayLighting
- VRayNormals
- VRayRawGlobalIllumination
- VRayRawLighting
- VRayRawReflection
- VRayRawRefraction
- VRayRawShadow
- VRayRawTotalLighting
- VRayReflection
- VRayReflectionFilter
- VRayRefraction
- VRayRefractionFilter
- VRaySampleRate
- VRaySelfIllumination
- VRayShadows
- VRaySpecular
- VRayTotalLighting
- VRayZDepth

8.71

8.72

More often than not some of the above-listed elements may not work well with the base render, depending on the overall lighting. However, the rule of thumb is to always add them, in case they are needed. ▶8.72

To work out the correct values for the *VRayZDepth* element, do a test render with the override material on and with low render settings.

The best Z-depth results often yield a smooth transition from white to black.

It is possible to achieve good results by tweaking the *zdepth max* values. For this scene, the *zdepth max* value of 3.0 m worked well. However, feel free to experiment with different values, if desired. ▶8.73

8.73

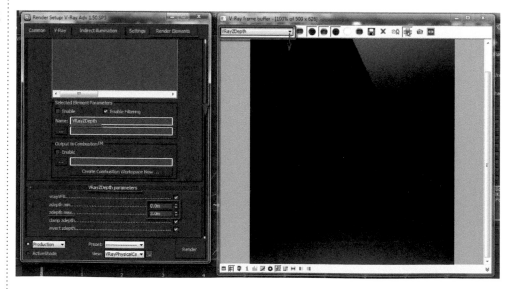

3D Photorealistic Rendering

Conclusion

This chapter guided users through the process of creating and setting up V-Ray lights such as the VRaySun, the dome light and plane lights.

Throughout the process, users were shown how to use chalk renders to quickly set up the overall lighting through a series of test renders at low resolution. Following that, users were also guided through the detailed step-by-step methodology of tweaking the materials and the lights to complement one another realistically.

Finally, once the lights and the materials were tweaked, the final render parameters were refined and sent for final render, with their respective render elements.

> **NOTE**
>
> Fox render Farm services were extensively used to render the final images, at a lightning speed.
>
> For more information about Fox Render Farm, please go to: http://www.foxrenderfarm.com/

9

Interior Daylight

Post-production

As the final phase of the entire process, post-production is also the most important phase. Its final execution often determines the success of an entire project. Furthermore, this is the phase where the artist can rectify and/or enhance materials, colours, skies, lights, etc., with great ease, without having to re-render the entire scene again. Finally, clients usually capitalize on this final opportunity to address new tweaks and incorporate last-minute changes.

9 Post-production

9.1

9.1 Post-production

Begin by opening and loading all the pre-rendered elements into a stack.

To do so, in Photoshop, click on *File* in the main toolbar. Choose the *Scripts* option from the drop-down list, followed by selecting the *Load Files into Stack* function. ▶9.1

The *Load Layers* dialogue should be prompted. Click on the *Browse* button to locate the files.

In the *Open* dialogue, select all the rendered elements. To do so, pick the first file from the top of the list then scroll down, holding down the Shift button and select the last file from the list.

Multiple files should be selected. Click *OK* to open them. ▶9.2

9.2

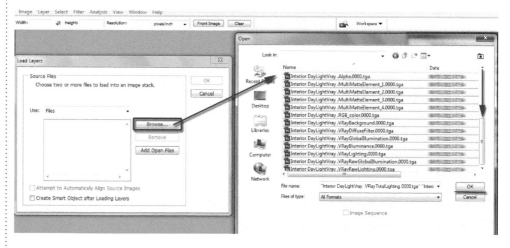

In the *Load Layers* dialogue, click *OK* to load all the files displayed in its list. ▶9.3

The beauty of this Photoshop script is that it stacks all rendered elements automatically, while retaining their original filenames.

Save the current file (Shift+Ctrl+S) as 'Interior DaylightVray start.psd'. ▶9.4

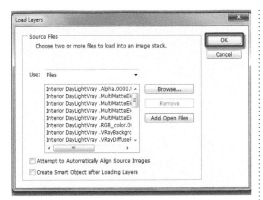

9.3

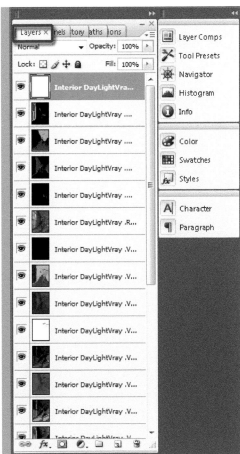

9.4

9.5

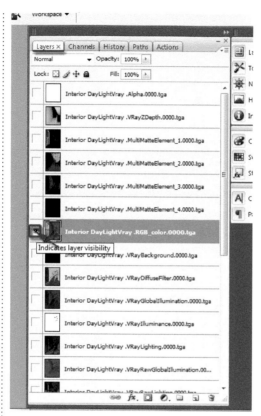

Start by enabling the visibility of only the layer under the name 'Interior DayLightVray.RGB_color.0000.tga' and disabling the visibility of the other layers automatically. To do so, hold down the Alt key and click on the relevant layer. ▶9.5

Next, open (Ctrl+O) the photo reference image file named '48.jpg'. This photo will be used to further match it with the render more closely.

Drag-drop the 'Interior DayLightVray.
RGB_color.0000.tga' layer to the
bottom of the layer stack. This step
will make it easier to blend other
layers on top of it. ▶9.6

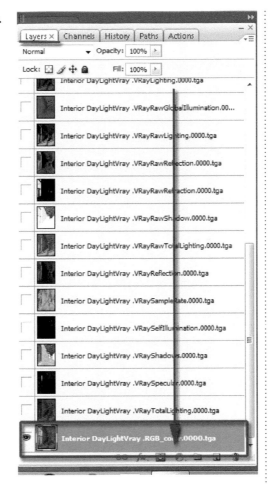

9.6

To add some brightness and contrast to the image, click on the *Create new fill or adjustment layer* button and choose the *Levels* function from its list. ▶9.7

9.7

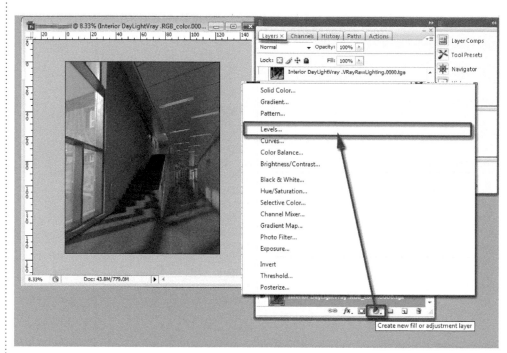

The *Levels* dialogue should appear. Begin dragging its middle slider to the left and the slider from the far left towards the right.

For this exercise, the following values worked well: left slider = 4; middle slider = 1.85; right slider = 255. However, feel free to experiment with different values, if desired. ▶9.8

9.8

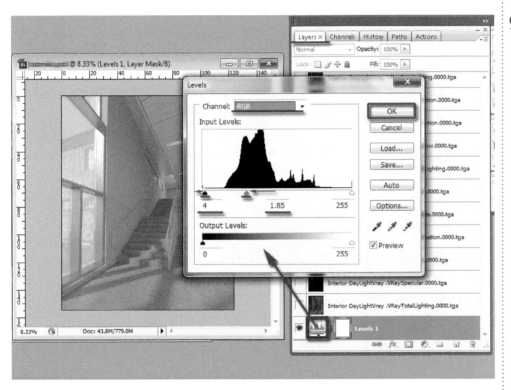

To give warmth to the render, add the *Photo Filter* adjustment layer, using some of the techniques covered earlier. In its dialogue, accept the default filter (Warming Filter (85)) and increase its density to 34% by dragging the slider to the right.

Although these values worked well here, experiment with different values, if desired.

9.9

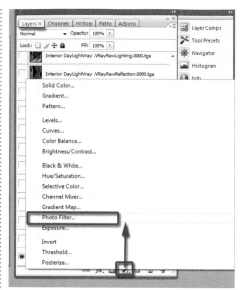

Click *OK* to close the dialogue. ▶9.9 and 9.10

While the photo filter made the render one step closer to the photo reference, the left areas require less of the filter and more of the sky colour. To begin omitting parts of the photo filter, select its adjacent mask thumbnail and enable the brush tool first (B).

With the mask thumbnail selected, in the tools sidebar, ensure the foreground colour swatch is black and the background colour swatch is white.

9.10

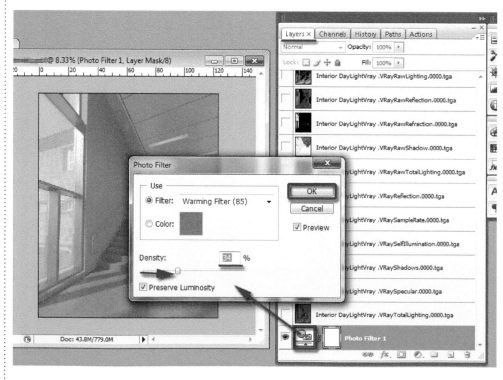

3D Photorealistic Rendering

In Photoshop, when brushing on layer masks, the black colour will omit pixels as one brushes away, and the white colour will do the opposite.

To prevent omitting large chunks of pixel while brushing, reduce the brush opacity slightly on the main toolbar. ▶9.11

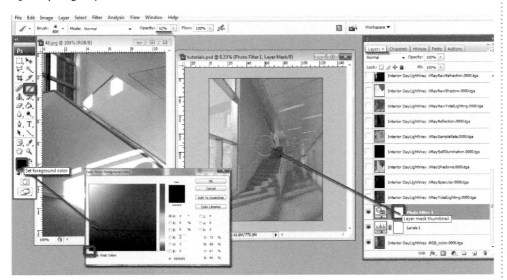

9.11

To pick and edit brushes, click on the brush preset picker button from the main toolbar. In its dialogue, reduce the hardness value to 0%. This will make the brush softer and easier to control while brushing away pixels. ▶9.12

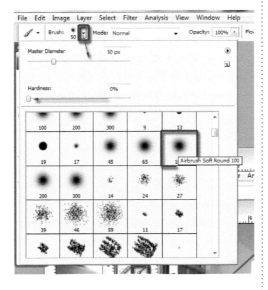

9.12

While the brush tool is enabled (B), use the right bracket key (']') to increase the brush size and the left bracket key ('[') to decrease it.

Use the zoom tool (Z) followed by (B) to brush pixels more closely. ▶9.13

9.13

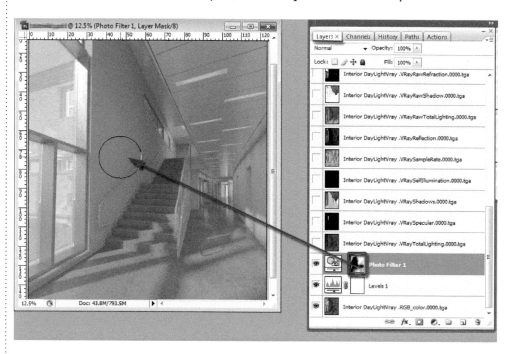

The next step is to put these two adjustment layers in one group (folder) to begin tidying up the PSD file. To create a group folder, select the *Photo Filter* layer first, followed by clicking on its button to create it.

By selecting the photo filter first, we've ensured the group folder was created on top of it. Rename the group folder 'Whole'.

The name 'Whole' was given because these adjustment layers are applied to the whole image. To rename the group folder, double-click on its text, type in the name and press Enter. ▶9.14

Move both adjustment layers inside this new group folder. To do so, select both layers (hold down Ctrl and click on one layer at time) and drag both layers into this new group folder. While dragging both layers into the group folder, you should see a rectangle indicating the layers are inside, once the drag cursor is on top of it.

9.14

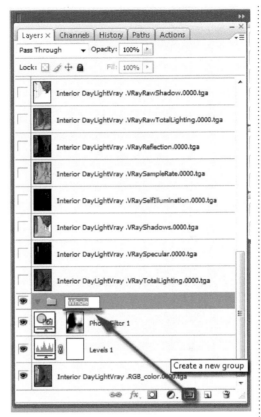

9.15

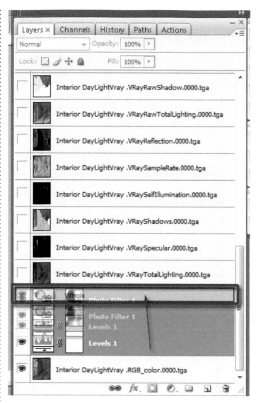

Once both adjustment layers are inside the group folder, click on its adjacent arrow to close or open it.
▶9.15 and 9.16

Create a folder mask to ensure that this group folder with adjustment layers doesn't affect the glass windows. To create a mask for this group folder, we need to select the glass material first. To do so, scroll up to where the 'Interior DayLightVray.MultiMatteElement_1.0000.tga' layer is. Make the layer visible by clicking on its visibility icon.

It is common practice to ensure all *MultiMatteElement* layers are positioned above all layers of the document.

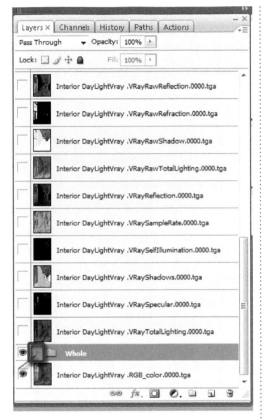

9.16

The selection of *MultiMatteElement* colours is more accurate when they sit above all the remaining layers. ▶9.17

9.17

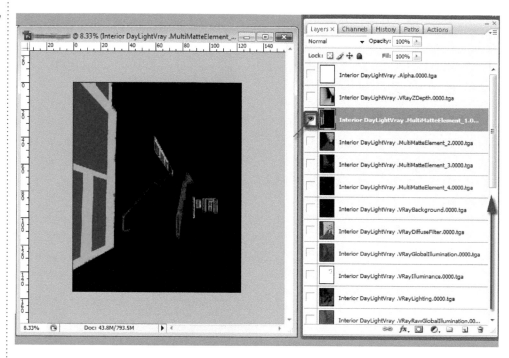

9.18

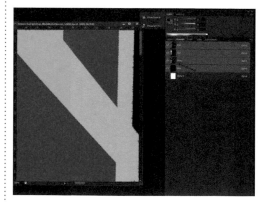

One of the most common methods of selecting any of the three channels (RGB), is to simple open the Channels' pallet, hold down the Ctrl key and left click on any of the three channels displayed (R, G or B) to enable its selection. ▶9.18

Alternatively, while the DayLightVray .MultiMatteElement_1.0000 layer is still selected, click on the *Select* main toolbar and choose the *Color Range* function from the drop down menu. ▶9.19

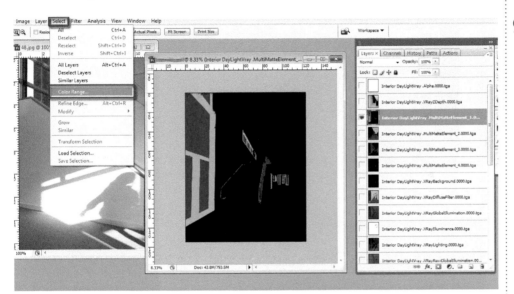

9.19

The *Color Range* dialogue should appear. In the *Select* group, choose the *Reds* from the drop-down list. All the reds from the layer should be selected automatically. This is one of many reasons why V-Ray *MultiMatteElement* is one of the best render elements used to select colours accurately and automatically.

9.20

9.21

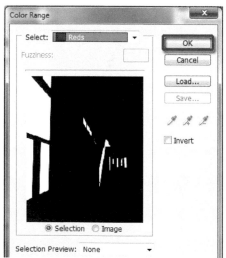

As mentioned earlier, when using the *MultiMatteElement* to select objects or materials, these layers need to be at the very top of all layers in order for the selection to be accurate. In addition, the relevant *MultiMatte* layer in question needs to be selected first. ▶9.20, 9.21 and 9.22

Turn off the *MultiMatteElement* visibility to see the selection in the render. The next step is to invert the selection (Shift+Ctrl+I), followed by selecting the group folder and creating the layer mask by clicking on its button. ▶9.23, 9.24 and 9.25

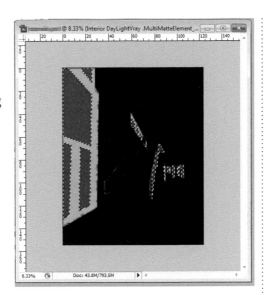

9.22

9.23

9.24

9.25

Use the *Layer Mask* in conjunction with the *Brush* tool (B) to mask/brush in areas affected by the mask. ▶9.26

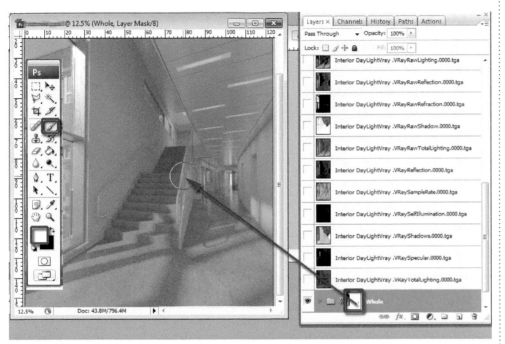

9.26

In addition, right-click on the *Layer Mask* and choose to disable it. This tool allows users to compare the effects of the *Layer Mask*.

9.27

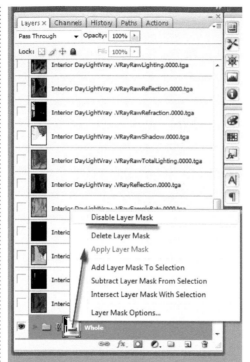

To enable the *Layer Mask* again, left-click on it. ▶9.27

The next step is to begin tweaking each material individually. Start with the hand rail.

Use some of the previous steps to select the blue colour range from the 'DayLightVray. MultiMatteElement_1.0000.tga' layer. ▶9.28 and 9.29

While the selection is still active, create a new group folder and name it 'Handrail'. Following that, create a layer mask as previously done.

9.28

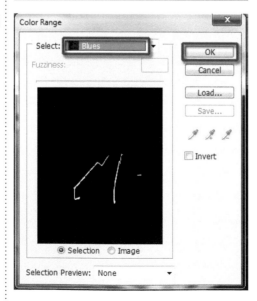

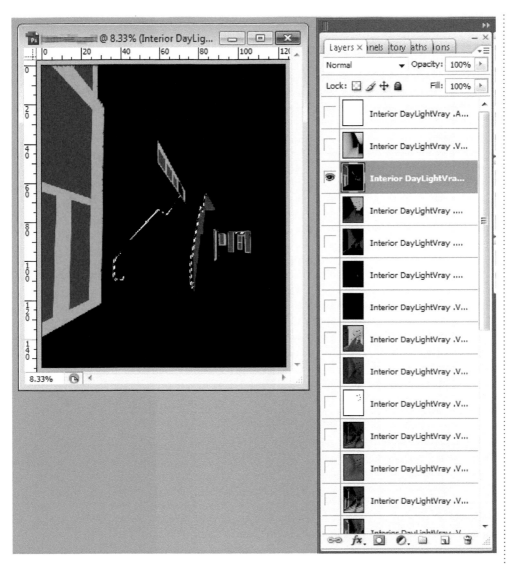

9.29

9.30

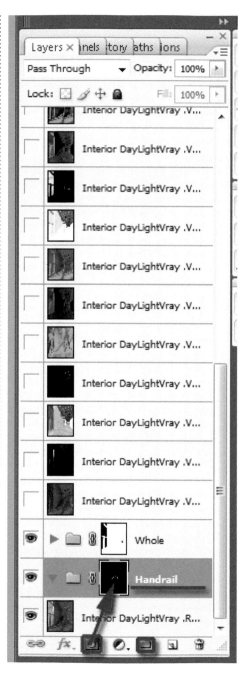

Ensure this new folder is above the layer named 'Interior DayLightVray.RGB_color.0000.tga'. ▶9.30

Next, select the layer named 'Interior DayLightVray.RGB_color.0000.tga' and create the *Levels* adjustment layer. ▶9.31

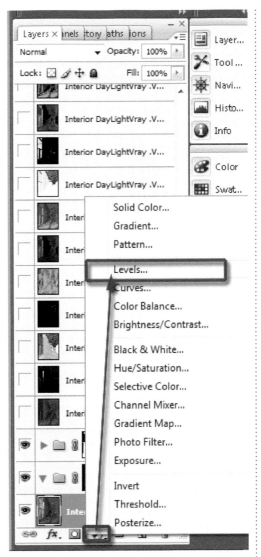

9.31

In its dialogue, set its middle slider to 0.78 and its left slider to 11. Try different values if desired. ▶9.32

9.32

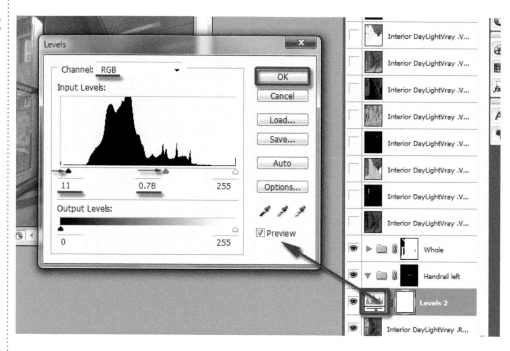

To ensure the *Levels* changes affect the handrails only, select the adjustment layer and move it into the pre-masked handrail group folder. Use some of the steps covered earlier to move the adjustment layer and see the before and after results. ▶9.33 and 9.34

With this masked group folder, now begin adding render elements such as *VRaySpecular* and *VRayReflection*.

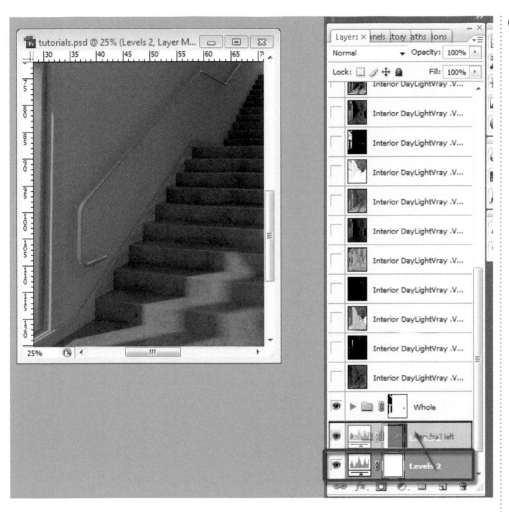

9.33

9.34

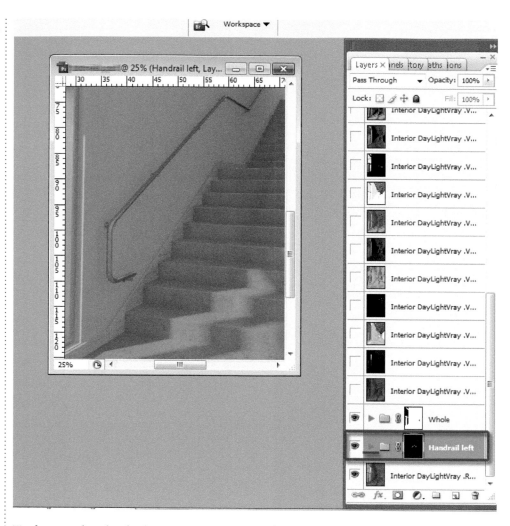

To do so, select both elements using some of steps covered earlier, then hold down the Alt key and move both layers into the handrail group folder. Release the Alt key once both layers are inside the handrail group folder. ▶9.35, 9.36 and 9.37

These two rendered elements will be used to help enhance their influence on this particular object/material (handrails).

9.35

9.36

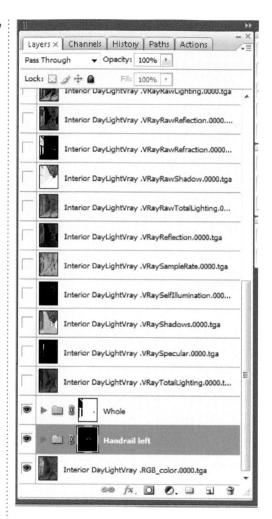

9.37

First, enable the *VRayReflection* layer visibility and choose the *Soft Light* blending mode from its drop-down list. After trying a number of different blending modes from the list, this one seemed to work best for this particular render element.

The rule of thumb is to always try different types of render elements and blending modes to see which ones work best for the final output. It's common for some film studios to use up to six different render elements for each group folder. ▶9.38

9.38

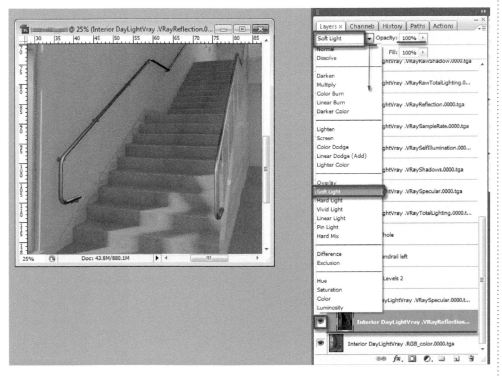

Next, turn on the layer visibility of the *VRaySpecular* and choose the *Screen* blending mode.

This blending mode worked best. However, experiment with a different one, if desired.

In addition, ensure the *VRaySpecular* layer sits on top of the *VRayReflection* layer. That particular position worked best after having tried the *VRayReflection* layer on top first. ▶9.39

9.39

Note how the element effects affect the masked handrail folder only. This unique technique allows users to control the effects of specific materials or objects without being forced to make compromises of the entire image.

Finally, colour code each render element according to its properties (i.e. VRaySpecular = Red; VRayReflection = Yellow, etc.).

To colour code a layer, right-click on the layer and choose the *Layer Properties* option from the pop-up list. In its dialogue, pick any colour from its drop-down list. Most recent versions of Photoshop allow users to pick colours without having to open the *Layer Properties* dialogue. ▶9.40 and 9.41

Use some of the techniques covered earlier to enhance other materials or objects in the image.

As previously mentioned, not every rendered element is useful for every single material or object in the image. It is a case of trial and error to see which rendered elements and blending modes work best for each image/object in the image.

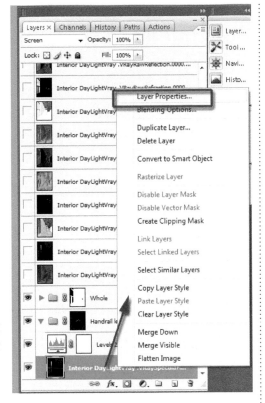

9.40

9.41

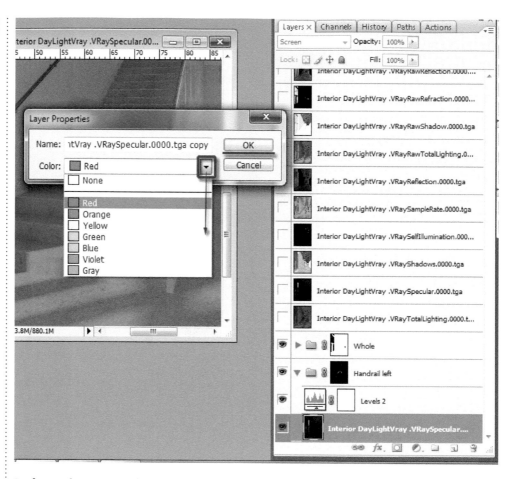

NOTE

To enable the selection of a layer mask, hold down the Ctrl key and click on the mask thumbnail.

Refer to the PSD under the name of 'Interior DaylightVray.psd' to see how each render element was used. ▶9.42

The next step is to create a glow for the *Ceiling Lights.* Start by selecting the ceiling lights. Use some of the techniques covered earlier. ▶9.43

9.42

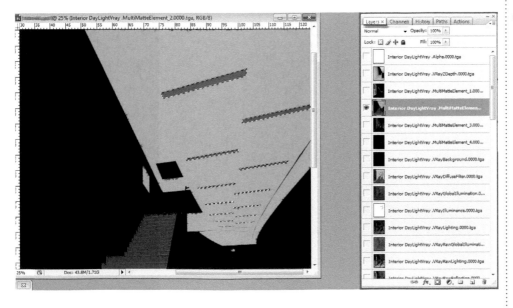

9.43

Once the selection is on, deselect the *MultiMatteElement* layer and scroll down. Before creating a new layer, select any of the top group folders to ensure the layer is created on top of it. Once a new layer is created, rename it 'Ceiling lights glow'. ►9.44 and 9.45

9.44

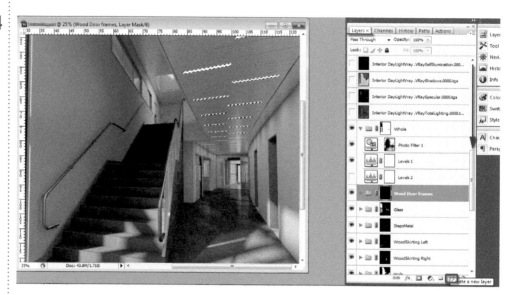

9.45

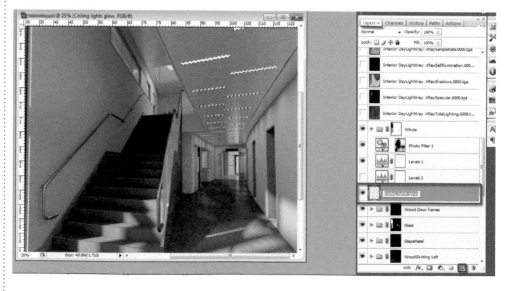

3D Photorealistic Rendering

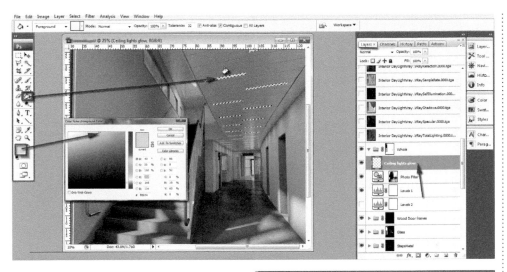

9.46

While the selection is still active, set the foreground colour to an orange tone and use the paint bucket tool (G) to fill out the selection layer.

If necessary, move the layer further up in order to be visible. ▶9.46

Following that, deselect the selection (Ctrl+D) and right-click on the 'Ceiling lights glow' layer. Choose the *Convert to Smart Object* option from the list.

This layer option allows users to record the parameters of filters applied. While useful, it also adds up to the PSD file size. ▶9.47 and 9.48

To begin adding the glow effect to the ceiling lights, click on the *Filter* main toolbar, followed by selecting *Blur* and

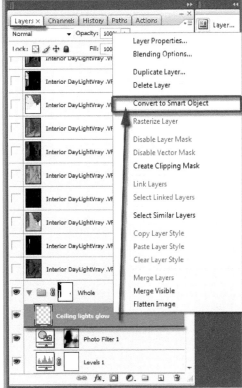

9.47

9.48

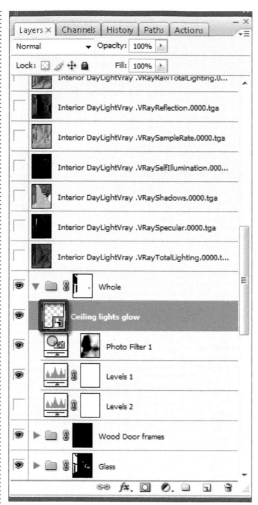

choosing the *Gaussian Blur* option from the drop-down list. ▶9.49

Its dialogue should appear; the radius of 21.4 worked best. However, try different values, if desired. ▶9.50

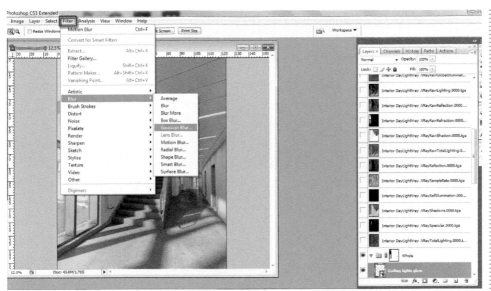

9.49

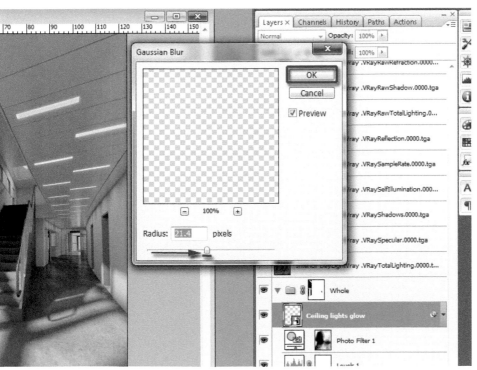

9.50

Use the *Lighten* blend mode to create the glow effect and reduce its *Opacity* to about 51%. Again, this blend mode and opacity value worked best. Experiment with different values and blend modes if desired. ▶9.51

9.51

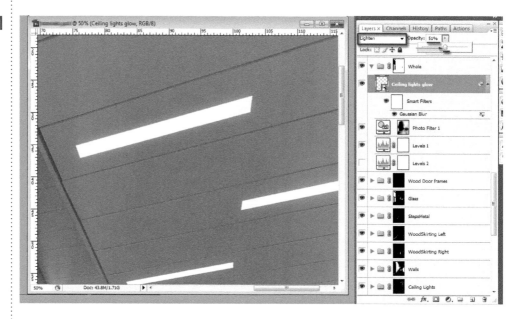

To edit the *Gaussian Blur* filter applied, expand the smart object layer by clicking first on its side arrow and then on its eye icon.

The same side arrow can be used to close the expanded layer palette.

Its adjacent mask thumbnail (*Smart Filters*) allows users to mask out areas with a brush tool. ▶9.52

9.52

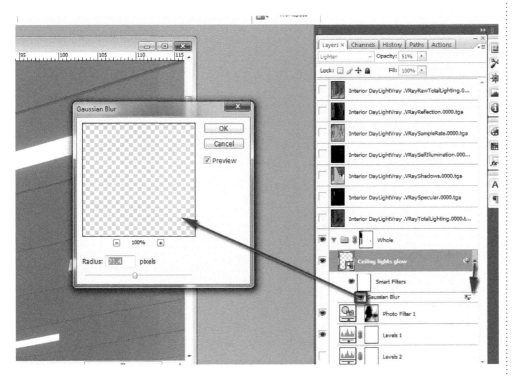

The next step is to create diffused shadows and the vignetting effect in random areas of the image.

Create a new layer inside the group folder under the name 'Whole' and name it 'Vignetting'. Ensure this layer is under the 'Ceiling lights glow' layer.

This is to ensure the vignetting effect occurs under the above-mentioned layer.

In addition create its layer mask thumbnail and change its colour to grey. Follow some of the techniques covered earlier to achieve this step. ▶9.53

9.53

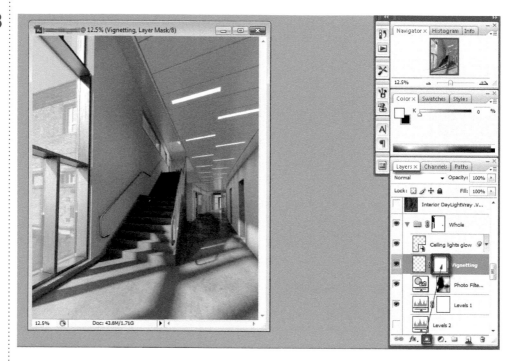

Next, ensure the layer is selected, as opposed to its mask, and select the *Paint Bucket Tool* from the side toolbar.

To select the *Paint Bucket Tool*, left-click and hold down the mouse button, then select its icon. ▶9.54

While the vignetting layer is still selected, paint the layer by clicking the paint bucket tool on it. Ensure its foreground colour is black. ▶9.55

Before we begin painting in the shadows, the black colour needs to be masked out first. To quickly mask out the black colour, select the vignetting layer mask and use the paint bucket tool to mask out the entire layer.

9.54

9.55

As mentioned earlier, the black colour on the mask hides pixels away and the white colour does the opposite. ▶9.56

9.56

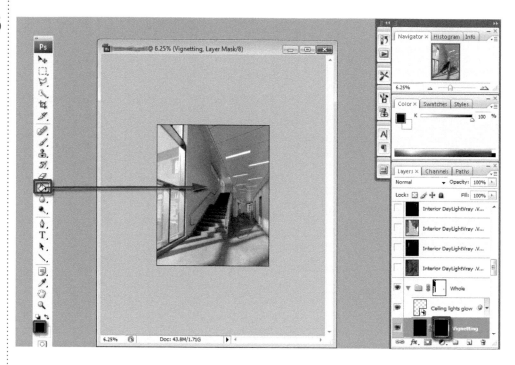

To begin creating the vignetting effect with the layer mask, select the brush tool (B) and set the foreground colour to white.

In addition, decrease the brush opacity to about 7% and begin brushing in the black colour on areas such as the corner of the document. With the brush opacity decreased to 7%, you can gradually control the amount of pixels to be brushed in. ▶9.57

The vignetting effect can also be achieved with adjustment layers such as *Levels* or *Curves*.

Instead of using the paint bucket tool on a layer, create a *Curve* or a *Level* adjustment layer to achieve this. ▶9.58

It's also common practice to tidy up and organize all the remaining layers and pass into group folders. To do, use some of the previous steps.

9.57

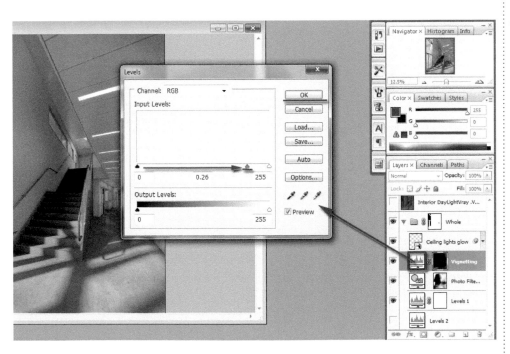

9.58

As mentioned earlier, ensure that all the *MultiMatte* layers/elements are placed above all the other layers from the document. ▶9.59

9.59

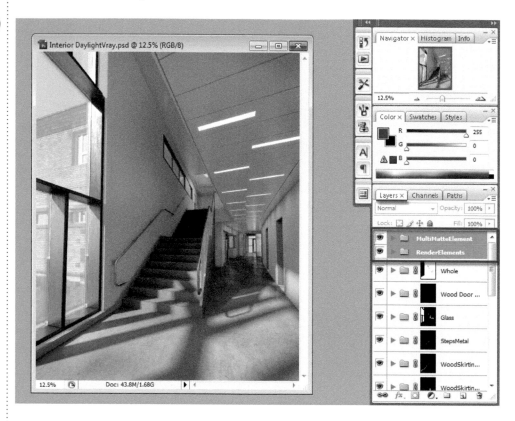

Finally, save your final file as a PSD and close it.

To see the final results, open the final PSD file under the name of 'Interior DaylightVray.psd'.

It's quite common for PSD files to grow to sizes larger than 2 GB when implementing some of the techniques covered earlier. When such occurs, Photoshop will generate an error and cancel the saving process. To override this artefact, save the PSD file as a PSB instead.

This large document format type allows Photoshop to save files larger than 2 GB, while retaining all the usual PSD document and layer properties. ▶9.60

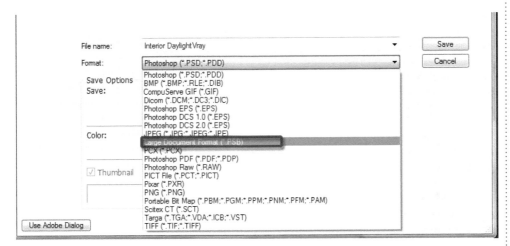

9.2 Adding People

If perchance you had Renderpeople (photo real 3d people) in your scene, this tutorial would have probably ended here; with your render looking more or less like the images ▶9.61 and 9.62.

There are often instances when there isn't enough time or/and resources available to add people in post.

In such cases Renderpeople assets (photo real 3d people) can work just as well, if not better than photoshoped 2d people; especially when working with crowds or/and aerial shots.

9.62

Presently, Renderpeople have some of the most realistic 3d models in the industry.

For more information about them, please visit: http://renderpeople. com/3d-people/

Adding 2d People in post

Adding people to visuals often help tell a story while giving a sense of scale and realism to the image.

Furthermore, the task of choosing the right type of people in the correct lighting environment, can be extremely time-consuming at times.

Having an extensive library of 2d people and background images/environments can help expedite this process immensely.

A very useful place to find 2d people, silhouettes and background images/ environments is, http://www.gobotree.com/. The website has a vast and diverse library.

In addition, the site offers a vast library of high resolution photos such as, grass, aerial shots, backgrounds, etc.

For more information about them, please visit: http://www.gobotree.com/

Back in your 3ds Max scene, create boxes that are 1.65/1.736 m in height and 0.332 m in width/length, to be used later as placeholders for human dimensions.

9.63

Place them around the scene, in areas where you plan to add people in post-production. ▶9.63

Next, click on the Print Screen key from your keyboard (PrtSc) and go back to Photoshop. In Photoshop, press Ctrl+N to create a new document and Ctrl+V to paste the printed screen. ▶9.64

Use the crop tool (C) to crop in the yellow areas (camera frame area) of the printed screen. To crop, click and drag the crop tool in the desired area, followed by double-clicking. ▶9.65

9.64

9.65

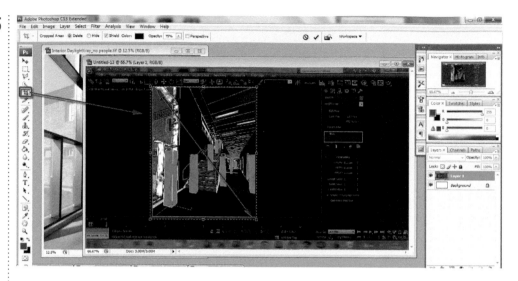

9.66

Next, enable the move tool (V) and select the cropped screen grab layer. Then drag-drop it onto the 'Interior DaylightVray_no people' document. ▶9.66

Use Ctrl+T to enable the transform tool handles. Next, hold down the Shift tool, grab the top left side of the layer and scale it up proportionally.

Use the layer opacity to match/line up the screen grab position against the 'Interior DaylightVray_no people'. ▶9.67

One of the most challenging parts about adding people in post-production is the process of selecting the correct types, with the appropriate lighting and at the right angle. Depending on the client or project, you may be asked to add casual or smartly dressed people.

It is common practice to place people in groups or pairs, utilizing key areas of the space.

Start by opening the file under the name of 'group of people.psd'.

This file was specifically chosen because it contains people at the right angle, with the correct lighting and dressed casually. ▶9.68

While the document comes with a variety of people, we'll focus mainly on the girl standing on the far right.

Start by enabling the *Polygonal Lasso Tool* and drawing it around the girl. To draw, click and move the mouse repeatedly while drawing around the entire body.

Once a full circle around her body is completed, a tiny circle should appear. Double-click to close the circle. A selection should be activated. ▶9.69 and 9.70

9.68

9.69

9.70

While the polygonal lasso selection is active, copy the selection (Ctrl+C). Next, select the document named 'Interior DaylightVray_no people' and paste it (Ctrl+V). ▶9.71 and 9.72

To begin editing/scaling the pasted image, enable the *Free Transform* tool (Ctrl+T), followed by holding down the Shift key and moving up the top left handle.

The image should scale proportionally. Ensure that it matches with one of the boxes from the screen grab.

9.71

9.72

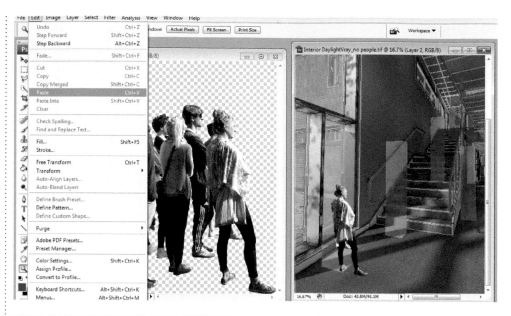

9.73

To exit the free transform tool, double click on the centre of the image being edited. ▶9.73 and 9.74

To ensure her direct shadows are falling in the right direction, we are going to flip the image (the girl) horizontally.

To do so, while *Layer 2* (the girl) is selected, select *Edit* on the main toolbar and choose the *Transform* option, followed by *Flip Horizontal*.

Also turn off the visibility of the screen grab underneath it. ▶9.75

The next step is to erase the unwanted pixels around the image. Rename *Layer 2* as 'Girl by the window' and duplicate it.

Turn off the visibility of the original layer. It is common practice to always keep the original layer intact, for reference purposes and as a precautionary measure.

9.74

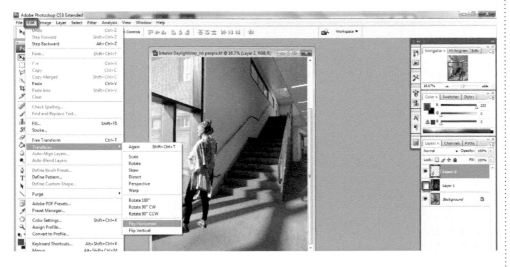

9.75

To quickly and accurately erase pixels use the background eraser tool. Enable this tool from the side toolbar and set the sampling type to *Once*.

This option allows users to sample the area/colour with a circle target, followed by clicking to erase a sampled area/colour.

Users can also click, hold down the mouse button and move the mouse to continuously erase similar sampled areas/colours.

Set the *Limits* type as *Contagious*, the *Tolerance* at 50% and the option to *Protect Foreground Color*.

In addition, zoom in to the document and begin erasing unwanted pixels around the selected layer ('Girl by the window copy').

Change different tolerance values, depending on the areas being erased. ▶9.76 and 9.77

9.76

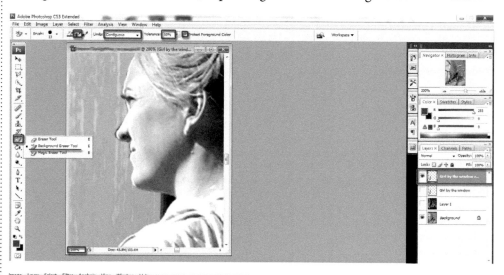

9.77

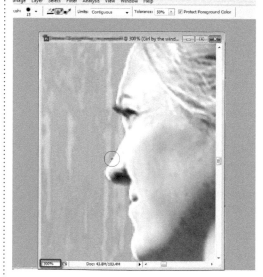

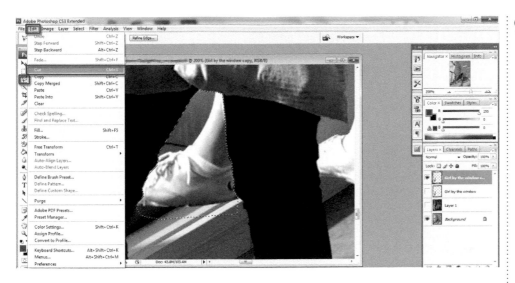

9.78

To remove other parts of the image, use the polygonal lasso tool to select and cut (Ctrl+X) unwanted pixels. ▶9.78

The next step is to add her shadows being cast along the corridor. When adding shadows, always match its direction and blurriness with the original base render.

Select the 'Girl by the window' layer and duplicate it. Rename the layer as 'Girl by the window shadows' and change its colour to grey.

By default the duplicated layer may sit on top of the original. Select and move it underneath the original layer, as shadows of a person are often cast under them.

9.79

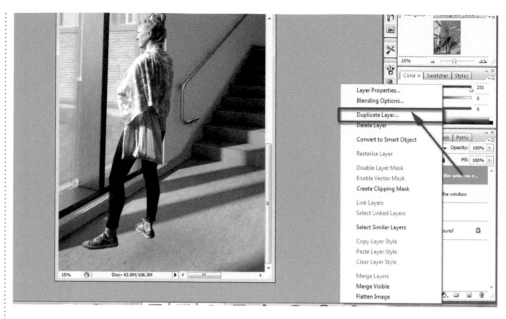

9.80

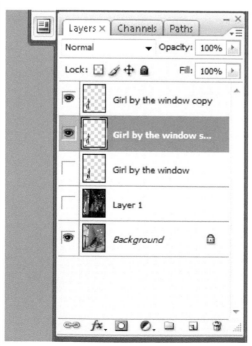

Use some of the techniques described earlier to achieve this. ▶9.79 and 9.80

To emulate a shadow start by darkening the layer underneath 'Girl by the window shadows'. To do so, select the layer and press Ctrl+L to bring up the *Levels* dialogue.

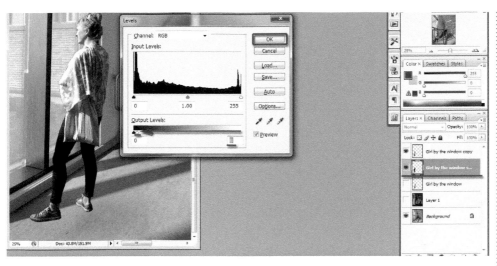

9.81

Move the *Output Levels* slider all the way to the left (to value 8 or less) to darken it; click *OK* to close its dialogue. ▶9.81

Before we begin modifying the shadow direction, convert the layer 'Girl by the window shadows' into a smart layer. Use some of the techniques covered earlier to do so.

As mentioned earlier, a Smart Objects layer records some of the layer's transformations/actions, which will later allow users to undo or edit actions. ▶9.82

To begin transforming the layer, press Ctrl+T to enable it, then move its top middle point downwards until it matches with the floor perspective. ▶9.83

While the layer is still selected, right-click and choose the *Skew* option from the pop up list. Begin pushing and pulling its four corner points individually to distort the layer horizontally. You may also use the middle point to move the layer.

9.82

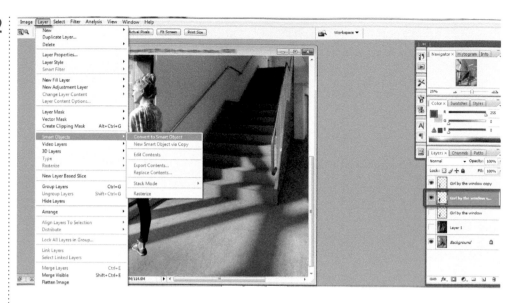

9.83

Note that the skew corner points can only be used/distorted once they go from black to grey/hatched. ▶9.84

Next, add the *Motion Blur* filter to match the blurriness of the shadows in the base render. ▶9.85

Set the *Angle* to 0.0 and the *Distance* to 171 pixels.

As mentioned earlier, these values worked well. However, feel free to use different and/or filters, if desired. ▶9.86

To match its shadow brightness to the ones depicted in the base render, decrease its *Fill* value to about 69% and add the *Levels* adjustment layer on top of it, using some of the techniques covered earlier.

In the *Levels* dialogue, move the leftmost slider of the *Output Levels* to 54. The brightness of the image should increase substantially.

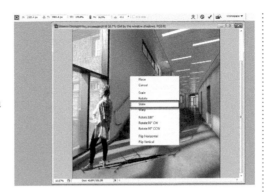

9.84

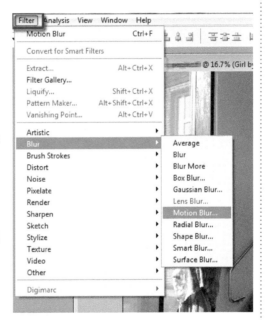

9.85

9.86

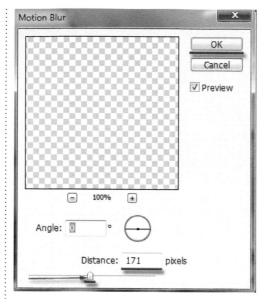

To ensure only the 'Girl by the window shadow' layer is affected by this *Levels* adjustment layer, hold down the Alt key and click on the middle line dividing the levels and the 'Girl by the window shadow' layer.

Once a small icon appears, create a clipping mask by clicking on it to restrict its influence on the entire document.

With the levels restricted to the layer below it, an arrow pointing downwards should automatically appear next to it. ▶9.87

9.87

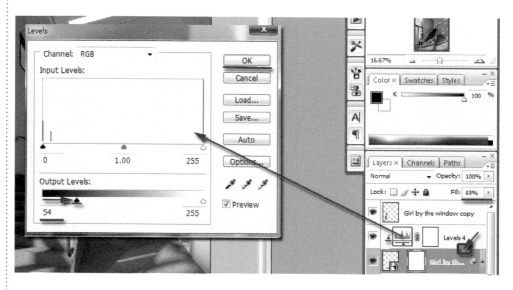

To blend areas where the shadows and the base render are overlapping, create a new layer mask and begin masking out the relevant areas.

Use some of the steps covered earlier to achieve this. ▶9.88

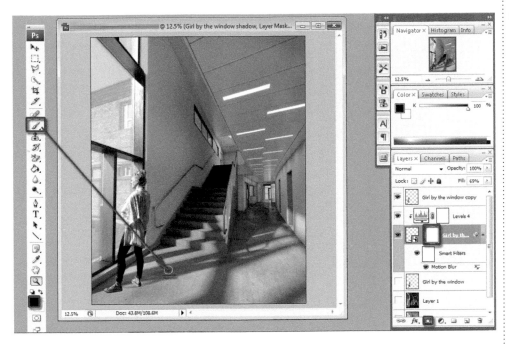

9.88

The next step is to add someone walking upstairs. Open a file under the name of 'Boy Walking up.psd'. This file was specifically chosen because it contains a person directly lit by sun and walking with his back to the camera.

Drag-drop the file into the working document and flip it horizontally using some of the techniques highlighted earlier. Following that, place him next to where the staircase begins and close to the large window on the left side.

9.89

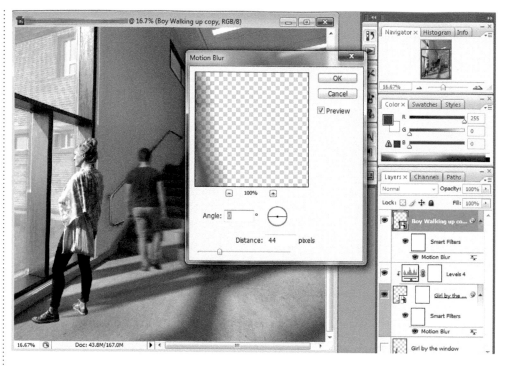

In addition, convert the layer into a smart object and apply a slight *Motion Blur* to it, to give it a sense of motion. ▶9.89

To match the layer brightness with the rest of the image, create an adjustment layer (*Levels*) and add a clipping mask to it, as previously done.

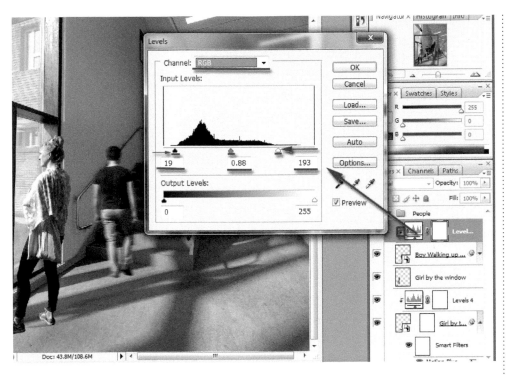

9.90

In the *Levels* dialogue, move its leftmost RGB slider to 19, the middle slider to 0.88 and the rightmost slider to 193. ▶9.90

Next, create its shadows while using some of the steps covered earlier. However, this layer should not be converted to a smart object due to the technique required to have its shadows cast over the first two steps of the staircase.

9.91

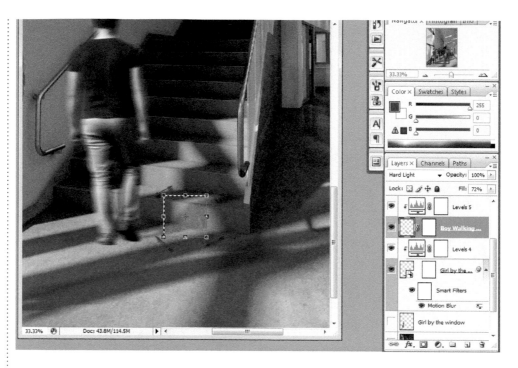

9.92

After the shadows are transformed and blurred, the first selection should be created and Ctrl+T enabled to rotate its direction upwards. ▶9.91

Following that, the second selection should be created and rotated to sit on top of the next step. ▶9.92

Use some of the approaches covered earlier to add more people in areas such as the corridor and walking up the stairs.

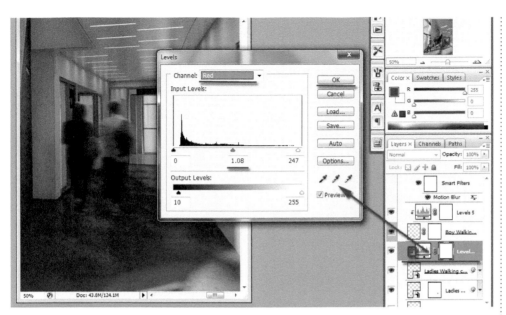

In addition, use adjustment layers such as *Levels* and *Hue/Saturation* to help integrate people and shadows. ▶9.93 and 9.94

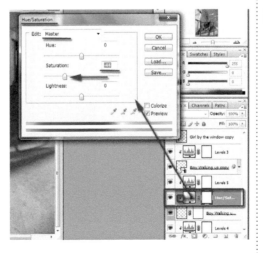

To help 'ground' the people in the scene, use the exact same technique previously implemented to create the vignetting effect and name it 'diffused shadows'.

Also ensure this layer is positioned under all layers in order to have the shadows below the people. ▶9.95

9.95

9.96

To emulate reflections of people walking in the corridor, select and duplicate the relevant layer, followed by moving it down and flipping it vertically.

To flip a layer, select *Edit* on the main toolbar, then *Transform* and *Flip Vertical*. ▶9.96

To match the reflection opacity with the rest of the image, reduce the layer opacity to about 34%.

To match its blurriness and slight unevenness with the rest of the image, convert the layer to a smart object as previously done; add *Motion Blur* and the *Ocean Ripple* filter to it. ▶9.97

3D Photorealistic Rendering

To see the final result, open the file named 'Interior DaylightVray people. psd'.

To finally make the whole image 'pop', add some key adjustment layers.

First, open the image named 'Interior DaylightVray.tif'. To create some contrast in the image, add the *Levels* adjustment layer. In its *RGB Input Level*, move the middle slider to about 0.34. In the *Output Levels*, move the leftmost slider to 5 in order to create an atmospheric effect.

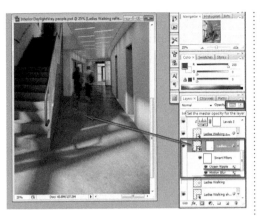

9.97

Use the layer mask to slightly brush away this effect on areas such as the wall. ▶9.98

To add a bit of colour to the image, create another *Levels* adjustment and choose the *Blue Channel*.

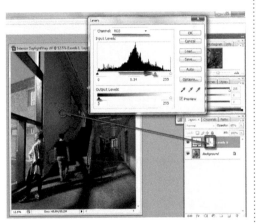

9.98

In its *Input Levels*, move the middle slider to about 0.52. In the *Output Levels*, move the left slider to 35 and the right point to about 123. ▶9.99

To brighten up the image and add more colour, create the *Curves* adjustment layer.

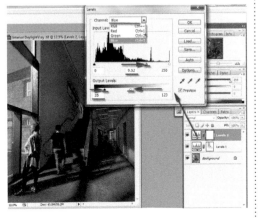

9.99

The lower part of the curve represents the dark areas of the image, and the upper part of the curve represents the brighter areas.

Choose its *Blue Channel* and add two point curves with the mouse target. The first curve point on the lower part of the curve line should have the following values, for example: *Output*, 93; *Input*, 94. The point on the upper side of the curve should be *Output*, 161; *Input*, 161.

Select the upper point curve and move it downwards slightly (*Output*, 142; *Input*, 187). Note the colour changes taking place. ▶9.100

9.100

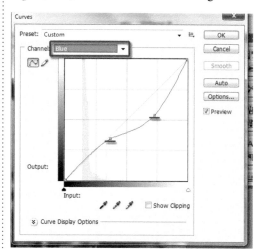

Next, choose the RGB channel, followed by creating and moving two curve points: first point, 92/43; second point 192/109. Note the brightness of the image changing gradually.

Finally, use the layer mask to brush away the curves' effects in areas such as the window on the left-hand side. ▶9.101

To see the final results, open the file under the name of 'SMESTOW_Interior_Lighting contrast.psd'.

9.101

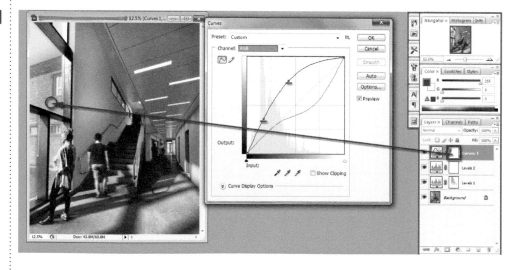

Conclusion

This chapter has taken users through the process of using render elements and Photoshop adjustment layers to control the display of numerous objects in the scene individually. Users were also shown how to add people in post-production realistically, to create a sense of scale, while utilizing the space to help sell the design. Finally, users were taken through the unique process of making an image pop while using key adjustment layers.

10

Interior Night Time

Pre-production

10.1 Client Brief

For this night shot, the main brief was to highlight the effect of the artificial lights in the corridor in the windows from the block outside and the effect of the sky/ambient light affecting the overall scene.

10.2 Photo References and Mood Board

The images below depict two of many photo references presented to the client. ▶10.1

10.1

Lighting and colour suggestions

First choice

Second choice

Conclusion

While this pre-production stage was notably more straightforward than the previous one, it was equally important to go through the process of selecting the best possible photo references related to the camera shot and the scene composition.

Furthermore, the photo references had to reflect the time of the day requested by the client (night).

11

Interior Night Time in V-Ray

Lighting

Lighting an interior night scene can be challenging at times, especially when dealing with multiple light sources and colours to achieve a balanced scene.

The following tutorial will help users set up and light an interior night scene quickly, while using industry standard techniques, as well as some new cutting-edge ones.

11 Interior Night Time in V-Ray

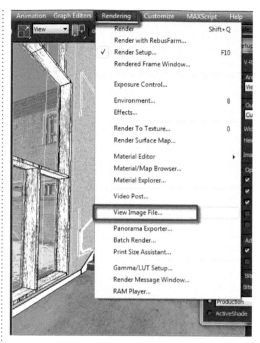

11.1

11.1 Getting Started

Open the MAX file under the name of 'SMESTOW_Interior Night Lighting_ Start01_.max'.

Follow some of the earlier steps to accept the *Gamma/LUT and Units Setup* dialogue and start by opening the photo reference named '49.jpg'.

The photo reference depicts everything that encapsulates a night interior shot: There's a cold blue tint from the skylight entering the space, balanced by the warm colours generated by the recessed lights.
▶11.1 and 11.2

11.2

11.2 Lighting

As is evident, this 3ds Max scene has all the lights that were created from the previous interior daylight tutorial. In addition, all rendering parameters have been set to draft/low resolution.

The following steps will help users transform the current daylight scene into a night one, while using the photo reference as a guide.

To start, enable the *Override mtl* as previously done and change the *VRaySun001* to the following values: $X = 95.966$; $Y = -400.493$; $Z = 0.146$.

The *VRaySun001* position was moved to emulate sunset or dusk and prevent direct shadows from being cast. ▶11.3 and 11.4

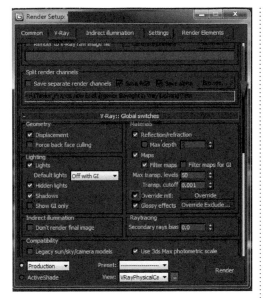

11.3

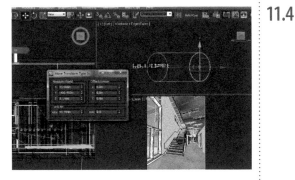

11.4

The following step is to change the light colours. Select the *VRayLight_Dome* and change its colour to blue, similar to the photo reference: *Hue* = 155; *Sat* = 234; *Value* = 60. ▶11.5

11.5

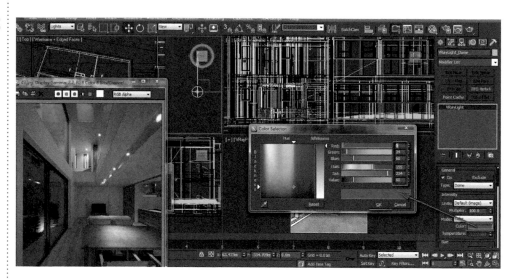

To keep all the external light colours consistent, copy the new colour from the *VRayLight_Dome* colour swatch and paste it onto the *VRayLight_Window*. Use some of the techniques covered earlier to copy and paste. ▶11.6 and 11.7

To reinvigorate the ceiling light colour, change it to a darker tone, similar to the photo reference. Select one of the ceiling lights in the scene and change its colour swatch to an orange tone: *Hue* = 13; *Sat* = 255; *Value* = 234.

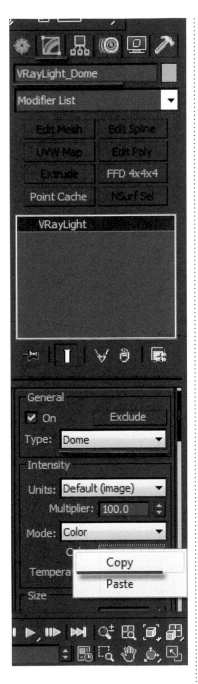

11.6

11.7

Because all the ceiling lights are instances, the changes applied to one light will affect all the other instanced copies in the scene. ▶11.8

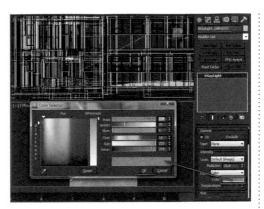

11.8

Also increase its multiplier value to about 75 to make it more noticeable in the render. ▶11.9

Finally, open the *Environment and Effects* dialogue. In the *Background* group, change its colour swatch to the same tone of blue as the dome light and disable the *Use Map* function. When the *Use Map* function is disabled, 3ds Max uses the background colour swatch automatically.

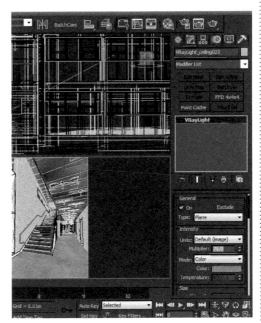

11.9

11.10

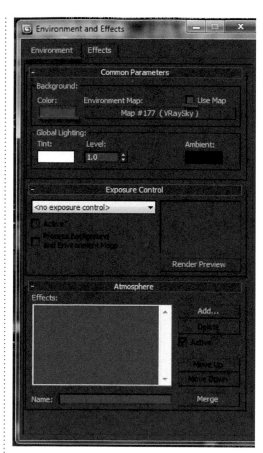

The sky colour should now be similar to the dome light. Do a test render (Shift+Q) for a quick preview of the recent changes. ▶11.10 and 11.11

The scene colours are now looking similar to the adjacent photo reference. The next step is to begin adding lights to the small windows seen directly outside the main glass window.

Use some of the techniques described earlier to create a new V-Ray plane light and rename it 'VRayLight_ Window house'.

With the *Move* tool, position the new light directly behind one of the building blocks seen through the main window.

Isolate some objects in the scene, if necessary. The following position worked well: $X = 31.202$ m; $Y = -339.028$ m; $Z = 3.306$ m.

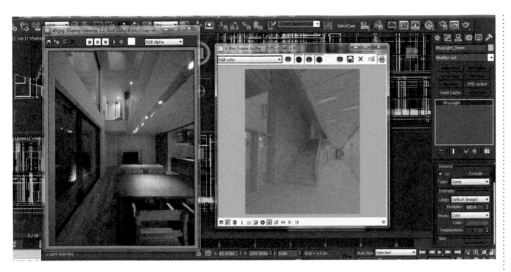

Set its size as follows: *Half-length* = 2.02 m; *Half-width* = 2.964 m. ▶11.12

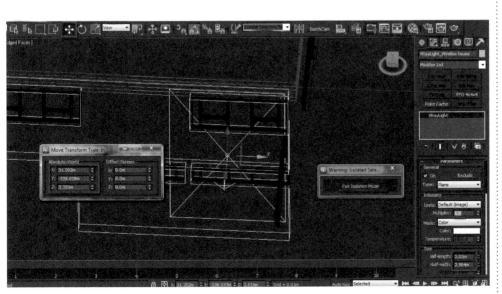

Next, we are going to use the photo reference bitmap as a source of colour and luminance to illuminate parts of the scene.

Set the new light parameter attributes in a similar way to the previous plane lights (i.e. *Affect diffuse*; *Affect specular*; *Ignore light normals*; *Invisible* and to *Cast shadows*).

Scroll down to the *Texture* group and click on the *Use texture* toggle to bring up the *Material/Map Browser* dialogue.

Under *Maps/Standard* choose the *Bitmap* option and pick the photo reference under the name of '49.jpg'. ▶11.13

11.13

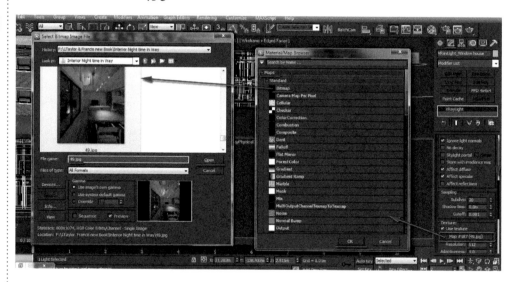

11.14

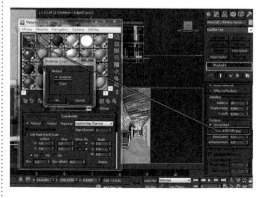

To edit '49.jpg', open the Material Editor (M) followed by dragging '49. jpg' from the *Texture* toggle onto the *Material Editor* slot.

Accept the Instance copy method and click *OK* to close the dialogue. ▶11.14

Because this image is being used as a light emitter, blur it slightly to avoid having the image source projected onto surfaces. Increase the value of the

Blur function to about 14.01, to start with. ▶11.15

11.15

To ensure a warm colour is being emitted from the bitmap, scroll down to the *Bitmap Parameters* roll-out and enable the *Cropping/Placement* function.

Next, click on the *View Image* toggle to bring up its dialogue. By default, the cropping area fits the exact proportions of the image. Select any of the corner handles and begin moving them to crop the image.

The final cropped area should encompass the warmest part of the image: $U = 0.582$; $V = 0.272$; $W = 0.418$; $H = 0.49$.

11.16

Once finished, close the dialogue by clicking on the close button (X). ▶11.16

The following step is to boost up *RGB Level* values, to emit light. To do so, scroll down and open the *Output* roll-out. Next, increase the *RGB Level* function to about 800.0.

Again, this value was achieved through a series of test renders.

11.17

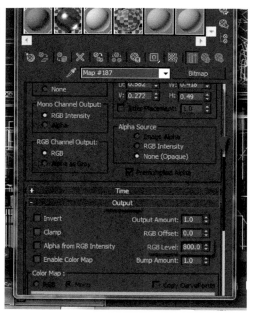

It's worth mentioning that the main intensity of the light multiplier was kept at 1.0, while its RGB level was increased to 800. This was done to ensure the bitmap colours were emitted onto the surfaces, as opposed to the intensity colour coming from the light multiplier. ▶11.17

The final step is to copy/instance this new light multiple times around the window areas. Place them strategically so they point towards the surfaces seen through the window (i.e. ceiling and walls). Use the *Move* and *Rotate* tools to position the lights accordingly. ▶11.18 and 11.19

11.18

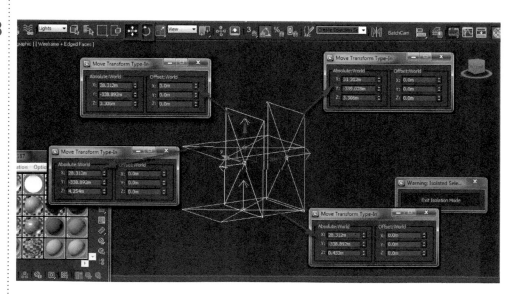

3D Photorealistic Rendering

Use similar techniques to create a light washing down the courtyard area outside. Disable the *Override mtl* and do a quick test to see the results. ►11.20

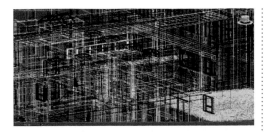

11.19

11.20

11.3 Setting Up for the Final Render

It's common for users to fine-tune materials when there are dramatic changes with the light in the scene. However, for this specific scene, despite the lights having been changed from day to night, it didn't seem to affect the materials much.

The final step is to increase the render settings, for high resolution renders.

As previously done, in the *Render Setup* dialogue, under the *Common* tab, increase the output size to 3500×4380. ►11.21

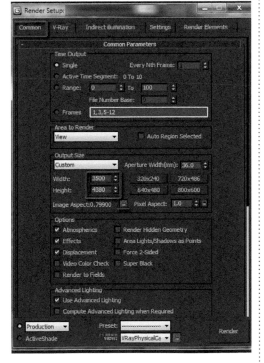

11.21

Next, open the *V-Ray* tab. Under the *V-Ray:: Frame buffer*, name the file 'Interior Night time in Vray_'. Use some of the steps covered earlier to name and save the final *Split render channels* as a TGA or TIFF. ▶11.22

11.22

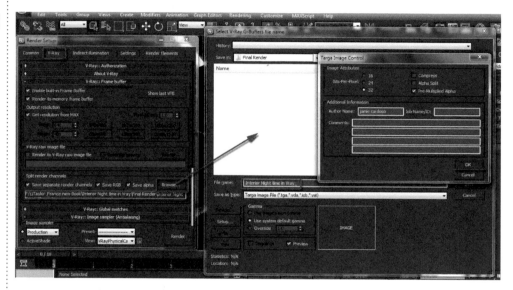

11.23

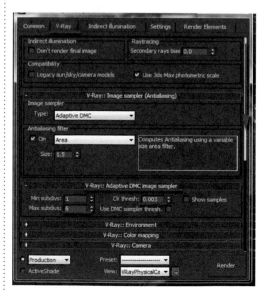

Scroll down further to the *V-Ray:: Adaptive DMC image sampler* roll-out and increase the *Max subdivs* value to 6. In addition, change the *Clr thresh* value to 0.003. While these two functions will increase the render times slightly, they will also increase the render quality dramatically. ▶11.23

In the *Indirect illumination* tab, increase the *V-Ray:: Irradiance map* preset to *Medium* and keep the *Interp. Samples* to 70.

While these values worked well, experiment with different values, if desired. ▶11.24

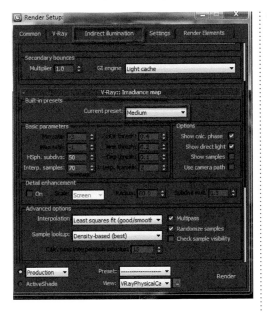

11.24

Scroll down further to the *V-Ray:: Light cache* roll-out and increase the *Subdivs* value to 1500. ▶11.25

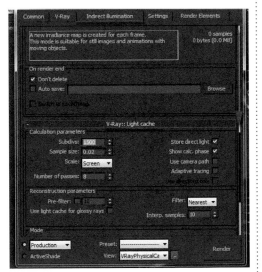

11.25

11.26

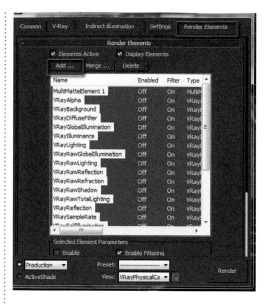

Finally, in the *Render Elements* tab, add all the elements previously used. ▶11.26

NOTE

Fox render Farm services were extensively used to render the final images, at a lightning speed.

For more information about Fox Render Farm, please go to: http://www.foxrenderfarm.com/

Conclusion

This chapter showed users how to set up an interior night scene using a photo reference as guide for lights, mood and ambient colours. Furthermore, users were introduced to new lighting techniques to create light emitters with bitmaps. Finally, the entire process enabled users to quickly create an appealing and relatively fast render.

12

Interior Night Time

Post-production

This last step of the production will take users through the process of putting together all the elements previously rendered in order to enhance the overall image and material details.

During this process, users will use some of the techniques previously covered in Chapter 9, while being introduced to new ones to achieve the final results.

12 Interior Night Time

12.1 Post-production

As previously done, start by using the *Load Files into Stack* script to select and load the rendered elements into a stack. ▶12.1 and 12.2

12.1

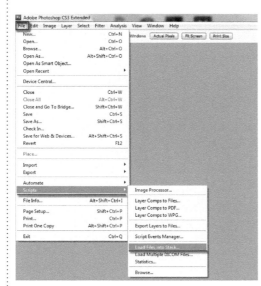

Save the document as 'Interior Night time Vray_tutorials.psd'.

Next, organize the *MultiMatteElement* and remaining render elements into two separate group folders and name each group folder accordingly. Ensure the *MultiMatte* elements are always on top of the stack. Keep the 'Interior Night time in Vray.RGB_color.0000. tga' layer as the base bottom layer and change its property colour to red.

It's a common practice to always have the base render at the bottom of the stack, in order to layer the remaining elements/passes on top of it.

12.2

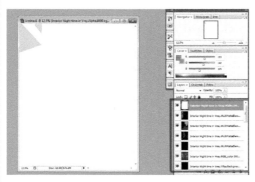

3D Photorealistic Rendering

Use some of the techniques described in Chapter 9 to do this. ▶12.3

The next step is to begin fine-tuning the overall interior contrast and colour of the image.

Before creating a new group folder for the overall interior contrast, enable the red colour range from the 'Interior Night time in Vray. MultiMatteElement_1.0000.tga' layer as previously done.

Use the rectangular marquee tool (M) in conjunction with the Alt key to subtract undesired selected areas. ▶12.4

Invert the selection (Alt+Ctrl+I), followed by creating a group folder and layer mask. As previously mentioned, creating a layer mask will confine subsequent adjustment layers to the group folder mask.

Rename the new group folder 'Whole Inside' and hide the visibility of the 'Vray.MultiMatteElement_1.0000.tga' layer. ▶12.5 and 12.6

Next, open the reference photo previously used to light up and render the scene.

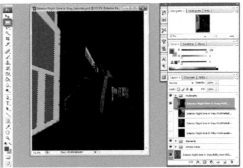

12.3

12.4

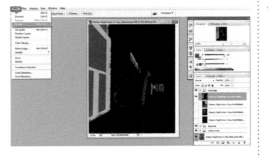

12.5

Create a *Levels* adjustment layer inside the new group folder. In the RGB channel, move the rightmost *Input Levels* slider to 155, the middle slider to 0.67 and the leftmost to 9.

12 Interior Night Time

12.6

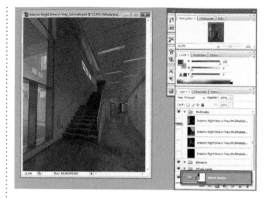

These values worked well to create a nice internal contrast. However, try different values, if desired. ▶**12.7**

12.7

To match the blue tones closely with the tones of the reference photo, add a *Hue/ Saturation* adjustment layer on top of the levels.

In *Edit colors*, select *Blues* and increase the saturation to about +30. Note how saturated the blue tones become.

Click *OK* to close the dialogue and decrease its *Opacity* value to about 36%, to tone down its colour a bit. ▶**12.8**

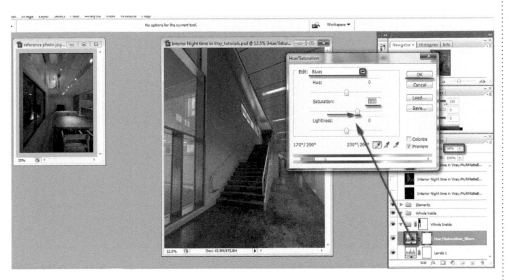

To further tweak the blue tones, add a *Selective Color* adjustment layer on top of the *Hue/Saturation* layer and add a clipping mask to it (Ctrl+Alt+G).

With a clipping mask added (an arrow pointing down), all changes made to the *Hue/Saturation* adjustment layer will only affect the layer below it (*Hue/ Saturation*).

In the *Selective Color Options* dialogue, choose *Blues* and increase the black values to +20%. Note how the black hues/tones of the image darken slightly. ▶12.9

12.9

To desaturate the yellow tones, add another *Hue/Saturation* adjustment layer and decrease the yellow saturation to –17. The yellow tones are now similar to the adjacent photo reference. ▶12.10

12.10

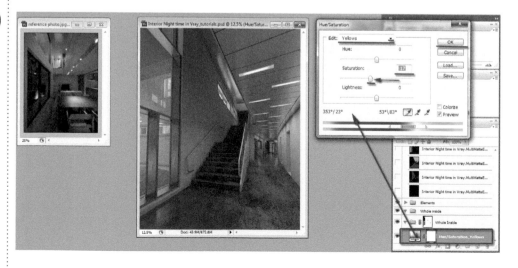

The next step is to create a glow effect for the ceiling lights, using the same techniques highlighted in Chapter 6.

Use the 'Interior Night time in Vray.MultiMatteElement_2.0000.tga' layer to select the ceiling light. Following that, while the ceiling light selection is still active, select the base render layer ('Interior Night time in Vray.RGB_color.0000. tga') and copy (Ctrl+C) and paste (Ctrl+V) the selection. ▶12.11

12.11

Next, rename the new pasted layer 'Ceiling Lights' and convert it to a smart object layer, using some of the techniques covered in Chapter 6.

Change its property colour to red and add a *Gaussian Blur* filter to it.

Increase its radius to about 27.0 and click *OK* to close its dialogue box. For better integration with the base render, change the *Blending* mode to *Screen* type and reduce its *Opacity* to about 65%.

Finally, move the 'Ceiling Lights' layer inside the 'Whole Inside' group folder. The light glow levels now look similar to the photo reference. ▶12.12

12.12

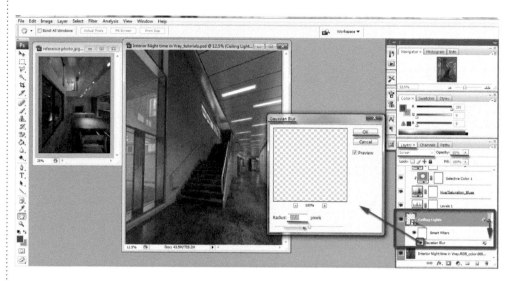

The next step is to adjust the external values using some of the techniques highlighted earlier.

To select the outside areas, hold down the Ctrl key and click on the 'Whole Inside' group folder mask. Invert the selection (Shift+Ctrl+I) and create a new group folder.

3D Photorealistic Rendering

Rename it 'Whole Outside' and create an adjacent layer mask while the inverted selection is still on. ▶12.13 and 12.14

12.13

To begin adjusting the outside levels, create the *Levels* adjustment layer. In the *RGB Channels*, move its rightmost *Input Levels* slider to 189 and the middle slider to 0.48. Note how the outside levels liven up.

Try different values, if desired.

12.14

In addition, use the brush tool in conjunction with the *Levels* mask, to brush away undesired areas. ▶12.15

12.15

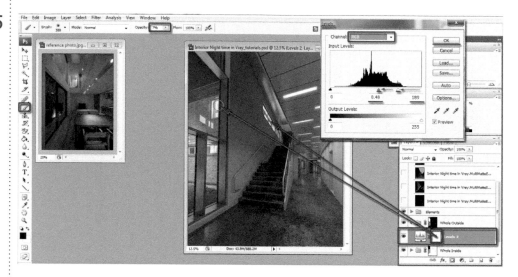

To add some warmth to the yellow tones outside, create a new *Hue/Saturation* adjustment layer.

In the *Edit Yellows* parameters, decrease the hue to about –15 and increase the saturation to about +19.

Note how new tones have been gradually added to the yellows. Although these values have worked well, try different values if desired. ▶12.16

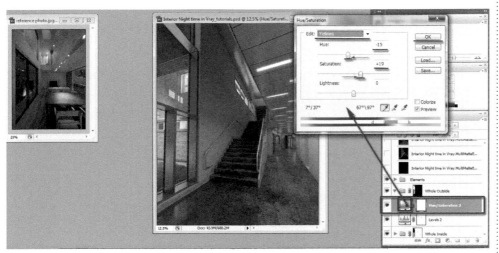

12.16

To accentuate the green colour on the grass outside, select the relevant area with the polygonal lasso tool (L) and create a *Color Balance* adjustment layer. Rename it 'Green areas'. Ensure this adjustment layer is immediately below the *Levels*.

In the *Color Balance* dialogue, move the *Cyan/Red* slider to +1, the *Magenta/Green* slider to +19 and the *Yellow/Blue* slider to –11.

A green tint is now more apparent on the grass.

As mentioned earlier, all these new adjustment layers should be confined to the 'Whole Outside' layer mask. If not, click on the little arrow to the right of the group folder to close it, followed by selecting and moving the relevant layers inside the group folder. ▶12.17

12.17

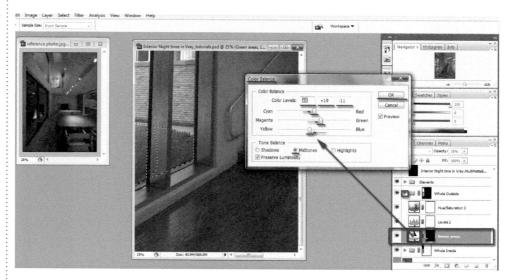

The next step is to balance the colour and contrast of the sky outside.

To select the sky outside, open the *Elements* group folder and turn on the visibility of the 'Interior Night time in Vray.Alpha.0000.tga' layer.

Next, select the *Magic Wand Tool* (W) from the main toolbar, set the *Tolerance* to 30 and select the sky area (grey colour). That area was easily selected due to the specific V-Ray glass refraction material set to affect the *Color+Alpha* channel. ▶12.18

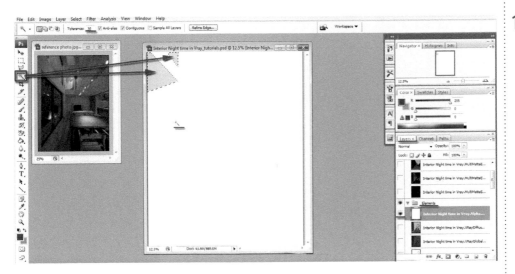

12.18

While the selection is on, turn off the 'Interior Night time in Vray.Alpha.0000. tga' layer and create a new *Levels* adjustment layer. Rename it 'Skies'.

In the *RGB Channel Input Levels*, move the leftmost slider to 21, the middle slider to 0.80 and the rightmost slider to 199. Note the sky contrast taking place. ▶12.19

12.19

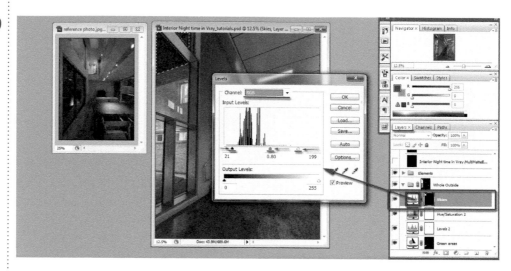

12.20

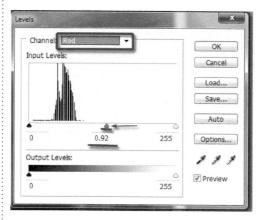

While the *Levels* dialogue is still open, open the *Red* channel and move its middle slider to 0.92. In the *Blue* channel, move the middle slider to 1.05 and click *OK* to close the dialogue. ▶12.20 and 12.21

The next step is to begin tweaking specific materials such as the floor and handrails.

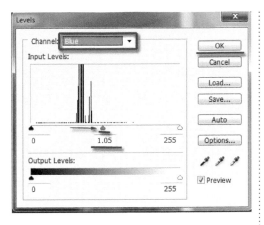

Select the floor material from the 'Interior Night time in Vray. MultiMatteElement_2.0000.tga' layer, using some of steps covered earlier. Create its group folder with a layer mask and rename it 'Floors'. ▶12.22 and 12.23

12.23

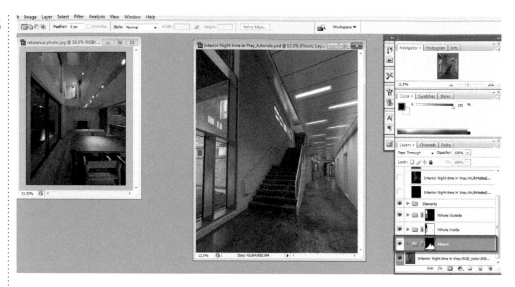

To add a bit of contrast to the floor material, create a *Levels* adjustment layer. In its RGB channel, move its rightmost *Input Levels* slider to 187 and its midpoint to 0.76. ▶12.24

12.24

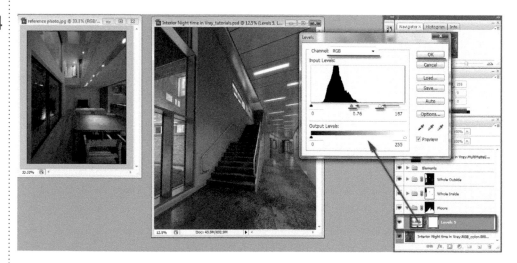

To make the floor more interesting, add more reflectivity to it by copying and moving the 'Interior Night time in Vray.VRayRawReflection.0000.tga' layer from the *Elements* group folder into the 'Floors' group folder. Use some of the techniques demonstrated in Chapter 6 for this step.

There are areas of the floor that will benefit from having fewer reflections than others. To control this, create a layer mask and brush away the undesired areas (represented in red).

In addition, reduce the *Opacity* to 30% to make it less prominent. ▶12.25 and 12.26

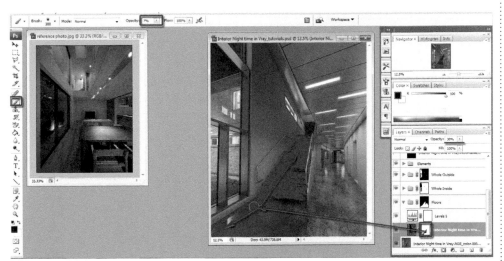

12.25

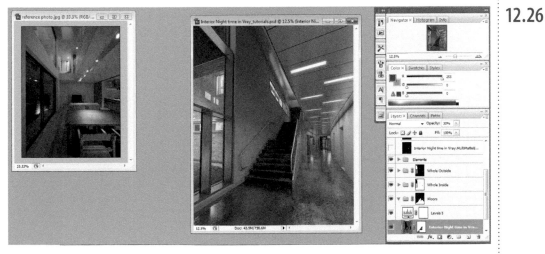

12.26

12.27

To add more depth to the floor, copy and move the 'Interior Night time in Vray.VRayRawGlobalIllumination.0000.tga' layer into the 'Floors' group folder. For better integration with the floor, choose the *Overlay* blending mode and reduce its opacity to 35%.

In addition, create a layer mask to brush away undesired areas. ▶12.27

Use Chapter 6 as a reference to tweak the remaining materials (i.e. handrails, metal frames, etc.). The final file should look similar to the 'Interior Night time in Vray.psd'. ▶12.28

12.28

3D Photorealistic Rendering

12.2 Adding People

We are going to start by using some of the same people and techniques previously used in Chapter 6.

Create a new group folder under the name of 'People' and place the 'Boy Walking up copy' layer inside it. Note that this layer is already a smart object with a motion blur filter applied to it from Chapter 6. ▶12.29

12.29

The first challenge is to fully integrate this person/layer into this new night environment.

Let's start by emulating the yellow/orange light coming from the right-hand side. The influence of this orange/yellow light can also be seen on the stairs' handrails. It's good practice to always look closely at the overall environment light, prior to beginning to integrate people in it.

Create a photo filter adjustment layer with a clipping mask, to restrict its effect on the layer below it (i.e. 'Boy Walking up copy'). This technique was discussed in Chapter 6.

In the *Photo Filter* dialogue, set its *Color* to orange, with 100% density, and click *OK* to close the dialogue. Use the photo filter layer mask to mask away everything, apart from right half side of the 'Boy Walking up copy' layer.

Note the slight orange colour on one half of the person. ▶12.30

To create highlights around the person's body, create a new *Levels* adjustment later and rename 'highlights'. Add a clipping mask to it and open its dialogue. In the *RGB Input Levels Channel*, move the rightmost slider to 148 to create bright areas.

12.30

12.31

To add blue tones to the bright areas, go to the *Blue Input Levels Channel* and move the rightmost slider to 169 and the middle point slider to 1.21.
▶12.31 and 12.32

12.32

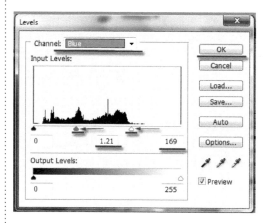

Close the *Levels* dialogue and begin masking out everything, apart from areas around the rim of the body. ▶12.33

To change the overall colour of the person, add a *Selective Color* adjustment layer with a clipping mask on top of it.

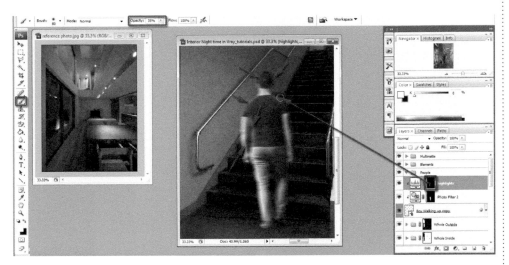

12.33

In the *Selective Color Options* dialogue, change the *Reds* to blue by moving the *Cyan* value to +2%, *Magenta* to –54%; *Yellow* to –76% and *Black* to +82%. ▶12.34

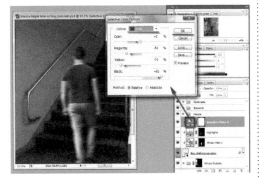

12.34

To fully integrate the overall levels of the person with its surroundings, create another *Levels* adjustment layer and move its *RGB Channel Input Level* slider to 0.55. The overall image of the person should go slightly darker. ▶12.35

12.35

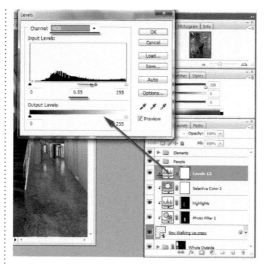

To add more blue tone to the person, go to the *Blue Channel* and move its middle *Input Levels* slider to 1.57. The overall person is now looking more integrated with the rest of the scene. ▶12.36

12.36

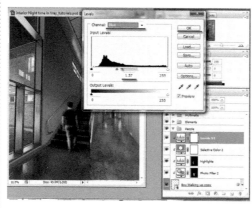

To further match the blue tones of the person with the rest of the environment, create a *Hue/Saturation* adjustment layer with a clipping mask. In its *Edit Blues* parameters, change its *Hue* to –25 and its *Saturation* to +4. Note how the blue tones are now perfectly matched with the rest of the environment. ▶12.37

12.37

To reinvigorate the yellow rim lights around the person's body, add another photo filter adjustment layer with a clipping mask. Use a strong yellow photo filter colour and mask out undesired areas, as previously done. ▶12.38

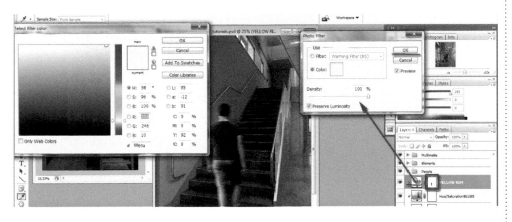

12.38

The remaining people and their reflections were added and the colour corrected using the same techniques discussed earlier in Chapter 9. Refer to the final PSD file under the name of 'Interior Night time in Vray.psd' to see the final results. ▶12.39

12.39

While the Chromatic Aberration (CA) effect on real photos is dimmed as a camera artefact, with CG images it can often add more realism.

While this effect can be achieved with a *Lens blur* filter in Photoshop, the following process will demonstrate how to achieve the same results, whilst providing more control over its general effect.

The CA effect can only be achieved on a separate flattened document/image. To do so, select the working PSD file and duplicate it, by clicking on *Image* on the main toolbar and choosing the *Duplicate* option.

The *Duplicate Image* dialogue should appear; name the duplicate 'CA' and click *OK* to close the dialogue. ▶12.40 and 12.41

12.40

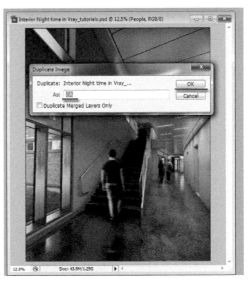

12.41

Once duplicated, select the base render image layer, followed by right-clicking on it and choosing the option *Flatten Image*. Note that this option is only available on image layers, *not* adjustment layers or group folders. ▶12.42

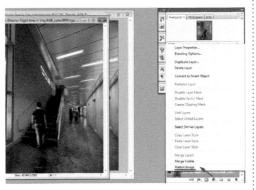

12.42

12.43

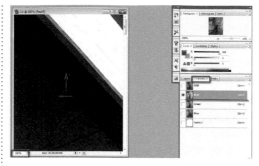

With a flattened image we can now begin to emulate the CA effect on it.

First zoom into the document at 100%, to ensure the nudging process is not overly done. Next, open the channels palette and select the *Red Channel* only. The remaining channels are turned off automatically.

12.44

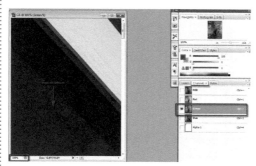

Following that, select the *Move* tool from the side toolbar (V). Nudge the red channel upwards once, with the up arrow from the keyboard. It should move up by one pixel. ▶12.43

Next, select the *Green Channel* and nudge it downwards, with the down arrow from the keyboard. ▶12.44

12.45

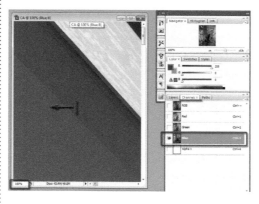

Lastly, select the *Blue Channel* and nudge it to the left. The idea behind this exercise is to have each channel going in a different direction. ▶12.45

Select the *RGB* channel to see the final result. The CA on the overall image is now very apparent and realistic. ▶12.46

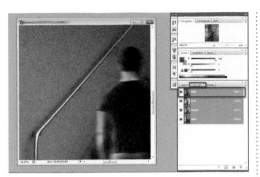

12.46

To drop this new CA effect into the main PSD document, first click on the CA's *Layers* palette and right-click on it to duplicate the layer. ▶12.47

The *Duplicate Layer* dialogue should appear. Set the destination document as 'Interior night in Vray_tutorials.psd', followed by clicking *OK* to close the dialogue. The CA image should automatically be dropped into the correct document ('Interior night in Vray_tutorials.psd').

12.47

In the 'Interior night in Vray_tutorials.psd' document, ensure the CA image is on top of the 'People' group folder and its fill value is set to about 80%. Its opacity was slightly reduced in order to decrease its prominence. ▶12.48 and 12.49

12.48

12.49

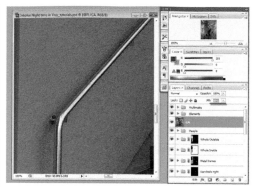

To see the final result, please open the file 'Interior Night time in Vray.psd'.

Conclusion

This chapter guided users through the initial intricacies adjusting the overall image in order to give it more impact, whilst using a photo as the reference. The following step was to fine-tune each material separately, to reinvigorate key physical properties that weren't originally apparent on the base render.

The next stage was to integrate the people with the overall surroundings, while using the general scene lighting as the main focal reference to help achieve seamless integration. Finally, a CA effect was used to help add a more photographic feel to the overall image.

13

Exterior Daylight

Pre-production

13.1 Client Brief

For this project the initial brief was to create a daylight shot, with the camera capturing the entire building entrance and the bike rack.

In addition, to help tell a story and emphasize important features of the building, people will be added, shown using the space/key facilities.

13.2 Photo References and Mood Board

After the brief, photo references were provided by the designers, to help describe their ideas and concepts, to the studio/visualizers. Furthermore, the studio/artists played a role in choosing some of the photo references for the overall lighting and 'feel' of the image.

As previously mentioned, designers/architects usually supply the studio/artists with mood boards depicting their furniture and materials. The studio/artist can find the respective 3D versions of the furniture from the manufacturer's website or from websites such as http://www.designconnected.com/.

Alternatively, if the requested furniture is bespoke, you can create your own photo realistic 3D model and materialize it. ▶13.1 and 13.2

13.1

Camera and lighting suggestions

Camera/colour

Lighting

Suggestions for materials and finishes

Paving

Bike rack metal

Red brick

Glass canopy

Conclusion

The pre-production phase is quite important to sign off on camera angles and scene details. In addition, the studio/artist frequently uses this process to agree on the art direction, materials, furniture, colours, etc., prior to commencing the production phase.

14

Exterior Daylight

Creating Materials

Having previously covered in detail the process of sourcing photos as references to create realistic materials in 3ds Max (e.g. Chapter 7), in this chapter we will quickly delve into creating similar materials for an exterior scene.

As such, the starting file has the V-Ray renderer loaded into the scene already, and the *VRayPhysicalCamera* has been set up.

This tutorial will focus mainly on materials such as pavement, window glass, metal, a wood bench and bricks.

Tip: https://www.arroway-textures.ch/ offers users a wide range of seamless and photorealistic textures.

14 Creating Materials

14.1 Getting Started

To begin, open the 3ds Max file under the name of 'fulbridge002 bound_Start.max'.

Follow some of the earlier steps to adopt the *Gamma & LUT Settings Mismatch* options.

14.1

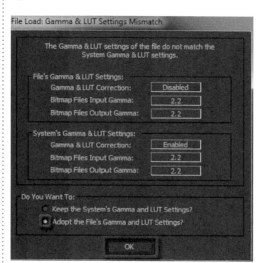

The opening scene has no materials or modifiers applied. The next step is to begin assigning materials, textures and modifiers to some of the objects in the scene. ▶14.1 and 14.2

14.2

14.2 Pavement

One of the most distinctive characteristics of pavement is its rough stone finish with a hint of diffused reflectivity. In 3ds Max, some users emulate its physical properties procedurally, most through a basic shader in conjunction with a realistic texture with specific shader parameters.

Start by selecting, in the scene, the object under the name of 'Pavement 004'. Next, open the Material Editor (M) and select an empty slot. Rename the new material slot 'a-paving00'.

The *VRayMtl* is already loaded because the *Custom UI and Default Switcher* was already chosen in Chapter 7. ▶14.3

14.3

Otherwise, load the *VRayMtl* by clicking on the *Standard* toggle and choosing the *VRayMtl* from the *Material/Map Browser* list dialogue. ▶14.4

▼14.4

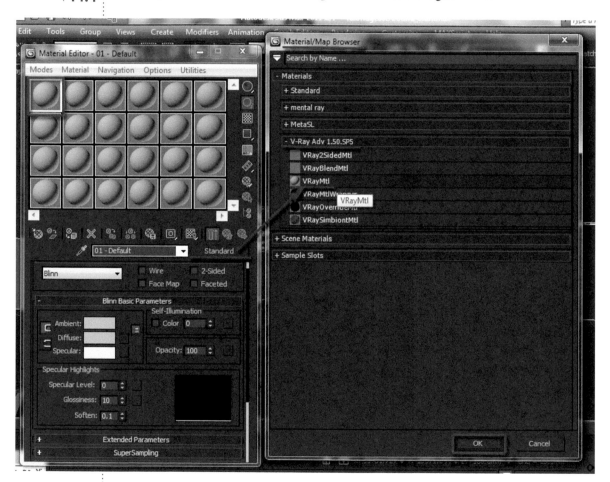

While the 'Pavement 004' object is still selected, assign it to the new slot and load the 'FloorsRegular0195_1_S.jpg' texture to its *Diffuse* toggle.

As mentioned earlier; a very good resource to find seamless high resolution textures is, www.arroway-textures.com

In the bitmap *Coordinates* roll-out, make the new texture visible in the viewport and apply a *UVW Mapping* modifier to it. Keep the *Mapping* as *Planar*.

Back in the bitmap *Coordinates* roll-out, sharpen the texture by reducing its *Blur* value to about 0.5.

To adjust the texture perfectly, rotate its *W* angle to 90 degrees and apply the *Cropping/Placement* to fit the texture perfectly to the surface.

The following cropping values worked well: *U* = 0.0; *V* = 0.008; *W* = 1.0; *H* = 0.982. ▶14.5 and 14.6

To add realism/life to the surface, copy the diffuse texture and paste it onto the *Reflect* toggle. Reflection and glossiness work best with greyscale textures. Because the diffuse texture is greyish, it will work well with the *Reflect* toggle.

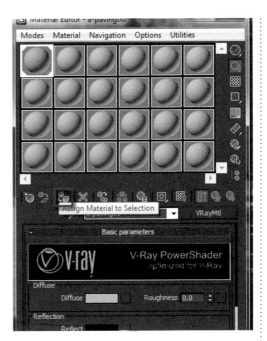

14.5

14.6

Enable *Fresnel reflections* and disable the *Hilight glossiness* padlock. Disabling the *Hilight glossiness* padlock will allow the reflect glossiness values to work independently.

At times, enabling Fresnel reflections is great for balancing out overly reflective surfaces. In this particular instance, it will give the impression of a dump and lively surface, which often makes a surface look very realistic.

Decrease the value of the *Refl. glossiness* function to about 0.4. This value will yield smooth/diffused glossy reflections. ▶14.7

14.7

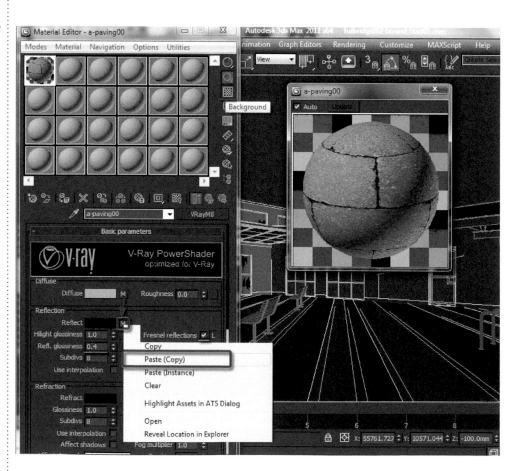

Next, reduce the reflectivity by scrolling down to the *Maps* roll-out and reducing the current texture appearance to 20.0%. Reducing the appearance of the texture will automatically force V-Ray to use 80.0% of the default *Reflect* colour swatch (e.g. black = 0.0.0). This will result in reduced reflection by 80%.

Also add the same texture to the *Bump* toggle. ▶14.8

14.8

Next, increase the brightness of the diffuse texture by first applying the *Color Correction* map to it. Use some of the previous steps to do so. ▶14.9 and 14.10

14.9
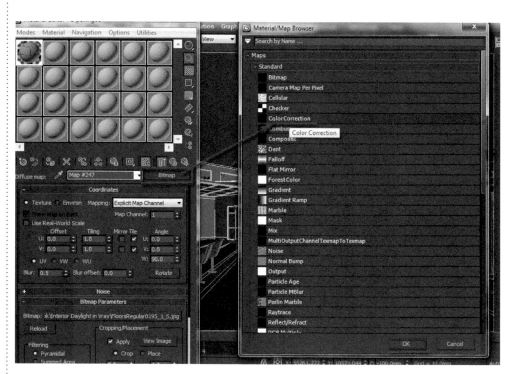

14.10

Scroll down to the *Lightness* roll-out and increase the *Gamma/Contrast* RGB value to 1.6. This value worked well. However, try different values, if desired. ▶14.11

Create a new material slot using some of the techniques covered earlier to create a red pavement material. Rename the new material slot as 'a-paving02' and apply a texture under the name of 'FloorsRegular0279_2_S long.jpg'. ▶14.12

In addition, apply the *Color Correction* procedural map and set its *Gamma/Contrast* value to 1.4. ▶14.13

Next, scroll down to the *Maps* roll-out and apply the texture 'FloorsRegular0279_2_S long reflect.jpg' to the *Reflect* toggle. Set the *Reflect* value to about 10 to reduce the texture's reflectivity effect.

14.11

14.12

14.13

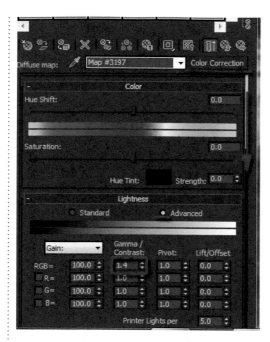

Finally, apply the texture 'FloorsRegular0279_2_S long bump.jpg' to the *Bump* toggle and assign the material slot to objects in the scene under the name of 'pavement 001'. ▶14.14

14.3 Texturing: Metal

As previously highlighted, one of the main characteristics of a metallic surface are its diffused/dark reflective surface and distinctive shine.

14.14

Start by creating a new material slot and renaming it 'Steel satin'. Ensure its *Diffuse* colour swatch is set to plain black ($R = 0.0$; $G = 0.0$; $B = 0.0$).

Next, set its *Reflect* colour swatch to an off-white colour ($R = 164$; $G = 164$; $B = 164$).

Finally, to diffuse its reflections, decrease the *Refl. glossiness* value to about 0.5 and the *Subdivs* value to 22. ▶14.15

In the scene, apply this material to the object under the name of 'bike parking rack'. All other metallic surfaces in the scene were derived from this material.

14.4 Window Glass

As previously discussed, the main characteristics of this material are its transparency and slight reflectivity.

Create a new material slot and name it 'Glass clear'. Next, to add colour to the glass material, change its *Diffuse* colour swatch to dark blue (R = 0.0; G = 0.0; B = 3.0).

To add a bit of reflectivity, in the *Reflection* group, change its colour swatch to light grey (R = 32.0; G = 32.0; B = 32.0). In addition, to add a bit of shine, decrease the *Hilight glossiness* to 0.9.

To add transparency, in the *Refraction* group, change its *Refract* colour swatch to almost white (R = 225; G = 225; B = 225). To ensure shadows are cast through the glass transparency, enable the *Affect shadows* function.

To emulate the IOR of window glass, reduce the IOR to about 1.1.

Finally, to ensure the transparency of the glass is displayed accurately in the render passes, change the *Affect channels* type to *Color+alpha*. ▶14.16

14.16

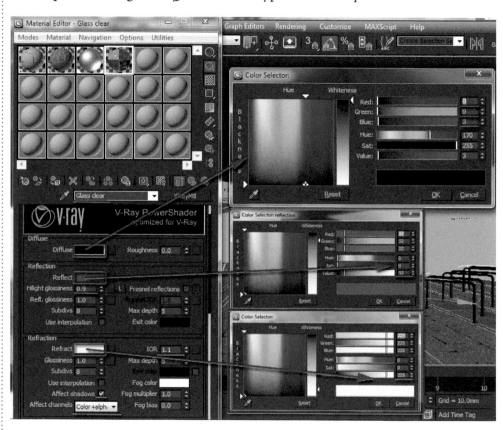

In the scene, assign this material to all objects under the name of 'Curtain Panels <System Panel : Glazed>'.

14.5 Brick

The appearance and properties of bricks differ, depending on what's required. In 3ds Max, users tend to emulate this material procedurally or by using a realistic texture in conjunction with the *VRayMtl* shader.

For this exercise we are going to use a standard *VRayMtl* shader in conjunction with a tileable realistic texture of a red brick, to emulate its intricate surface.

Start by creating a new V-Ray material slot as previously done. Rename this new material slot 'a-wall red brick'.

Next, locate and apply the tileable/realistic texture under the name of 'Brick2.jpg' to the *Diffuse* toggle.

In the scene, select the object under the name of 'Walls <Basic Wall : Cav - 25rs 170i 19l 154SFS-27.5p : Cav - 25rs 170i 19l 154SFS-27.5p>'. This object is part of one of the building facades.

In addition, assign this material and apply a *UVW Mapping* modifier to the object. ▶14.17

14.17

14 Creating Materials

Generally, the brick dimensions are 215 mm in width and 65 mm in height. To ensure the tiling is close to real dimensions, use the *Tape* helper to measure to help tile the texture realistically. ▶14.18

▼14.18

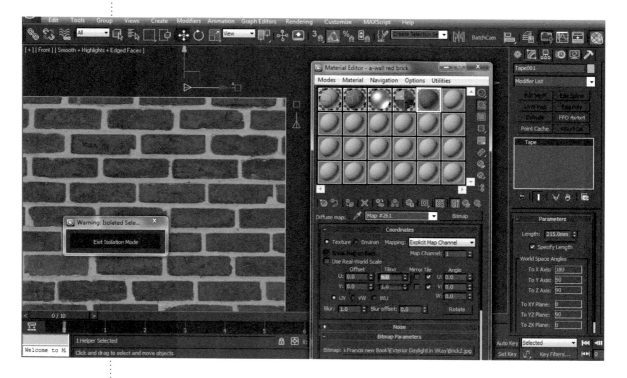

To use the *Tape* tool, open the *Create* command panel and click on the *Helpers* group/button. Following that, select the *Tape* button and drag it into the viewport.

Users can also preset the *Tape* length from its parameters. ▶14.19

14.19

14.20

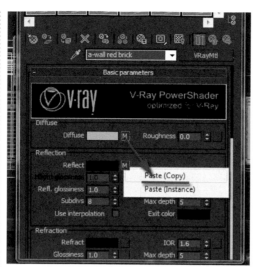

To add a bit of shine to the brick, first copy the texture from the *Diffuse* toggle and paste it into the *Reflect* toggle. ▶14.20

Next, open the copied texture and replace it with a pre-created texture under the name of 'Brick2_gloss 1.jpg'. ▶14.21

14.21

The subsequent step is to create diffused glossy highlights by decreasing its *Hilight glossiness* to 0.5. Also, copy and paste/instance the *Reflect* map into the *Refl. glossiness* toggle.

In addition, set the *Subdivs* value to 20. ▶14.22

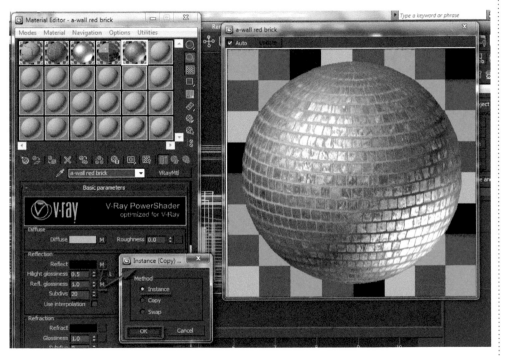

14.22

Next, reduce the brick reflectivity by scrolling down to *Map* roll-out and decreasing the *Reflect* map percentage to 25%.

To add detail to the brick material, apply the 'Brick2_bump.jpg' texture to the *Bump* toggle. Use the same tiling coordinates as the *Diffuse* texture. ▶14.23

14.23

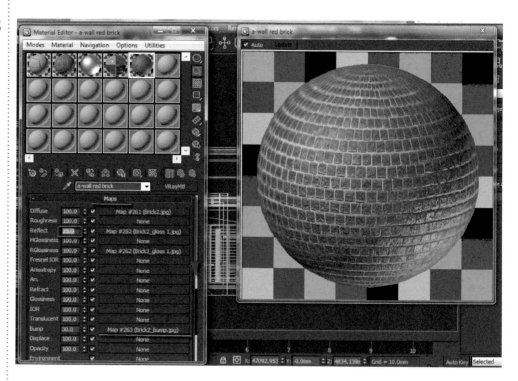

Finally, enable Fresnel reflections in the *Reflection* group.

14.6   Polished Wood

As covered earlier, this material consists mainly of wood planks with a nice polished finish to them. In addition, the surface holds a hint of shine and reflectivity.

As previously done, start by creating a new *VRayMtl* slot and renaming it 'wood polished oak'.

Next, apply a map under the name of 'white_oak_natural.png' to its *Diffuse* toggle and reduce the *Blur* value to 0.01. ▶14.24

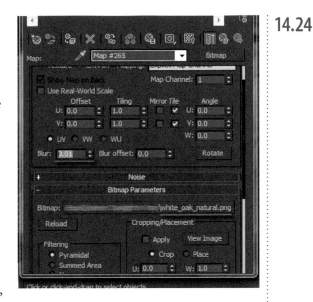

14.24

To make its colour display with more contrast, add a *Color Correction* procedural map to it as previously done. In the *Color Correction* parameters, scroll down to the *Lightness* roll-out and enable the *Advanced* function. In the *RGB* values, reduce the *Gamma/Contrast* value to 0.7. ▶14.25

14.25

Back in the *Basic* parameters, increase the *Reflection* colour swatch to about 126. Widen its *Hilight glossiness* by decreasing its value to about 0.5. To blur the reflections, decrease its *Refl. glossiness* value to about 0.8. Finally, increase the *Subdivs* value to about 22.

▼14.26 In the scene, assign this material to all the wooden bench objects and apply a UVW mapping modifier to them individually. ▶14.26

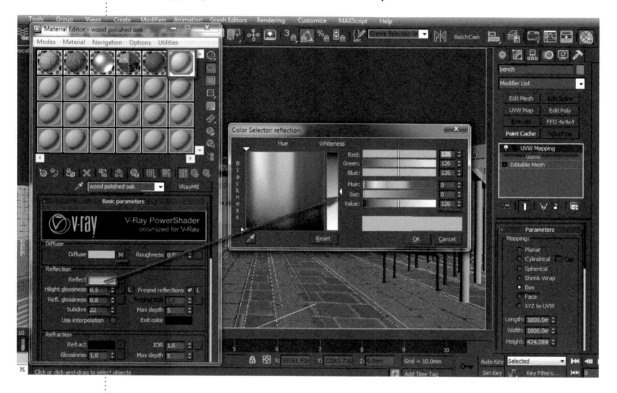

Conclusion

Because most of the materials have already been covered in the previous chapters, this chapter delved quickly into the detailed process of creating and assigning materials in a scene.

This chapter covered materials such as pavement, window, glass, metal, a wooden bench and bricks. During the process of creating and applying these materials, users revisited some of the previously described techniques involved in creating and fine-tuning shaders to emulate specific surface effects.

Some of these techniques involved having to tweak texture settings and parameters and functions such as reflection, glossiness, refraction and bump.

15

Exterior Daylight

Lighting and Rendering

Lighting exteriors is often a straightforward process. However, the camera and scene composition, object details, material properties, colours, shadow direction and render contrast can ultimately determine whether the final output will be successful.

The initial scene for lighting consists of a camera with the composition already set up. The overall composition consists of numerous tree proxies and foreground items such as benches and fences.

All of the above-mentioned elements will be crucial in making the final render more appealing and realistic.

15 Lighting and Rendering

15.1

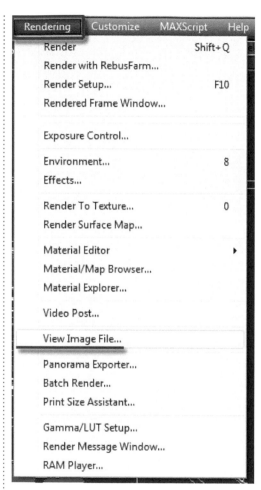

15.1 Getting Started

Open the 3ds Max file under the name of 'fulbridge002 bound_Lighting start.max'.

Follow some of the earlier steps to accept the *Gamma/LUT and Units Setup* dialogue and open the photo reference under the name of '47.jpg'.

The photo reference clearly illustrates how direct sunlight affects the lit areas and how the shadows help define the scene. ▶15.1 and 15.2

15.2 Lighting

The first step is to create the daylight system. Ensure all four viewports are visible on screen (e.g. top, left and front). This action will help you visualize and create the daylight system very quickly.

15 Lighting and Rendering

15.3

Click on *Create* on the main toolbar and choose the *Lights* option from the drop-down list, followed by selecting *Daylight System*. ▶15.3

A target cursor should appear in the viewport. Left-click, hold the mouse button down and drag the mouse in the top viewport to create the compass. While dragging the mouse, you should see the compass being created.

Once the compass object has become big enough in the top viewport, release the mouse button and move the mouse to begin creating the daylight object. As you move the mouse, you should see the daylight object being created vertically in the left and front viewports.

Once satisfied, left-click to stop creating and right-click to exit creation mode. ▶15.4

15.4

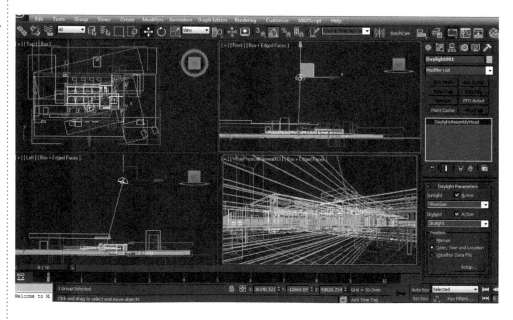

The next step is to open the *Modify* command panel and change the default sunlight to *VRaySun*.

The *V-Ray Sun* environment map dialogue should appear. Click *Yes* to create it automatically. ▶15.5

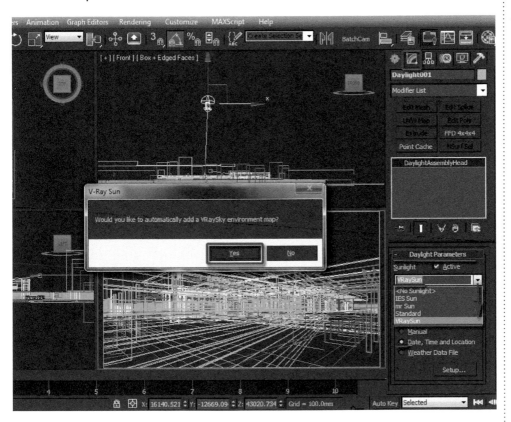

15.5

The following step is to set up the sunlight position and location.

While the daylight object is still selected, open the *Motion* command panel and click on the *Get Location* button. The *Geographic Location* dialogue should be prompted. In the *Map* group, choose *Europe* and select *London, UK*, from the *City* list.

Once satisfied, click *OK* to close the dialogue. ▶15.6

15.6

Before we begin test rendering the shadow directions, we're going to first create an off-white *VRayMtl* override as previously done.

Repeat some of the steps covered earlier to copy/instance the new material into to the *Override mtl* toggle of the *V-Ray:: Global switches* roll-out parameters. ▶15.7

As mentioned earlier, shadows can help make an exterior shot look more interesting and detailed, especially when they are long and dark.

To quickly achieve this, first enable the *Hardware* shading and shadows in the camera viewport. This will help visualize the shadow direction in the viewport. Use some of the techniques covered earlier to do this.

Next, open the *Motion* command panel while the daylight system is selected. In the *Time* group, set the *Hours* to about 7. Also set the *Latitude* value to about 21.6 and the *Longitude* to about –4.417.

The shadows being cast by the sunlight now look long and are covering key areas of the foreground and the building.

It's worth mentioning that these values were achieved after much tweaking with the parameters. ▶15.8

Finally, set the daylight compass size to about 150.0 mm and its position to the following coordinates: X = 14281.791 mm; Y = –1641.782 mm; Z = 0.0 mm. ▶15.9

15.8

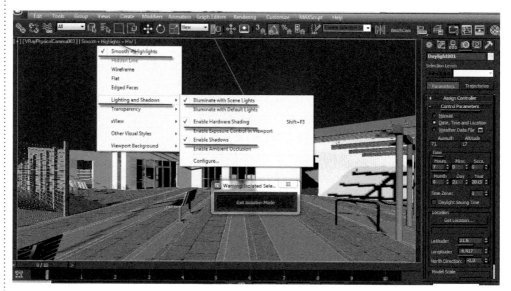

15.9

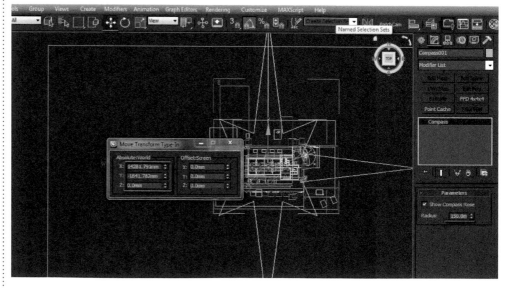

The next step is to open the *Render Setup* dialogue and begin adjusting some of its key render parameters prior to initiating the test renders. Note that most of the following steps will be similar to ones covered in Chapter 8.

In the *V-Ray* tab, open the *V-Ray:: Frame buffer* roll-out and switch on the *Enable built-in Frame Buffer* function. ▶15.10

Scroll down and open the *V-Ray:: Adaptive subdivision image sampler* roll-out. Set the *Min. rate* to 1 and the *Max. rate* to 4.

Next, open the *V-Ray:: Color mapping* roll-out and enable the *Sub-pixel mapping* function.

In addition, set the colour mapping type to *Linear multiply* and the gamma to 2.2. ▶15.11

Select the *Indirect illumination* tab, open its roll-out and turn it on. Also switch on the *Ambient occlusion* and set its radius to about 300.0 mm and the *Subdivs* value to 16.

In the *Secondary bounces* group, choose the *Brute force* GI engine.

15.10

15.11

15.12

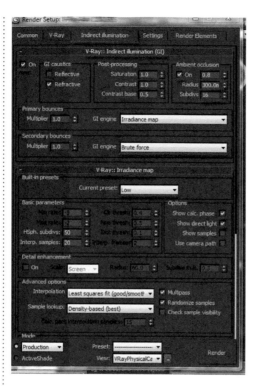

Further down, open the *V-Ray:: Irradiance map* roll-out and set the *Current preset* to *Low*. In the *Options* group, enable *Show cal. phase* and *Show direct light*. ▶15.12

To speed up the precalculation and render times, open the *Settings* tab. In the *V-Ray:: System* roll-out, increase the dynamic memory limit to 2000 MB or higher.

A value of 0.0 sets the dynamic memory to limitless. However, it may ultimately crash the render, if *V-Ray:: System* ends up using more memory than available in your computer. ▶15.13

15.13

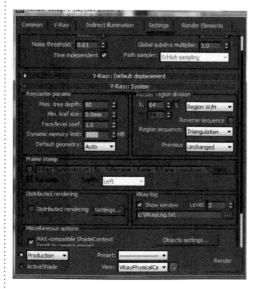

Test render (Shift+Q) to see the first draft. Ensure the *SRGB* button is enabled in the V-Ray frame buffer. ▶15.14

While the overall lighting is looking good, the ambient/diffused light could be improved further.

The first step towards this goal is to disable the current skylight from the daylight object and create a new V-Ray dome light object. Use some of the steps covered earlier to accomplish this step.

Once the new V-Ray dome light is created, rename it 'VRayLight_Dome' and set its colour to light blue: $R = 0$; $G = 41$; $B = 117$. This colour will help make the indirectly lit areas slightly blue (e.g. areas in shadow).

15.15

Also increase the intensity multiplier to about 30. This will help invigorate the dome light colour in the scene. ▶15.15 and 15.16

Next, scroll down to the *Options* group and use similar dome light parameters to the ones covered in Chapter 8.

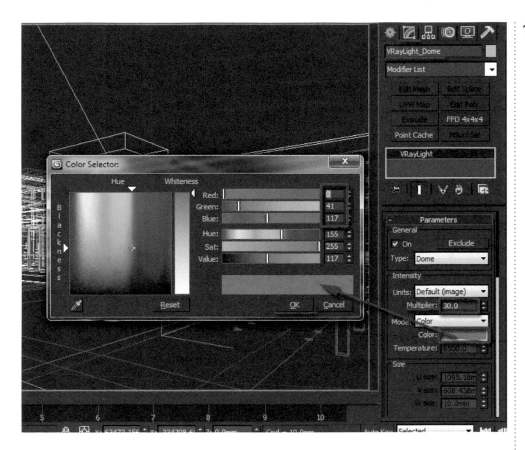

15.16

15.17

Before test rendering the latest changes, duplicate the current V-Ray frame buffer. This action will enable you to cross reference between different test renders. ▶15.17 and 15.18

15.18

3D Photorealistic Rendering

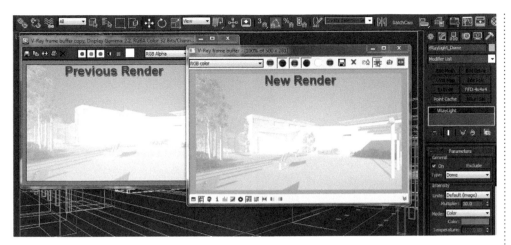

15.19

Test render the new dome light changes (Shift+Q). The new render is visibly less 'scorched' than the previous one, and it has more of the skylight colour on its indirectly lit areas. ▶15.19

The next step is to test render the scene without the *Override mtl*. ▶15.20 and **15.21**

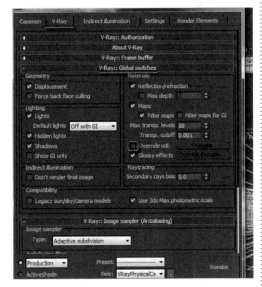

15.20

15.21

The first render without the *Override mtl* is looking good. However, a few materials could benefit from further tweaks.

Start by spreading out/diffusing the pavement reflection. To do so, reduce its *Refl. glossiness* value to about 0.7. ▶15. 22

15.22

Next, select the 'a-paving02' material slot and reduce its *Bump* value to about 15.0. ▶**15.23**

To make some of the glass reflections more interesting, first add a nice reflection map to the environment reflection.

To do so, go to the *Render Setup* dialogue and open the *V-Ray* tab. Scroll down to the *V-Ray:: Environment* roll-out and enable the *Reflection/refraction environment* override.

Next, click on its *Multiplier* toggle and load the bitmap under the name of 'BLUU SKY01 backgrnd.jpg'. ▶**15. 24**

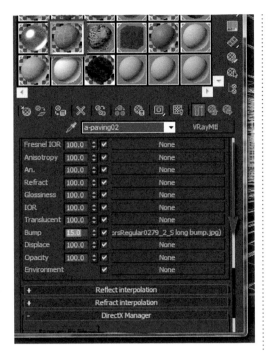

15.23

15.24

15.25

15.26

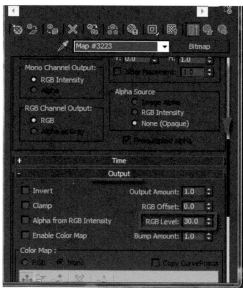

To edit the recently loaded bitmap, drag-drop the *Multiplier* toggle content into a material slot and choose the *Instance* method, when prompted with the *Instance (Copy)* dialogue. ▶15.25

Following that, to ensure the bitmap is visible enough in the reflections, scroll down to the bitmap *Output* roll-out and increase the RGB level to 30.0 or higher. ▶15. 26

After a few tweaks and test renders, the following bitmap coordinates worked best: The bitmap was set to *Environ* and the *Mapping* type to *Screen* mode. In addition, the *U offset* value was set to 0.11 and the *V offset* to −1.18. ▶15.27

15.27

Finally, select the 'Glass top bit' material slot and increase its reflection from the *Color Selector* to the following values: $R = 119$; $G = 119$; $B = 119$.

This material slot was originally assigned specifically to the top glass panes of the main building, to capture more reflections.

Test render the recent tweaks. Once satisfied with the latest draft render, begin setting up the scene for the final render. ▶15.28

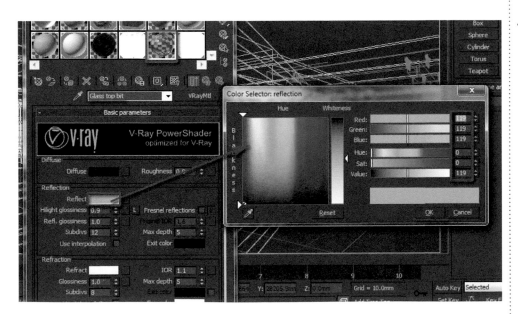

15.28

15.3 Setting Up for the Final Render

Open the *Common* tab from the *RenderSetup* dialogue and set the output size to 5500×3091 pixels. ▶15.29

15.29

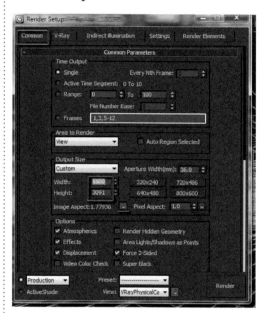

Following that, in the *V-Ray* tab, enable the *Split render channels* group and click on the *Browse* toggle to save the render output.

In the *Select V-Ray G-Buffers file name* dialogue, set the filename as 'Exterior Daylight' and select the file type *TIF Image File (*.tif)*.

Next, click on the *Setup* toggle to bring up the *TIF Image Control* dialogue. Choose the 16-bit colour image type, with no compression and 300.0 DPI.

Click *OK* to close the dialogue and click *Save*. ▶15.30

15.30

Scroll further down and open the *V-Ray:: Image sampler (Antialiasing)* roll-out. Change the *Image sampler* type to *Adaptive DMC* and pick the *Area* antialiasing filter.

In the *V-Ray:: Adaptive DMC image sampler* roll-out, increase the *Max subdivs* value to 6 and *Clr thresh* to 0.003. ▶15.31

Next, open the *Indirect illumination* tab and change the *Irradiance map Current preset* to *Medium*. This built-in preset should be sufficient to achieve good results in exterior scenes. However, try different presets, if desired.

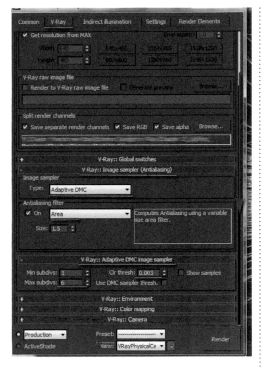

15.31

15.32

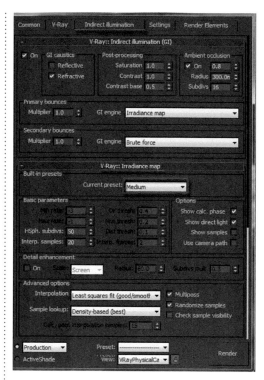

The default brute force parameters should yield good results for exteriors. ▶15.32

The last step is to open the *Render Elements* tab and click on the *Merge* toggle.

Locate and select one of the previous final scenes such as 'SMESTOW_ Interior Night Lighting_Final.max'.

The *Merge Render Elements* dialogue should appear. To select multiple elements, first click on any of the displayed elements, then hold the mouse button down and drag the mouse down to select multiple files from the list.

Once all the elements are selected, click *OK* to load them. ▶15.33, 15.34 and 15.35

Finally, render the final high resolution image.

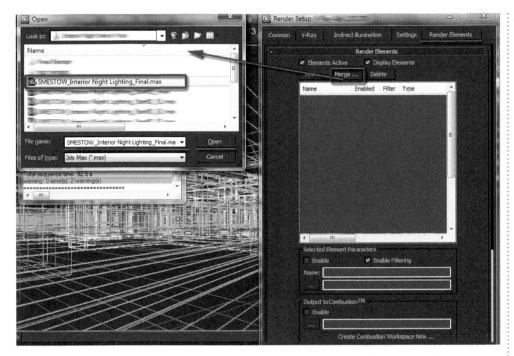

15.33

15.34

15.35

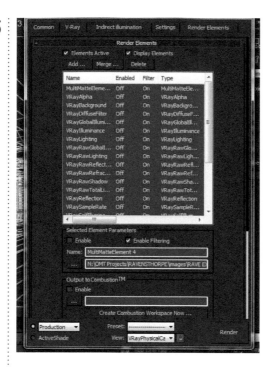

Conclusion

This chapter guided users through the unique process of creating a daylight system to illuminate an exterior scene and utilize the shadow direction to help make the render and composition more interesting and detailed.

In addition, users were also shown the importance of using a V-Ray dome light to help reinvigorate the colour and contrast of areas in shadow (indirectly lit areas).

Furthermore, this chapter also highlighted the need to continuously tweak the materials to react realistically to the added lights prior to setting up the final render parameters with its elements/passes.

Finally, the entire process helped users understand the different challenges and techniques involved in texturing and lighting an exterior scene realistically.

NOTE

Fox render Farm services were extensively used to render the final images, at a lightning speed.

For more information about Fox Render Farm, please go to: http://www.foxrenderfarm.com/

16

Exterior Daylight

Post-production

This final stage of the production will take users through the process of enhancing the overall image by using key render elements/passes previously included in the output settings.

In addition, key Photoshop tools and techniques previously highlighted in Chapter 6 will be reused in order to achieve the desired results.

16 Post-production

16.1 Post-production

Open the *Load Files into Stack* script, to select and bring the rendered elements into a stack. Use some of the approaches covered in the previous chapters.
▶16.1 and 16.2

16.1

16.2

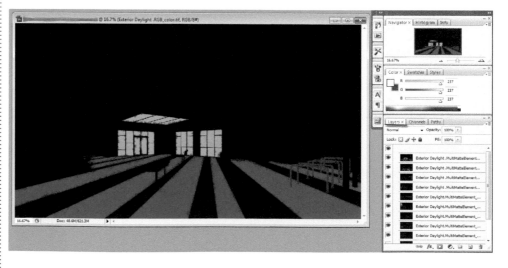

Save the document as 'Exterior Daylight in Vray_tutorials.psd'.

Next, organize the *MultiMatte* element and the remaining render elements into two separate group folders. Name each group folder accordingly.

Ensure the *MultiMatte* elements are always on top of the stack. Keep the 'Interior Night time in Vray.RGB_color.0000.tga' layer as the base bottom layer and change its property colour to red. In addition, disable the visibility of all layers inside the group folders and keep the visibility of the 'Interior Night time in Vray. RGB_color.0000.tga' layer.

It's common practice to always have the base render at the bottom of the stack, in order to layer the remaining elements/passes on top of it. Use some of the techniques described in Chapter 9 to do this. ▶16.3

16.3

The first step is to begin replacing the sky/background image. This process will involve creating a group folder with a layer mask, followed by inserting a sky inside it.

16.4

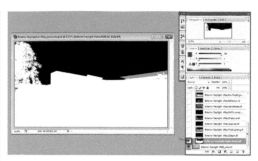

Start by opening the *Element* group folder and enabling the visibility of the 'Exterior Daylight.Alpha.0000.tif' layer. ▶16.4

To select its black and white alpha channel, go to the *Channels* palette, hold down the Ctrl key and click on its RGB channel. A selection should appear. To select the background, simply invert the selection (Shift+Ctrl+I), then create a group folder with its adjacent layer mask.

Rename the new group folder as 'Background'. ▶16.5 and 16.6

16.5

The correct sky image can sometimes turn a boring image into a very interesting one. For this reason the selection process should be carried out diligently. It is common for users to choose skies with clouds following the vanishing/ perspective lines of a building.

This can be achieved by choosing one 'hero' sky image or by simply creating a proprietary one. Proprietary skies can be created in Photoshop, by layering multiple sky images with layer masks and adjustment layers.

3D Photorealistic Rendering

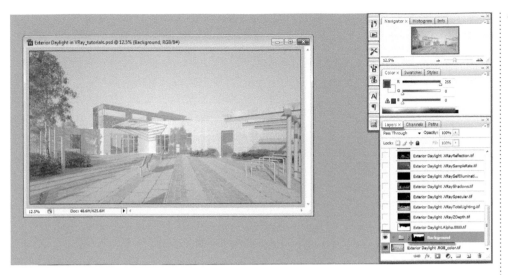

16.6

For this project, I sky has already been chosen. So the next step will be to insert a sky into the background group folder.

Open a document under the name of 'Sky.jpg'. ▶16.7

16.7

Insert the 'sky.jpg' document into the *Background* group folder, using some of the techniques covered in Chapters 9 and 12.

Move (V) and scale the document (Ctrl+T), if necessary, to make the sky fit accordingly. Rename the layer 'Sky_bright'. ▶16.8

16.8

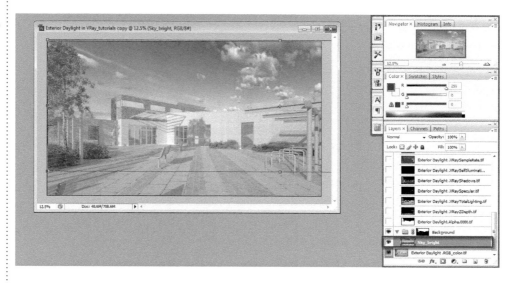

The next step is to emulate the gradient between bright and dark areas commonly seen in skies.

To achieve this, add a *Levels* adjustment layer and move its rightmost *Input Levels* slider to 88. Use a clipping mask (Alt+Ctrl+G) to restrict its influence on the layer below it ('Sky_bright'). ▶16.9

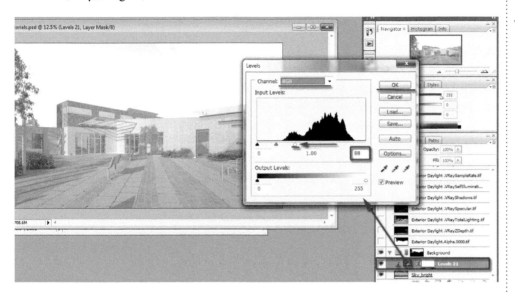

Next, make a copy of the 'Sky_bright' layer by selecting it first, then holding down the Alt key and moving the layer down to copy it.

Rename the new copied sky layer 'Sky_dark'. ▶16.10

16.10

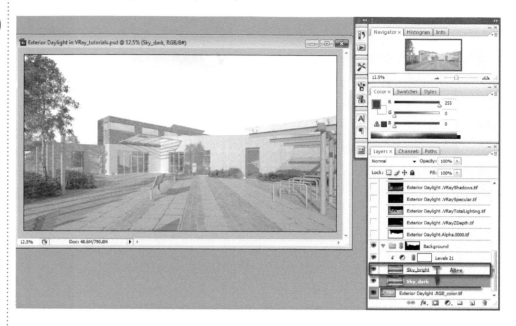

To build the gradient between the 'Sky_bright' and 'Sky_dark' layers, create a layer mask for 'Sky_bright' and select it, and then enable the *Paint Bucket Tool* (G).

Ensure the foreground colour palette is black and use the paint bucket tool (G) to paint the 'Sky_bright' layer mask as black. Note how the 'Sky_bright' layer went suddenly invisible. ▶16.11

16.11

To control the gradient between the layers, simply enable the brush tool (B), set its opacity to about 7% and begin brushing in areas of the bright sky that were previously made invisible with the paint bucket tool.

As mentioned earlier (Chapter 9), the brush hardness should always be set to 0% (very soft), unless stated otherwise.

16 Post-production

When brushing in areas of the bright sky, focus mainly on the areas around the edges of the building. This effect is commonly seen in photos, and it brings more focus to the building. Use some of the techniques previously covered in Chapters 9 and 12 to do this. ▶16.12

16.12

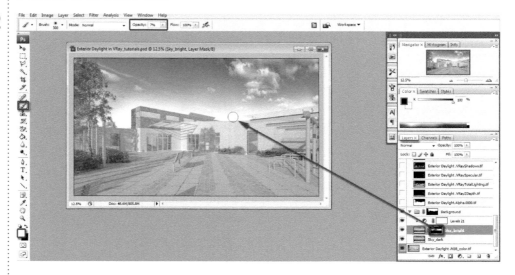

To desaturate the sky slightly, simply add a *Hue/Saturation* adjustment layer on top and reduce the *Master Saturation* to about −29. ▶16.13

16.13

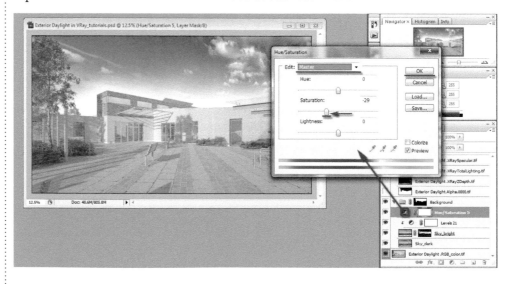

The next step is to create a new group folder to adjust the levels of the entire scene, apart from the skies.

To do so, use some of the previous steps to enable a selection of the alpha channel. Create a new group folder under the name of 'Whole' with a layer mask. ►16.14

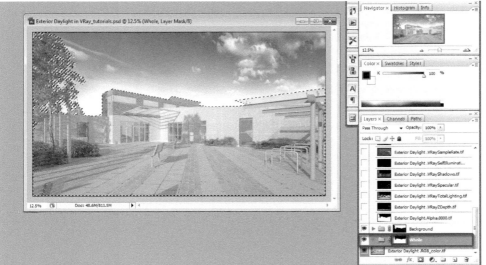

16.14

The next stage is to reinvigorate some of the shadows. To do so, simply copy and move the 'Exterior Daylight.VRayRawTotalLighting.tif' layer from the *Elements* group folder, into the 'Whole' group folder.

Choose the *Overlay* blending mode and reduce its opacity to 35%. Create and use a layer mask to omit this effect in areas such as the trees in the foreground (the areas shown in red).

As mentioned earlier, it's only through trial and error that we can determine the appropriate blending mode to use with each rendered element or other layers. ▶16.15

16.15

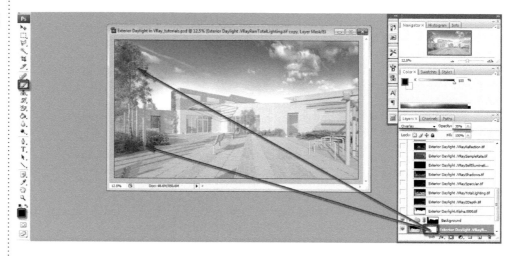

Add another *Levels* adjustment layer inside the 'Whole' group folder to increase the contrast of the image. In the *Levels* RGB channel *Input Levels* group, move the leftmost slider to 15, the middle slider to 0.72 and the rightmost slider to 219.

Use a layer mask in conjunction with the brush tool to mask away areas where the *Levels* adjustment layer is scorching the image (areas shown in red with arrows). Desaturate the image by adding a *Hue/Saturation* adjustment layer and decrease its *Master* saturation slider to −12.

Note again that all these changes are affecting only the 'Whole' group folder, due to its layer mask. ▶16.16 and 16.17

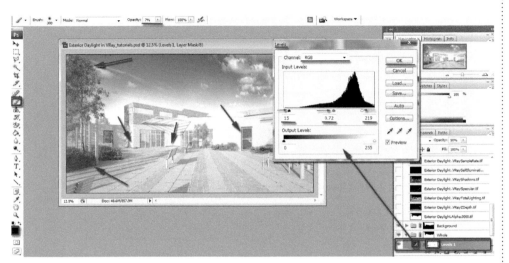

16.16

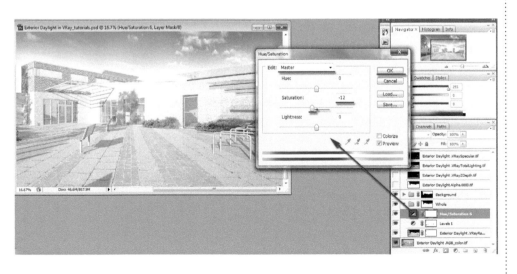

16.17

To correct the overall gamma (apart from the skies), add the *Exposure* adjustment layer and reduce its *Gamma Correction* slider to 0.40. ▶16.18

16.18

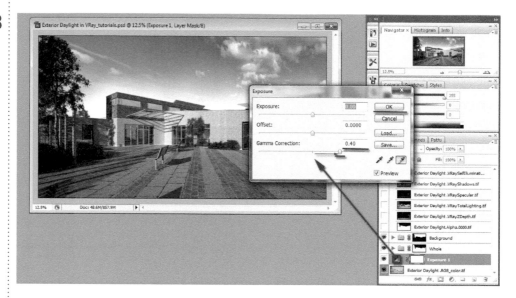

The next step is to begin tweaking each material individually, as previously done in Chapters 9 and 12.

3D Photorealistic Rendering

Start with the concrete material in the foreground by selecting its *MultiMatte* layer ('Exterior Daylight.MultiMatteElement_1.tif') and creating a new group folder with its layer mask. Rename the group folder 'Concrete'. ▶16.19 and 16.20

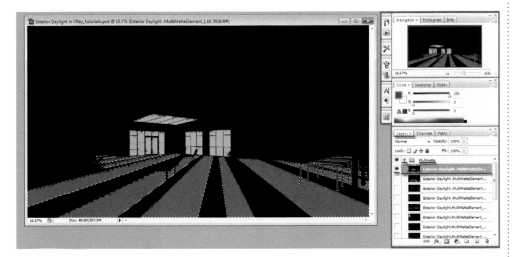

16.19

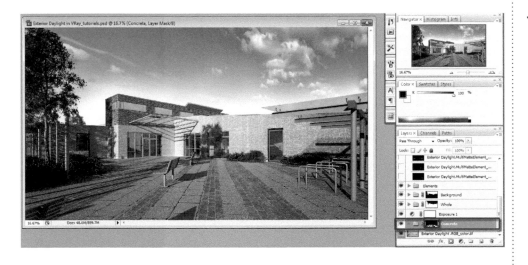

16.20

To help reduce the concrete reflection, copy and move the 'Exterior Daylight. VRayTotalLighting.tif' layer from the *Elements* group folder into the 'Concrete' folder.

Use the *Darker Color* blending mode to help integrate the layer. Also create and use its layer mask to omit areas where shadows may overlap (shown in red). ▶16.21

16.21

3D Photorealistic Rendering

To add some specularity to the concrete, copy and move the 'Exterior Daylight. VRaySpecular.tif' layer into the 'Concrete' group folder. Use the *Screen* blending mode to integrate it more seamlessly. ▶16.22

16.22

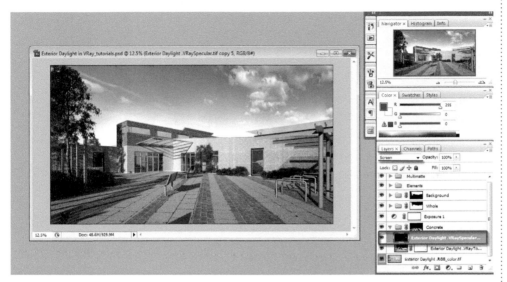

Create a *Levels* adjustment layer to add contrast to the concrete. In its *RGB Input Levels*, move the middle slider to 0.93. ▶16.23

16.23

Similar techniques were used to tweak most of the materials in the scene. ▶16.24

16.24

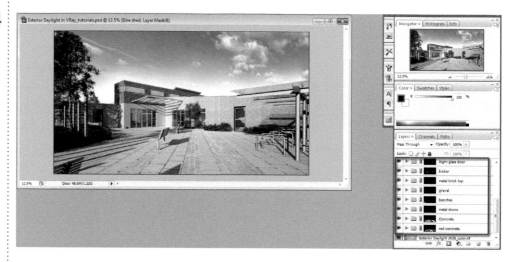

The door glass materials were tweaked using the 'Exterior Daylight. VRayReflection.tif' layer with the *Overlay* blending mode and levels. ▶16.25

16.25

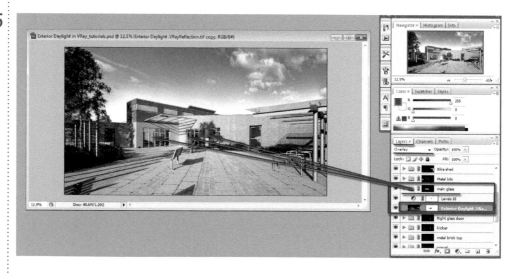

The glass windows at the top were tweaked with the *Selective Color* and *Levels* adjustment layers. ▶16.26

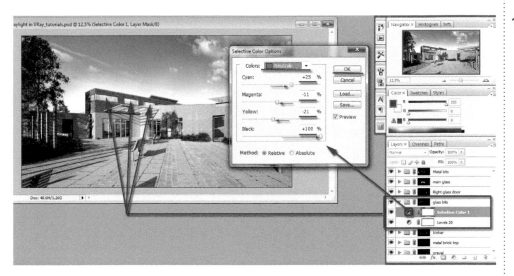

To make the tree on the far left side of the camera more realistic, a new group folder was created with its mask, followed by inserting a real photo of a tree inside it. To adjust the tree, adjustment layers such as *Hue/Saturation* and *Levels* were added to the 'Foliage 1' group folder.

In addition, the 'Exterior Daylight.VRayLighting.tif' layer was copied in and integrated with the *Darker Color* blending mode. Its layer opacity was reduced to 46%. ▶16.27

16.27

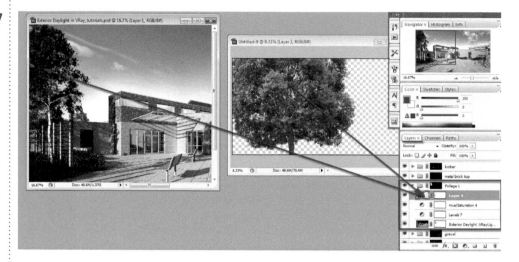

To tone down the bump material on the wall, the 'Exterior Daylight. VRayShadows.tif' layer was copied in and its image colour inverted (Ctrl+I). To integrate the layer, a *Luminosity* blending mode was chosen and its layer opacity reduced to 10%.

Following that, the 'Exterior Daylight.VRayDiffuseFilter.tif' layer was also copied in and integrated with the *Lighten* blending mode. The opacity layer was set to 70%. ▶16.28

16.28

Refer to the final document named 'Exterior Daylight in VRay.psd' to see the final results.

16.2 Adding People

The process of choosing and adding people to an external scene can sometimes be time-consuming. Depending on the building and context, users often choose people with the following attributes:

1. Dressed according to the surroundings (i.e. if it's an office, people should look smart; if it's a school, people should look more casual)

2. People engaged in some sort of activity

3. People using the space (i.e. looking/photographing an art piece, sitting, walking up the stairs, using facilities, etc.)

4. People at the correct camera angle

5. People with the correct lighting (i.e. if it's a directly lit scene, the people need to have direct shadows on them; if it's an overcast scene, the people need to have diffused shadows on them)

6. People in groups and alone

7. People evoking motion

8. Other attributes

Start by adding someone using the bike shed facility first.

Open the file under the name of 'vp_casual_v4_434.psd' (provided by http://www.viz-people.com/). The PSD document should come with a cut-out figure of a person and its alpha channel.

Next, create a group folder under the name of 'People' and insert the cut-out person into it. Also insert a screen grab highlighting the average height of people, as previously done.

Before scaling down the cut-out person, convert the layer into a smart object first and scale it down proportionally thereafter (Ctrl+T). Rename the layer as 'woman on the bike'.

3D Photorealistic Rendering

As mentioned earlier, a smart layer allows users to scale a layer up or down without losing pixel quality. In addition, a smart layer records most filters and transforms applied to the layer. ▶16.29

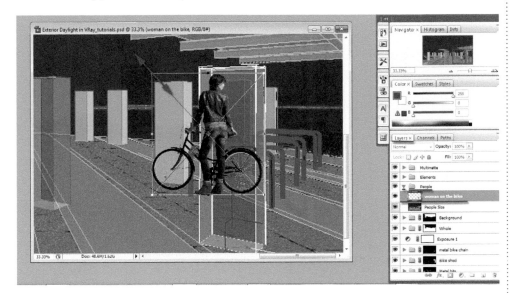

16.29

To create the illusion that the woman on the bike is behind the metal bike rack, create a layer mask and mask out the relevant areas with the brush tool (B) and a layer mask. In addition, use the polygonal lasso tool (L) to select the bike rack metal. ►16.30

16.30

To begin integrating the woman with the rest of the environment, add a *Hue/ Saturation* adjustment layer (with a clipping mask Alt+Ctrl+G) and reduce its *Edit Master* saturation to about −48. This value should bring the colours of the woman on the bike closer to the overall environment.

In addition, add a *Levels* adjustment layer on top, with a clipping mask. In *Input Levels*, move its middle slider to 0.80 and its rightmost slider to 195. To add a linear brightness to the woman on the bike, move the left slider of the *Output Levels* to about 18. ▶16.31

The final step is to add a motion blur to the 'woman on the bike' layer (smart layer), as previously done. Set the *Motion Blur* distance pixels to about 7. ▶16.32

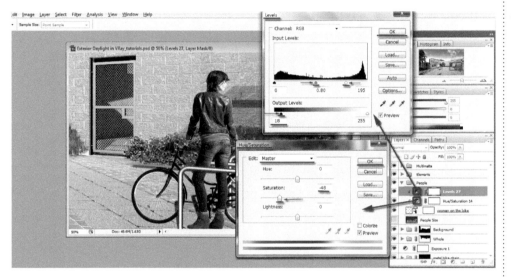

16.31

16.32

Create the direct shadows from the woman on the bike using some of the techniques covered in Chapter 9. In addition, ensure the direct shadows layer is converted into a smart object, with a motion blur applied to it.

Following that, use the *Smart Filters* layer mask to omit the blurriness in areas near the origin of the direct shadows. This is to emulate the direct shadows from the rendered scene (i.e. the shadows start sharp and gradually blur towards the end). ▶16.33 and 16.34

16.33

To change the colour of the shadows, add a photo filter adjustment layer with a clipping mask on top, followed by increasing its density to 100% and changing its colour to purple. ▶16.35

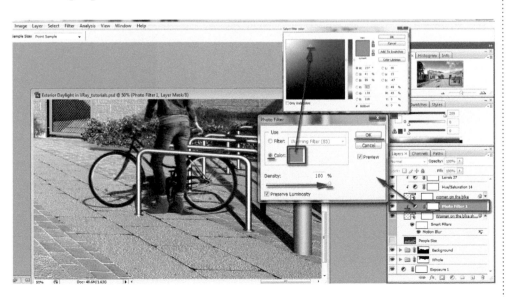

The remaining people and direct shadows were created using the same techniques. The diffused shadows (connecting shadows) were created using the same approach as described in Chapters 9 and 12. ▶16.36

16.36

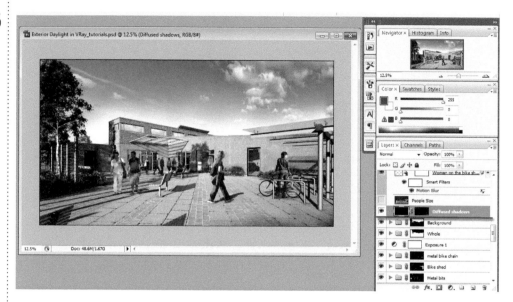

3D Photorealistic Rendering

To integrate the sky background with the foreground, select the group folder mask and begin to brush in slightly the areas that divide the background from the rendered foreground. ▶16.37

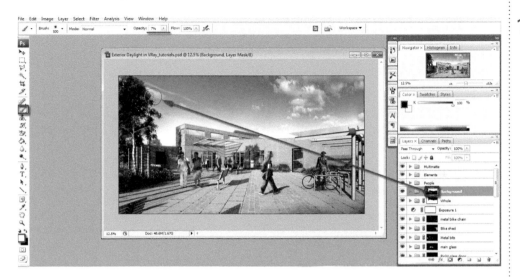

16.37

Finally, to add a bit of ambient light and haze to the whole image, add a *Levels* adjustment layer on top of the 'People' group folder. In its *Levels* dialogue, move its left *Output Levels* slider to around 35. ▶16.38

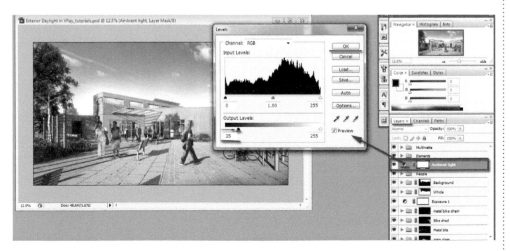

16.38

Finally, create the chromatic aberration effect (if desired), using some of the techniques described in Chapter 12.

As mentioned earlier, to see the final result, refer to the document under the name of 'Exterior Daylight in VRay.psd'.

Conclusion

This chapter has taken users through the process of using raw renders and some of its key elements/passes to enhance the overall image with help of Photoshop and its unique tools.

In addition, this chapter has shown users how to replace and manipulate the sky and the trees, in order to make the overall image more appealing.

Finally, users were introduced to techniques involved in choosing and integrating people and their shadows into the final scene.

17

Exterior Night Time

Pre-production

17 Pre-production

17.1 Client Brief

In this night exterior shot, the brief was quite similar to the interior night scene. The initial task was to accentuate the effect of the exterior and internal artificial lights against the overall sky/ambient light.

In addition, the final composition needed to have people utilizing some of the key facilities of the space.

17.2 Photo References and Mood Board

The images below depict two of many photo references presented to the client. ▶17.1

17.1

Lighting and colour suggestions

First choice   Second choice

Conclusion

As mentioned earlier, the second pre-production process for the same scene is usually easier than the first one. However, it's equally important to go through the same exercise of selecting the best photo references related to the camera shot, the scene composition and the overall lighting.

18

Exterior Night Time in V-Ray

Lighting and Rendering

Lighting and rendering an exterior night scene is often easier and more rewarding than most scenes, especially when the composition is relatively good. Some of the most appealing exterior shots consist mainly of two colour tones: blues and yellows. The blue hues usually represent the diffused skylight colour cast on indirectly lit areas. The yellow tones often indicate artificial light sources in the scene. With that in mind, this tutorial focuses primarily on emulating these two light sources, while ensuring the two colours complement each other creatively throughout the scene composition.

Finally, this tutorial is a follow-up from Chapter 15 and the previous chapters. Hence, techniques, materials and lights previously created will be used to emulate the exterior night shot.

18 Exterior Night Time in V-Ray

18.1

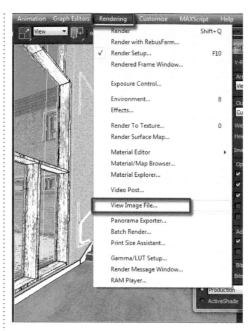

18.1 Getting Started

Open the 3ds Max file under the name of 'fulbridge002 bound_Lighting Night time start.max'.

Follow some of the earlier steps to accept the *Gamma/LUT and Units Setup* dialogue and open a photo reference named '87.jpg'.

The photo reference portrays a typical hero night shot in all its glory. Note how the skylight colour guides the eye towards the yellow hues being generated from the artificial light sources in the scene. Also note how the scene colours truly complement one another in the most captivating way. ▶18.1 and 18.2

18.2

3D Photorealistic Rendering

18.2 Lighting

The scene should contain lights from Chapter 15. In addition, the rendering parameters are set to draft/low resolution. The subsequent steps will take users through the process of turning the current scene into a night one, using the current photo reference as a guide.

Start by deleting the daylight system and selecting the VRayLight_Dome object in the scene. The next step is to match the dome colour closely to the photo reference. To do so, open the *Modify* command panel while the dome light is still selected.

In the *Intensity* group, select its colour swatch and set it to a light tone of blue: $R = 0$; $G = 6$; $B = 250$. Note that this colour was achieved after a few test renders to closely match it with the photo reference.

To change the sky to a colour similar to the photo reference, open the *Environment* dialogue (8). In the *Environment* tab, also change the background colour swatch to blue: $R = 0$; $G = 36$; $B = 250$.

In addition, disable the *Use Map* function. This action disables the *Environment Map* and uses its colour swatch instead.

As mentioned earlier, this colour was also achieved after a few test renders to closely match it with the photo reference. Test render the latest tweaks (Shift+Q). ▶18.3 and 18.4

To emulate some of the artificial lights seen in the photo reference, we're going to merge some of the interior lights previously created in Chapter 11.

To do so, click on the 3ds Max icon and choose the *Import* option from the drop-down list, then select the *Merge* function. Locate and choose the MAX file under the name of 'SMESTOW_Interior Night Lighting_Final.max'.

18.3

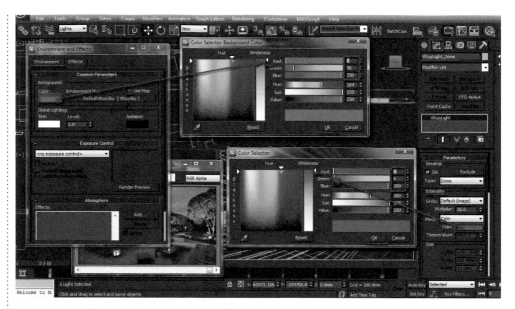

18.4

The *Merge* dialogue should open. To quickly select the lights, in the *List types* group, deselect the *Lights* type, followed by clicking on the *Invert* button. This action allows only the lights to be displayed in the list.

Select the following lights from the list: VRayLight_ceiling032; VRayLight_ courtyard light; VRayLight_Window house; VRayLight_Window house002;

VRayLight_Window house003 and
VRayLight_Window house004.

This is one of many reasons why is
very important to name relevant
objects in the scene accordingly. Click
OK to merge the selected lights.
▶18.5 and 18.6

Once the lights are merged, filter the
selection type to *Lights* and move them
towards the centre of the scene, in the
top viewport. Filtering selection types
makes it easier to select specific objects
in the scene. ▶18.7

As depicted in the photo reference, the
external lights beam up the trees, green
areas and walls. To emulate this, begin
positioning the lights under the name
of 'VRayLight_courtyard light' outside
the building.

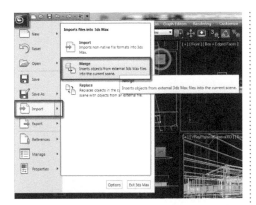

18.5

18.6

18.7

18.8

While lighting up areas in the foreground, copy/instance and move the 'VRayLight_ courtyard lights' to areas such as the trees, shrubs and the bike shed on the right-hand side. Use the *Light Size* group to change its original dimension. ▶18.8

Move some of the lights up and rotate them downwards to illuminate the shrubs. Rotate some of the other lights upwards to affect the trees.

In addition, use the *Select and Uniform Scale* from the main toolbar to change the dimension of the lights beaming up the shrubs against the building (far right-hand side).

The *Select and Uniform Scale* was used because all lights under the name of 'VRayLight_courtyard' are instanced to one another. Thus using the *Select and Uniform Scale* will only affect the selected lights individually.

3D Photorealistic Rendering

Use the lights under the name of 'VRayLight_Window house' to illuminate the interior of the building. It's worth mentioning that all lights under the name of 'VRayLight_Window house' are instances of one another.

Move, rotate and position the lights in areas close to the doors and windows of the building, to help make those areas seem lit up. If the lights seem too intense, use some of the techniques covered earlier to edit the texture being used for light intensity.

The RGB level intensity of the interior lights was set to 250.0. ▶18.9

Refer to the final 3ds Max scene under the name of 'fulbridge002 bound_ Lighting Night time start.max' to see how and where each light was positioned in the scene. As mentioned earlier, numerous test renders were carried out in order to determine the best position/rotation and parameters for each light in the scene. ▶18.10 and 18.11

The scene is now at a stage where it can be fully rendered and taken into post-production for final tweaks.

18.9

18.10

18.11

18.12

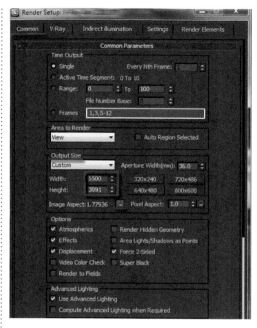

18.3 Setting Up for the Final Render

As previously done, open the *Common* tab from the *Render Setup* dialogue and set the *Output Size* to 5500×3091 pixels. ▶18.12

Next, in the *V-Ray* tab, switch on the *Split render channels* group and open the *Browse* toggle to save out the render output. In the *Select V-Ray G-Buffers file name* dialogue, set the filename as 'Exterior Night' and the file type as *TIF image File (*.tif)*.

Following that, click on the *Setup* toggle to open the *TIF Image Control* dialogue. Choose the *16-bit Color* image type, with no compression and 300.0 DPI. Click *OK* to close the dialogue and then click *Save*. ▶18.13

18.13

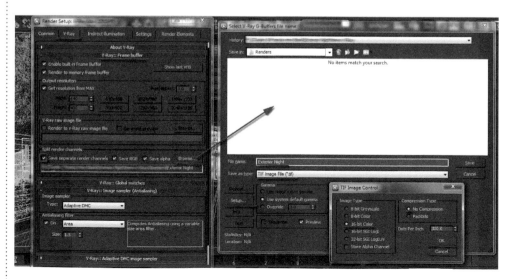

Scroll down to the *V-Ray:: Image sampler (Antialiasing)* roll-out and change the *Image sampler* type to *Adaptive DMC*. Set the antialiasing filter as *Area*.

In the *V-Ray:: Adaptive DMC image sampler* roll-out, increase the *Max subdivs* value to 6 and *Clr thresh* to 0.003. ▶**18.14**

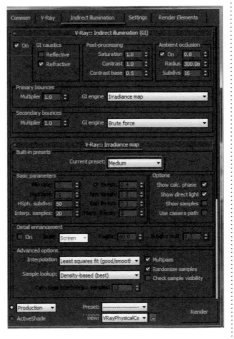

18.14

Next, open the *Indirect illumination* tab and change the *Irradiance Current preset* to *Medium*. As mentioned earlier, the default preset is often enough to achieve good results in exterior scenes. However, try different parameters, if desired.

The current brute force parameters should yield good results for exteriors. ▶**18.15**

18.15

18.16

The last step is to open the *Render Elements* tab and enable all its listed elements. ▶18.16

Finally, render the final high resolution image.

Conclusion

This chapter navigated users through the intricate process of lighting an exterior night scene.

NOTE

Fox render Farm services were extensively used to render the final images, at a lightning speed.

For more information about Fox Render Farm, please go to: http://www.foxrenderfarm.com/

A photo was used as a point of reference for light intensity and its colours. Furthermore, users also learnt the importance of fine-tuning the light colours and intensity, in order to balance the cohesion of both ambient light and the artificial lights in the scene.

Finally, old and new techniques were implemented in order to achieve the end result.

19

Exterior Night Time

Post-production

This last stage of the production will guide users through the steps of utilizing key render elements to enhance materials in the scene. A nice and balanced night mood will be created to make the general lighting more appealing. Numerous Photoshop tools, filters and techniques from previous chapters will be reused to improve the overall image and help integrate people into the scene.

19 Exterior Night Time

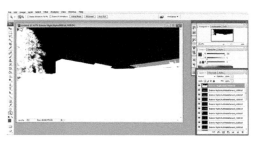

19.1 Post-production

As previously done in Chapter 9, open the *Load Files into Stack* script, to bring the rendered elements into a stack. ▶19.1

Next, create two group folders under the names of 'Multimatte' and 'Elements'. The 'Multimatte' group folder should have all the rendered *MultiMatte* passes. The 'Elements' group folder should have all the remaining rendered passes.

In addition, move the base render ('Exterior Night.RGB_color.0000.tif') to the bottom of the stack and change its property colour to red.

Finally, save the document as 'Exterior Nighttime in VRay_Tutorials.psd'. Use some of the techniques covered earlier in Chapter 9 to do this. ▶19.2

The next step is to replace the current environment colour with a striking dusk image.

19.2

In the *Elements* group folder, enable the visibility of the 'Exterior Night. Alpha.0000.tif' layer, and then open the *Channels* palette. In the *Channels* palette, hold down the Ctrl key and click on the RGB channel, to select the alpha channel. ▶**19.3** and **19.4**

19.3

19.4

Back in the *Layers* palette, while the selection is still on, create a new group folder under the name of 'Background' and generate its adjacent layer mask with inverted selection (Shift+Ctrl+I). ▶**19.5**

19.5

Next, open a sky image in Photoshop named 'night sky.jpg' and insert the image into the 'Background' group folder. ▶19.6 and 19.7

19.6

19.7

3D Photorealistic Rendering

Use the Ctrl+T tool to move and scale the background image proportionally, as previously done. Hold down the Alt key to scale the image proportionally. ▶19.8

19.8

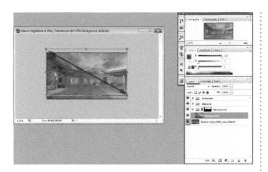

The next step is to create a compelling sky colour using some of techniques covered in Chapter 16. First duplicate the background layer and rename it 'Background darker'.

To make the sky more coherent with a night scene, add a photo filter adjustment with a clipping mask (Alt+Ctrl+I). In the *Photo Filter* dialogue, change its colour to light purple and increase its density to 100%. ▶19.9

19.9▼

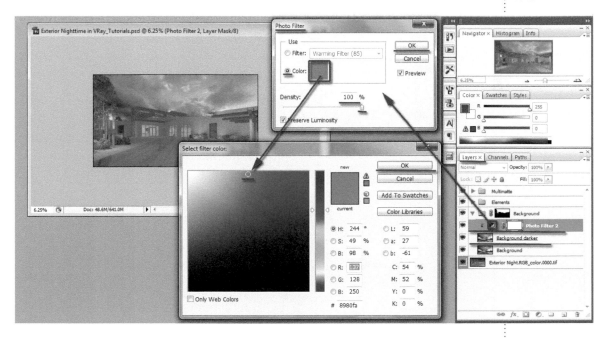

19.10

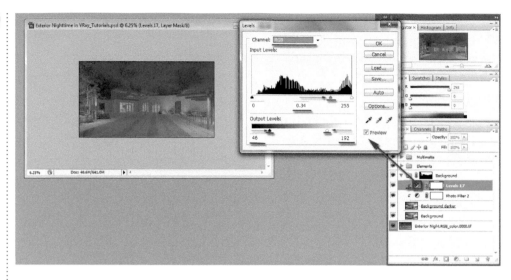

19.11

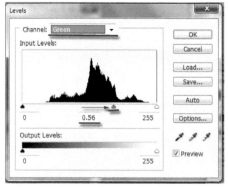

To make the sky colour more compelling, add a *Levels* adjustment layer on top of the photo filter. In its *RGB channel Input Levels*, move its middle slider to about 0.34, to add more contrast. In the *Output Levels*, move its leftmost slider to 46 and the right slider to 192. ▶19.10

To change the sky colour slightly, open the *Green Input Levels Channel* and move its middle slider to about 0.56. Note how the blue tones become darker. ▶19.11

19.12

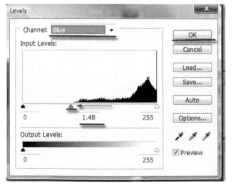

Finally, open the blue channel and move its middle slider to 1.48. ▶19.12

To desaturate the colours slightly, add a *Hue/Saturation* adjustment layer and decrease its *Saturation* value to –18. ▶19.13

To accentuate the line between the building and the sky, increase the brightness of the 'Background' layer by adding *Levels* on top.

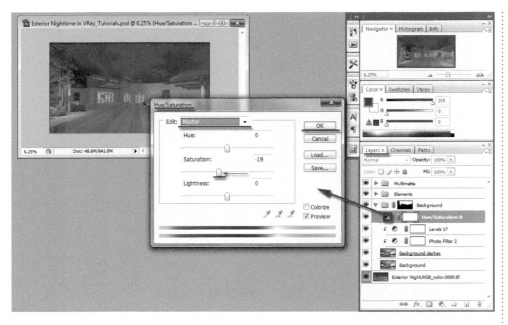

Following that, add a new layer mask to the 'Background darker' layer and begin brushing away areas around the building line, to reveal the brighter layer underneath it ('Background' layer). Use the same technique used in Chapters 9 and 16. ▶19.14

The next step is to begin adjusting the foreground levels.

To do so, start by creating a new group folder and renaming it 'Whole'. Ensure this new group folder is positioned underneath the 'Background' group folder, to make sure changes only affect the foreground.

Inside the 'Whole' group folder, create a *Levels* adjustment layer. In its *RGB channel Input Levels*, move its middle slider to 0.39 and its rightmost slider to 226. Note how the contrast in the foreground becomes more pronounced.
▶19.15

19.15

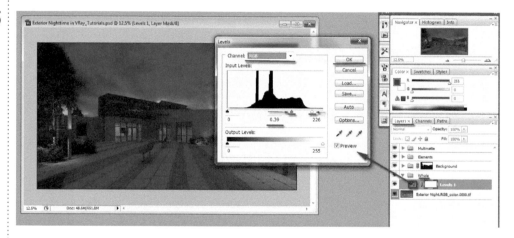

To control mainly the blue tones, add a *Selective Color* adjustment layer on top. In the *Selective Color Options* dialogue, set the colours to *Blues* and change the *Black* value to +2%; *Yellow* to –60%; *Magenta* to –4% and *Cyan* to +98%.

Note how the blue tones of the image begin changing with each parameter changed. ▶19.16

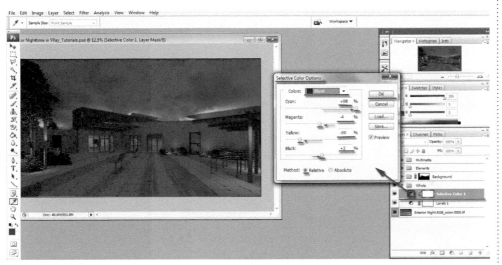

To desaturate the colours slightly, add a *Hue/Saturation* adjustment layer on top and reduce the master saturation value to –19. ▶19.17

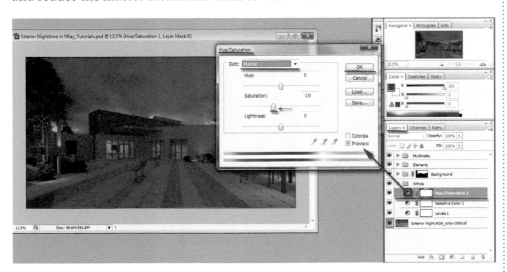

The following step is to make the windows a bit more interesting.

Use the 'Exterior Night.MultiMatteElement_1.0000.tif' layer to select and create a group folder for the windows in the middle. Rename the new group folder 'Windows middle'.

To add reflections to the windows, copy and move the 'Exterior Night.VRayRawReflection.0000.tif' layer into the 'Windows middle' group folder.

Use the *Darker Color* blending mode to help integrate the layer. Reduce its opacity to about 35%. ▶19.18

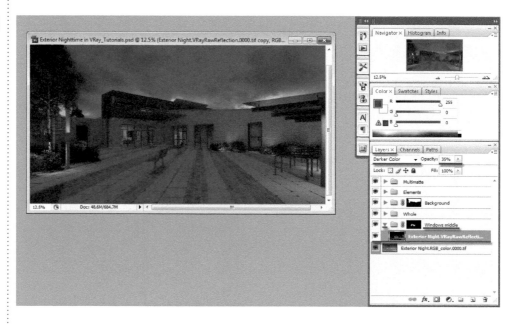

Next, copy and move the 'Exterior Night.VRayRawRefraction.0000.tif' layer into the 'Windows middle' group folder. In addition, change the blending mode to *Screen* and reduce its opacity to 20%.

Note how the glass becomes more interesting. ▶19.19

To increase the brightness of the lights inside the windows, add the *Levels* adjustment layer. In its *RGB Input Levels*, move the middle slider to about 0.81 and the rightmost slider to 189. Note how bright and interesting the windows become.

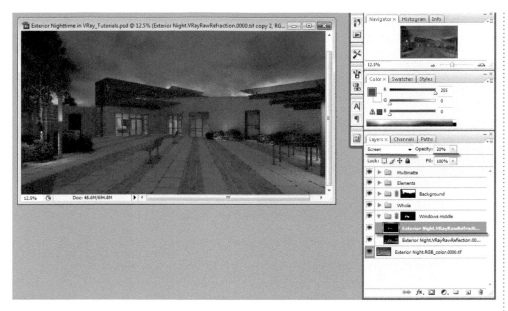

19.19

To uneven the levels, use the *Brush Tool* (B) in conjunction with the *Levels* mask layer to brush away parts of the window brightness, seen in red. ▶19.20

To add some warmth to the lights inside the windows, append a photo filter on top. Choose the orange filter and increase its density to about 78%.

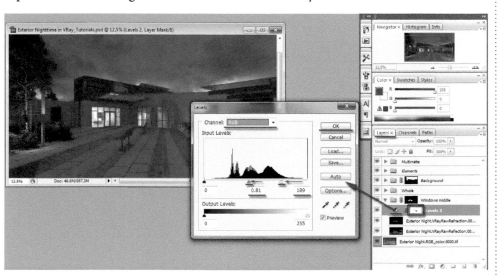

19.20

Finally, use the brush tool in conjunction with a layer mask to omit parts of the window mask being affected by the two adjustment layers. ▶19.21 and 19.22

19.21

19.22

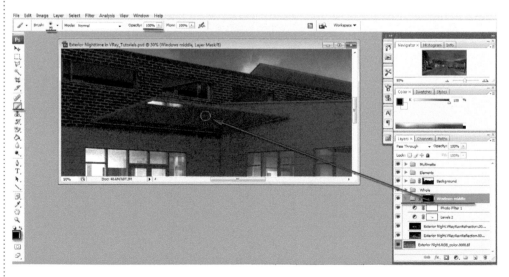

Use some of the previous steps to create similar effects in other windows. ▶19.23

19.23

The subsequent step is to select and create a new group folder for the tree on the foreground. Use some of the steps covered earlier to do this.

To increase the brightness on areas being affected by the upward-pointing lights, add a *Levels* adjustment layer and tweak it accordingly, using some of the steps covered earlier.

Add *Color Balance* and a photo filter to create tones of blue on indirectly lit areas of the tree.

To see the final results, please refer to the PSD file under the name of 'Exterior Nighttime in VRay.psd'. ▶19.24

19.24

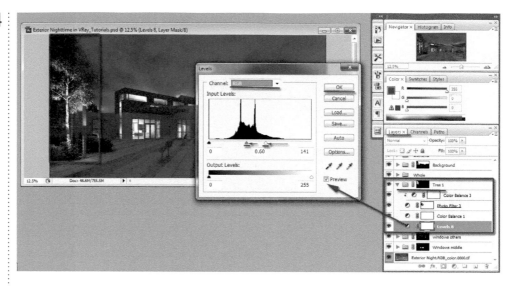

Tweak the remaining materials by using some of the techniques covered in the earlier steps of this chapter and the previous ones.

Again, refer to the PSD file under the name of 'Exterior Nighttime in VRay.psd' to see the final results. ▶19.25

19.25

Add people and diffused shadows, using the techniques described in detail, in Chapters 12 and 9. ▶19.26

19.26

To reduce the saturation of the overall image, add a *Hue/Saturation* adjustment layer. Decrease its *Saturation* slider to about –52.

Ensure this layer is on top of all group folders and adjustment layers previously created. ▶19.27

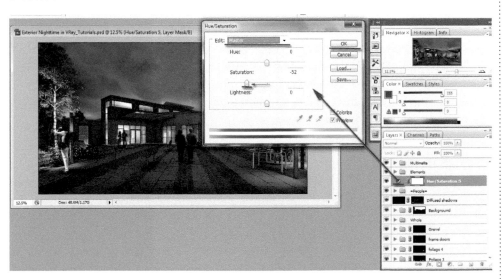

19.27

Depending on personal taste, you can create an ambient light/volumetric effect in the overall scene.

To do so, add a *Levels* adjustment layer and move its *RGB Output Levels* left slider to 40. Rename this layer as 'Ambient light'. ►19.28

19.28

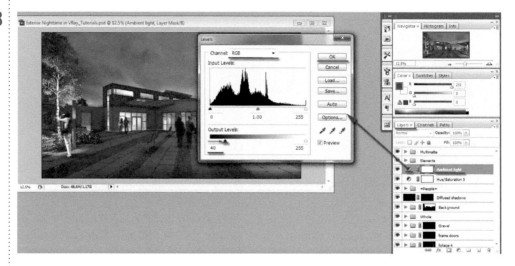

Conclusion

This final chapter guided users through the process of using key render elements to enhance materials and the overall lighting in the night exterior scene. While the final image differed from previous ones, most of the techniques and tools implemented in this tutorial were similar to ones previously covered in earlier chapters.

Finally, throughout this chapter and the previous ones, users were navigated through the intricacies of texturing, lighting, rendering and enhancing the renders in post-production. While each shot had its unique challenges, users were consistently steered through the process of delivering each shot successfully.

Index

Index

Index

Index

Index

Index